P9-ECT-508

Scenes of
EDWARDIAN LIFE

SIR CHARLES PETRIE
Bt, C.B.E., M.A.(Oxon), F.R.Hist.Soc.

SEVERN HOUSE PUBLISHERS LTD

First published by Eyre & Spottiswoode
(Publishers) Ltd 1965

© 1965 Charles Petrie

Severn House edition 1975
ISBN 0 7278 0019 1

Printed in Great Britain by Flarepath Printers
Ltd, St. Albans, Herts

Contents

Air. Curzon succeeds Goschen. His Strength and Weakness. His Red Book. Two Eccentric Dons. E. P. Warren. Undergraduate Life. A Rough Age. College Customs. 'The Britter.' The University Clubs. The Union. The Canning Club. Contrasts with Cambridge. An Anecdote of Sir John Squire. Some Cambridge Characters. 'The O.B.' Sir Shane Leslie's View of Him. Sir Austen Chamberlain's Opinion. Cost of Living at the Two Universities. Work and Religion at a Discount.

VI
IRELAND
page 135

State of the Country at Queen Victoria's Death. George Wyndham. The Land Conference. The Land Act. Arrival of Sir Antony MacDonnell. A Curious Appointment. The King's Approval. A Royal Visit. The Irish Reform Association. Unionist Dismay. Wyndham's Resignation. Walter Long as Chief Secretary. The Irish Party in the House of Commons. The Irish Administration. Long's Differences with Dudley. The Prime Minister's Ruling. The Liberals and Home Rule. Growing Disillusionment with the Parliamentary Party. Drift to Sinn Fein. The National Theatre. The Abbey. *The Playboy of the Western World*. Professor Starkie's Experience of its First Night. Lady Gregory and Yeats. Edwardian Ireland in Retrospect.

VII
SCOTLAND
page 172

The State of the Presbyterian Church. Formation of the United Free Church. Position of the 'Wee Frees'. Subsequent Legislation. Balfour's Views. Strength of Presbyterianism. Scottish Education. Some Lingering Superstitions. Edwardian Argyllshire. The Problem of Emigration. Social Conditions in the Highlands and Islands. The Deer Forests. Bad Housing. The Case of St Kilda. Its Vicissitudes. Final Evacuation. High Level of Illegitimacy in Scotland. Prevalence of Drunkenness. Comparison with England and Ireland. Drinking of Methylated Spirit. Reasons of This. A Cruise with King Edward VII. Scottish Adherence to Liberalism.

Illustrations

Foreword

———◦———

LIKE its predecessors, *The Stuarts*, *The Four Georges*, and *The Victorians*, this book makes no pretence of covering the whole field with which it deals, but it is claimed on its behalf that when the reader has perused it he or she will have a good, working idea what the Edwardian era was really like, what were its problems, and how it regarded them. Much of relevance has admittedly been omitted, and in order to paint in the background it has sometimes been necessary to stray into the Victorian age. The gay, as well as the grave, has been included in the narrrative.

For information and advice upon various points I wish to acknowledge my debt to Sir Kenneth Pickthorn, Bt, M.P.; Sir J. A. L. Duncan, Bt; and Mr D. Holland, Assistant Librarian of the House of Commons: none of them, I may add, is in any way responsible for the opinions expressed in these pages.

I should like to express my thanks to Mr S. C. Holliday, Chief Librarian of the Royal Borough of Kensington and Chelsea, for his kind readiness in procuring for me, often at very short notice, the many books on which this present work is based.

CHARLES PETRIE

April, 1965

Acknowledgements

———◦———

The right to reproduce the following plates is gratefully acknowledged: Dr Phillis Cunnington, nos. 10 and 11(b); William Gordon Davis, nos. 1, 2(a), 2(b), 3, 4, 5(a), 5(b), 6(a), 6(b), 7(a), 7(b), 8(a), 8(b), 11(a), 12(a), 12(b), 13, 14(a), 14(b), 15(a), 15(b), 15(c) and 16(a); The Raymond Mander and Joe Mitchenson Theatre Collection, no. 16(b); The Museum of British Transport, no. 9.

CHAPTER I

The Centre of Gravity

———•◦•———

THE impact of King Edward VII upon his age was greater than that of any of his successors upon the throne, and he touched his subjects' lives at many more points, but his exact influence is not easily defined, in spite of the recent publication – at long last – of his official biography. Across his earlier years lay the shadow of George IV. His father and mother were continually working themselves into a panic in case he should go the way of 'Prinny', and when, at the age of fifteen, he kissed a pretty girl in a moment of light-heartedness during a holiday on the Continent the news was rapidly passed to the Chancellor of the Exchequer, no less a person than Gladstone himself, who described it as 'this little squalid debauch'. When he was stationed at the Curragh four years later a few of his brother officers smuggled a young actress of the name of Nellie Clifden, who was going the rounds of the Brigade of Guards at the time, into his quarter, and when the Prince Consort heard of the incident he lost all sense of proportion. He declared himself too heart-broken to see his son, and sat down to write 'with a heavy heart upon a subject which has caused me the greatest pain I have yet felt in my life'. In retrospect, it is difficult to share Prince Albert's surprise that a healthy young man of nineteen should have a normal sexual appetite, and the most significant – and encouraging – aspect of the whole episode is surely the fact that the Prince of Wales, as he then was, refused to disclose the names of the friends who had led him astray.[1] The example of the First Gentleman took a good deal of living down, and on the morrow of the Tranby Croft Case one

[1] *Cf.* Magnus, Sir Philip: *King Edward the Seventh*, pp. 21, 47 and 51.

ecclesiastic went so far as to declare that 'among us has arisen a second George IV in the heir to the throne of this vast Empire'.

His reign, brief as it was, coincided with the last of Great Britain's prosperous years, and for long there was a not unnatural tendency to regard it as a golden age, much as that of Edward the Confessor was, quite wrongly, regarded by the generation that suffered under the first two Norman sovereigns. We know now that this was not the case, and that the British Empire, in spite of appearances, was passing her zenith when Queen Victoria died: her commercial and industrial rivals were steadily overtaking her, and the progress of scientific invention was undermining her position as mistress of the seas. While King Edward was still on the throne Blériot flew the Channel, and that was the end of many things, as well as the beginning of many more. All this, however, was hidden from most contemporaries and the succeeding generation, so that for long there was a tendency to view King Edward VII and his age in the wrong perspective.

Socially, the Court counted for a great deal more during his reign than it had done in that of his mother, and for the first – and last – time since the Revolution it was the centre of social life. When the Queen died there was a good deal of apprehension among those in whose memory the Tranby Croft scandal was still vivid with regard to the type of person who would henceforth be found at Court, but, on the whole, these fears were not realized. Society was itself becoming very mixed, and for the Court to have maintained the aloofness of the Victorian era would only have made matters worse instead of better, even if the King had been the man to follow in his mother's footsteps in that respect, which was certainly not the case. He firmly believed that Royalty should show themselves, and as early as 1869 he had written to Queen Victoria strongly on the subject.

If you sometimes even came to London from Windsor – say for luncheon – and then drove for an hour in the Park (where there is no noise)[1] and then returned to Windsor, the people

[1] One of the reasons which the Queen had adduced for not coming to London was that the noise was bad for her nerves.

would be overjoyed – beyond measure. It is all very well for Alix and me to drive in the Park – it does not have the same effect as when you do it; and I say thank God that is the case. We live in radical times, and the more the People see the Sovereign the better it is for the People and the Country.[1]

He knew that the British people in particular like to see their Sovereign, and he himself appeared before them more frequently than any of his predecessors since the fall of the Stuarts, with the result that the man-in-the-street, who had respected his mother, came to love him as 'Teddy' just as their ancestors had loved Charles II as 'Old Rowley', and for the same reason.

Sir Philip Magnus, in his recent biography of the King, takes the view on the evidence which he has consulted that relations between mother and son were a great deal better than has generally been assumed, but all the same it is impossible to dismiss the suspicion that she was jealous of him, as all the monarchs of the House of Hanover had been of their heirs. Instead of rejoicing that he should take the place of his dead father she resented the fact, and tried to keep him in the background. At this distance of time it would appear that she would have done better to have abdicated in his favour in the nineties, and it has puzzled many historians, as well as not a few contemporaries, to account for her failure to do so: if, however, she was jealous of him that would explain everything.

The position of Queen Alexandra is also open to misconstruction. Of her popularity from the moment of her arrival in England until the day of her death there can be no question, and Tennyson never expressed the mood of his fellow countrymen more accurately than when he wrote:

> Sea King's daughter from over the sea,
> Alexandra!
> Saxon and Norman and Dane are we,
> But all of us Dane in our welcome of thee,
> Alexandra!

If, however, the old Queen felt any jealousy of her heir then the

---

[1] *Cf.* Magnus, Sir Philip: *King Edward the Seventh*, pp. 101–102.

popularity of her daughter-in-law was not likely to lessen it, and it is to be noted that she did not go out of her way to allow the Princess of Wales to represent her.

Of the King's relations with his wife a great deal has been written, but very often without any allowance being made for human nature, which is the same in the case of Royalty as in that of lesser mortals. He fell in love with his Danish bride from the moment he met her, and there is no shred of evidence that he ever fell out of it. Whether he was attracted to her physically is another matter, but there is no proof that he was ever in love with anybody else. That he had innumerable affairs with other women is incontrovertible, but it does not affect the issue: he went with them not because he was in love with them, but solely for the purpose of fornication. His mistresses had no influence over him, save in a sexual sense.

What is clear is that Queen Alexandra did have considerable influence over her husband, especially in the matter of foreign politics – certainly a much greater influence than that of more recent Queens whose consorts were models of conjugal fidelity. Her hatred of Prussia, and later of the Hohenzollern Reich, was the guiding political motive of her life, and although it would obviously be an exaggeration to say that she was the cause of the King's aversion to Kaiser Wilhelm II – 'William the Great' – as his uncle called him – she was definitely a contributory factor. Whether she, too, sought consolation elsewhere is a matter upon which it would be rash to dogmatize, nor does it greatly matter, but the student of their times would do well to realize that in essentials King Edward and Queen Alexandra were a much more united couple than is usually accepted.

On the King's political influence there will always be considerable difference of opinion, and it is not easy to ascertain his real views on more than one important problem of the day. His biographers have tended to attach too much importance to what he wrote or said on the spur of the moment, and he was by nature a good deal of an extrovert, though in later life he learnt largely to control the outward manifestation of his feelings. The domestic scene did not much attract him, and rightly or wrongly he tended

4

to regard internal politics as smacking of the 'parish pump',[1] but this attitude in no way contrasted with that of the vast majority of his subjects: the Press and the politicians have always tended to exaggerate the average Englishman's interest in politics, and the constitutional crisis of the last months of the reign was never a popular crisis: to compare it with the agitation over the Reform Bill in 1832 would be to draw a false analogy.

His work for hospitals, particularly London ones, on the other hand, was as outstanding as was that of the Queen in the field of nursing. Possibly one reason for this, apart from his natural humanity, was the fact that more than most men in his position he had been brought closely into touch with death: not only had his father and his eldest son died early, but his favourite sister, the German Empress, and her husband, the Emperor Frederick III, had met agonizing deaths from cancer. From his youth he had taken a keen interest in medicine and therapeutics, and this continued until the end of his life, for his last public philanthropic function was to lay the corner-stone of a new wing of the Norfolk and Norwich Hospital at Norwich in October, 1909. As King he continued to concern himself with the progress of King Edward's Hospital Fund, which he had inaugurated as Prince of Wales, and during his reign its annual income was increased from fifty to nearly one hundred and sixty thousand pounds. Especially was he interested in the prevention and cure of cancer, and in 1908 he is found writing to Sir Frederick Treves, 'My greatest ambition is not to quit this world till a real cure for cancer has been found'.[2]

In all aspects of the international situation the King took the deepest interest, and he had a real flair for diplomacy which the wisest of his ministers frankly recognized. Evidence of this was forthcoming in 1908 when he paid a visit to Germany, and Sir Edward Grey provided him with two memoranda about the naval building programme, for use when he met his nephew. 'This,' Lord Hardinge has put on record, 'was really a very in-

---

[1] One is reminded of the third Marquess of Salisbury, the King's Prime Minister at the beginning of his reign, who once said that he preferred foreign to domestic politics, for the former concerned personalities and the latter dealt with issues, and he was more interested in people than in problems.

[2] *Cf.* Lee, Sir Sidney: *King Edward VII, A Biography*, vol. II, pp. 403–404.

teresting innovation, since for the first time in history the British Government briefed the King to act as their spokesman in an interview with the Head of a Foreign State, and it serves as an indisputable proof of the confidence they felt in the wisdom and tact of the Sovereign in dealing with such matters.'[1] The same sentiments had been expressed in the previous year by the Belgian chargé d'affaires in London when writing to Brussels:

> The English are getting more and more into the habit of regarding international problems as being almost exclusively within the province of King Edward, for whose profound political instinct and fertile diplomacy they very rightly feel great respect. The most obvious proof of this attitude of mind is the total absence of discord between the two great historic parties in all matters relating to England's political destinies. It is this fact which makes it possible for Sir Edward Grey to carry on Lord Lansdowne's work without hesitation and without incident.
>
> Confiding, on the one hand, in the enlightened judgement and happy tact of the King, and relying besides upon the capacity of the minister entrusted with the care of its international interests, public opinion is disinteresting itself more and more from questions of high policy, knowing by experience that the destinies of the Empire are in good hands.[2]

It is not, of course, suggested that the King controlled the foreign policy of the country as the Tudors and Stuarts had controlled it, but, to give a single example, it is doubtful whether his ministers could have carried through the Entente with France without him, for during his visit to Paris in May, 1903, he unquestionably created the atmosphere in which the statesmen of the two countries were able to collaborate. In fact he had some claim to have originated the term itself, for as early as 1878 in a speech in the French capital he referred to the '*entente cordiale* which exists between this country and our own', while after he was dead Poincaré said of him in connection with the Anglo-French Agreement, 'Not one of my fellow countrymen has forgotten the happy im-

[1] *Old Diplomacy*, p. 158.
[2] Quoted by Morel, E. D.: *Diplomacy Revealed*, p. 74.

petus given on that decisive occasion by His Majesty King Edward VII to the work of concord which has outlived him.'

The new reign was to see four Prime Ministers, namely Salisbury, Balfour, Campbell-Bannerman, and Asquith, and the first of these was a legacy from the old Queen. At the turn of the century the Conservative Government, with Salisbury as Prime Minister, had been five years in office; the worst of the South African War seemed to be over; and Salisbury and his colleagues felt that the moment had arrived for an appeal to the country, which duly took place in the autumn of 1900. That they were not mistaken was proved by the fact that they lost a mere nine seats, for their propaganda had been in the astute hands of Joseph Chamberlain, and the slogan 'A Vote for the Liberals is a Vote for the Boers' had been used with telling effect. When the victory had been won the reconstruction of the administration became a problem of the day. That Salisbury would continue as Prime Minister was unquestioned, but whether he would also remain Foreign Secretary was another matter. The Queen had come to the conclusion that he should no longer combine the two offices, and was prepared to advise him to that effect; but her advice was not required, for he appreciated the situation himself, and the Marquess of Lansdowne replaced him at the Foreign Office.

The reconstituted administration had as its primary task the winning of the war in South Africa, but that conflict was also having repercussions elsewhere which were ominous of what the future had in store. One of these was the growing Anglophobia in Germany as evidenced by the attitude of the Press in that country. At home the Opposition was divided on the question of the war, to which fact was to no inconsiderable extent due its poor showing at the General Election, but this did nothing to prevent the use by one section of it of an intemperate language which, in its turn, did not a little to exacerbate party feeling. In the middle of 1901 Lord Kitchener, who had succeeded Lord Roberts as Commander-in-Chief some six months before, erected, with a view to arresting the guerrilla activities of the Boers, a long chain of blockhouses along the railway lines and the banks of the rivers. At the same time he removed the dependents of the enemy to concentration camps in

Natal, and this policy, which today would be regarded as a normal operation of war, became the object of the most violent criticism on the part of a section of the Liberal Party. For example, on May 31st, 1901, Campbell-Bannerman at a meeting in Edinburgh denounced 'the most unworthy policy of enforcing unconditional surrender upon those who were to be their legal and contented subjects in the new colonies'. A fortnight later in London he taunted the Government with having described the war as 'not yet entirely terminated', and added, 'A phrase often used is "war is war", but when one came to ask about it one was told that no war was going on – that it was not a war. When was a war not a war? When it was carried on by methods of barbarism in South Africa.' The House of Commons, too, in those days was a place where quarter was neither asked nor given. On one occasion Joseph Chamberlain was interrupted by John Dillon, who called out that a certain Boer commander was a traitor for advising his men to surrender. 'Ah!' said the Colonial Secretary quietly, 'the honourable gentleman is a judge of traitors.'

No holds were barred either at Westminster or in the country. Before Parliament was dissolved it had been alleged in the House of Commons that the firm of Kynochs had been favoured by the War Office in the matter of contracts because Arthur Chamberlain, Joe's brother, was its chairman. 'I have nothing whatever to do with his private concerns,' said the Colonial Secretary, 'any more than he has anything to do with my public concerns, and it is a gross abuse to attack a man through his relatives for whom he is not responsible.' Nevertheless this did not put a stop to the stream of abuse, and *Punch* remarked that 'the more the Empire expands, the more the Chamberlains contract'. The campaign was carried on in this vein, and the registers at Somerset House were searched to reveal the investments of the Chamberlain family and its Kenrick relatives, and to connect these with Government contracts. It was also suggested that Austen Chamberlain, then Civil Lord of the Admiralty, had been allocating orders to a firm in which he and his brother Neville, the future Prime Minister, were interested. Throughout the General Election campaign Opposition candidates repeated these insinuations up and down the constituencies, though of course they always disclaimed any other motive than a zeal for the purity of public life. It was a foretaste of the Marconi scandal, though with the rôles reversed.

When the new Parliament met matters came to a head with an amendment to the Address, moved by Lloyd George, to the effect that ministers 'ought to have no interest direct or indirect in any firm or company competing for contracts with the Crown'. This gave Chamberlain an opportunity of turning upon his traducers, and he referred to the indictment as a 'dreary flow of petty malignity'. He denounced the 'conspiracy of insinuation', and he reminded the House that his family represented two centuries of unblemished tradition in business. He made, however, no secret of the fact that he had been hurt:

> If the object of those who entered in this conspiracy was to give pain I must admit that they have succeeded. . . . They have not injured me. They have not injured my cause. I have never received so many kindly letters and assurances of support and sympathy as I have done during the last few weeks. But they have introduced into our public life methods of controversy which are unworthy, and have made it more difficult for honourable, sensitive men to serve the State.

When the vote was taken on Lloyd George's amendment it was rejected by 269 votes to 127, and in view of the fact that the Liberal strength was 186 and the Irish (of whom, to their credit, hardly any voted) 82, the result of the division was the more significant. Outside Parliament it was not so easy for the Chamberlains to deal with the 'conspiracy of insinuation', for the attacks were so contrived that Joseph Chamberlain was advised that he had no legal remedy, but his brother and his younger son took the matter into court and obtained damages.[1]

On May 31st, 1902, the struggle in South Africa came to an end with the complete surrender of the Boers, and on the morning of Friday, July 11th, the retiring Prime Minister, Salisbury, restored his seals of office to the King, but no public announcement was made until after the week-end; indeed, he would not appear either

---

[1] *Cf.* Garvin, J. L.: *Life of Joseph Chamberlain*, vol. III, pp. 601 and 613-616.

to have consulted his colleagues or even to have notified them in advance of his decision to resign. It was the end of an era, and the British Empire was no longer to be subject to remote control from Hatfield and Osborne: the new problems were to be faced by new men.

What rendered Salisbury's decision the more extraordinary was that he chose the moment when his strongest colleague, Chamberlain, was in the early stages of recovering from a serious carriage accident. On the afternoon of July 7th the Colonial Secretary left the Colonial Office in a hansom cab to go to the Athenaeum, where an election of members was taking place, and he wanted to assist a friend who was a candidate. The day had been very hot, and the glass window, fitted in the front of the cab to protect the occupant from rain, was folded back under the roof and secured by a leather strap. Whitehall, which was festooned with bunting in honour of the coming Coronation, had been watered shortly before to lay the dust, and the wood pavement was in consequence slippery. The driver, therefore, proceeded slowly, but as he came to the great Canadian arch, the horse shied at the fluttering decorations, slipped on the wet pavement, and fell. Chamberlain was thrown violently forward, and at the same moment the strap which secured the window gave way, with the result that the heavy glass pane crashed down on his forehead. Half stunned and with blood pouring into his eyes, he stumbled from the cab and asked a passer-by to help him to the Colonial Office. A policeman, however, arrived on the scene, bound up the wound with a handkerchief, and hurried the statesman off in another cab to Charing Cross Hospital.

The cut was found to be a deep one, stretching for three and a half inches from the centre of the forehead towards the right temple. The glass pane had penetrated to the bone and caused a slight indentation of the skull. Three stitches were put in at once, but Chamberlain refused an anaesthetic. The loss of blood was regarded as serious – 'I never knew I had so much blood to lose,' he said – but the pulse was normal, and at first it was thought that he had escaped shock or concussion. His private secretary and his P.P.S. at once went to the hospital and found their chief inclined to make light of the incident, for he held out his hand and said, 'See, it does not shake.' Mrs Chamberlain arrived soon afterwards: she had been driving in the Park with her mother and had been alarmed to see a poster announcing 'Chamberlain in Hospital'.

On the following day a curious incident occurred which throws an interesting light upon the easy-going methods of Edwardian hospitals. Chamberlain was to have attended a dinner given by the Prince of Wales in honour of the Colonial Premiers, and in his absence Mrs Chamberlain went alone. On her way home she called at Charing Cross Hospital to see her husband. The rest of the story is best told in Mr Julian Amery's words:

> There was no porter at the door, and, though the coachman rang the bell several times, no one answered. Deciding to investigate for herself Mrs Chamberlain pushed the swing-door open and walked in. There was no one about. Trusting to her memory, she made her way through the wards to her husband's room. There was no night nurse to be found; but Chamberlain was fast asleep; and, after sitting by him for half an hour, she returned to the carriage. A weird picture this, of the Edwardian lady driving from a Royal banquet to watch over the statesman, asleep in a deserted hospital.[1]

As had been generally anticipated the new Prime Minister was Arthur Balfour, the nephew of his predecessor; and he included so many of his relatives in the Government that it became known as the 'Hotel Cecil'. After he was dead Austen Chamberlain wrote of him, 'Things which seemed important to him often appeared of little consequence to his followers, and to his opponents (as for instance in the tariff controversy) a mere splitting of hairs, a quibble unworthy of the ingenuity with which he sustained it and of the serious issues at stake. He was not content to make a broad statement of his views without at the same time giving expression to all the qualifications which, to his mind, it required.'[2] Such being the case it is hardly surprising that with two exceptions Balfour should have been the worst Prime Minister that the Conservative Party has inflicted on the country.

---

[1] *Life of Joseph Chamberlain*, vol. IV, p. 450.   [2] *Down the Years*, pp. 214–215.

He was admirable as a second-in-command, but he did not possess the gifts of a leader. As the lieutenant of his uncle, and particularly during his tenure of office as Chief Secretary for Ireland, he was often brilliant, and he did some good work in his later days, but he was not the man to place at the head of affairs: in a crisis he either failed to take a decision at all, or else he took the wrong one. Nor was his loyalty to his colleagues always above suspicion, though it must be remembered that from the sixteenth century onwards there had been a dash of the Borgias about many of the Cecils, and he was a Cecil on his mother's side. As a leader he had the most frustrating effect on the rank-and-file of his party; times innumerable he would address a meeting when it was confidently expected that he would give a lead in some moment of crisis, but no lead would be forthcoming. He was a master of the type of speech which sounds impressive but really says nothing, while it was widely believed that he retired to his bed under pretext of illness whenever there was a difficult problem to be solved. As a debater in the House of Commons he was in the front rank.

The truth is that Balfour is one of the most difficult characters in recent history to assess. A man of great charm, a philosopher, and a scholar, he was also a good deal of a lecher, though in a rather detached and superior way. He was careful, according to a recent biographer, 'to spread his emotional interests over a wide field', but the centre of his private life was Mary Wyndham, who early became the wife of the eleventh Earl of Wemyss, whom he originally met with her mother at Lord Leighton's studio: Balfour helped the husband politically, and in the process he helped himself to the wife. The liaison was particularly active during his Chief Secretaryship, but it lasted for a number of years after that, for as late as 1898 the lady was corresponding with him about a self-induced abortion.[1] It is given to few men to rouse such different feelings as those expressed in the nicknames 'Prince Arthur' and 'Bloody Balfour', yet the fact is illustrative of his paradoxical nature. No man could be so far-sighted, yet on more than one occasion he proved unable to see what was close at hand. At the same time it must be admitted that as leader of the Conservative

[1] *Cf.* Young, K.: *Arthur James Balfour*, p. 138.

Party he had difficulties to face which might well have proved too much for one who possessed greater talents in that particular direction. The division of opinion among the ranks of his followers on the subject of Tariff Reform more than once threatened to disrupt the Conservative Party altogether, and he felt it to be his duty to prevent this at all costs. The not unnatural consequence was that he came to be mistrusted both by the Protectionists and the Free Traders. That he did prevent a split on the tariff issue must be conceded, but in so doing he was very often the despair of those who were called upon to collaborate with him. In the House of Commons his qualities showed to greater advantage than on the platform, where he too often gave the impression of not having made up his own mind.

The late Sir John Squire's parody of a speech by Balfour was not very far from the truth:

> But even allowing – which I am far from allowing, I shall come to that presently – that we have been superficially inconsistent, are honourable gentleman opposite so ignorant of the most elementary forms of our constitutional practice, of that Parliamentary custom which in the opinion of many of us has a higher sanction even than the laws of the land, as to think that the speeches of the Opposition ten years ago either are, or should be, or should be expected to be, valid criteria of the actions of a Government today?

His tenure of the Premiership came to an end in the closing weeks of 1905 when, against the wishes of many of his colleagues, he resigned. The King disagreed with his action, and wrote that he could not 'help regretting that Mr Balfour should not have abandoned his idea of resignation, and that he should not have instead decided on meeting Parliament'. The reason for this pusillanimous line of conduct would seem to have been that he thought that it would involve the Liberals in taking over and producing a policy before going to the polls. This tortuous reasoning proved to be completely beside the point, for Campbell-Bannerman, having formed his Government, went to the country in January, 1906, without a policy at all, and the Conservative Party sustained the biggest defeat in its history. An administration that had begun life in 1900 with a majority of some 130 now found itself in Opposition with only 157 seats in all. Nevertheless, it was not until Balfour had lost three General Elections in succession that his long-suffering followers came to the conclusion that it was time they found another leader.

His successor as Prime Minister, namely Campbell-Bannerman, possessed none of the shining qualities which had marked the five previous holders of the office. 'Among his colleagues were men superior to him in power of speech; in talent for grasping great masses of administrative difficulty; and up to a certain time, but not after his worth was fully measured, even in striking or interesting the popular imagination. And yet he was indispensable, the only man possible, and the time came when the popular interest in his personality rose to enviable heights, and good-will passed into cordial admiration and affection.'[1] He was an admirable chairman, anticipating Attlee in this respect, and he knew exactly how to make his very difficult team work. Campbell-Bannerman also possessed a very considerable fund of common-sense, which came both to the House of Commons and to the electorate as a welcome relief after the metaphysical approach of his predecessor to the problems of the day. When he instantly followed one of Balfour's ingenious flights of dialectic with the blunt exclamation that we had 'best have done with all this foolery', he echoed the sentiments of many far beyond the ranks of his own party. He also had a great deal to live down, for, as we have seen, some of his remarks during the South African War were hardly calculated to pour oil on troubled waters. 'I never could have believed that a man who had used that language could ever become Prime Minister of England,' one of the Conservative leaders remarked to Morley, yet the apparently impossible was achieved, and the fact is an eloquent tribute to Campbell-Bannerman's merit and ability.

His relations with the King were a great deal better than those of Balfour had been; indeed, the two men had much in common, for however widely they might differ on points of domestic and foreign policy, neither of them was in the least insular. Campbell-

[1] Morley, Viscount: *Recollections*, vol. II, pp. 140–141.

Bannerman, like the Sovereign, appreciated the French character, spoke the language fluently, and found most of his recreation in reading French novels. He knew French men and women in all walks of life, and, again like his master, enjoyed the friendship of General Gallifet and had frequented the *salon* of the Princess Mathilde. Soon after his arrival in Downing Street the new Prime Minister became personally congenial to the King, who came to appreciate the pawky humour and the general kindliness of temper of 'the gay old dog with a twinkle in his eye'. He had a knack of amusing King Edward with good stories, but he never made any secret of his political views, with which, however, the King probably agreed anyhow. Above all his comments on his colleagues were amazingly frank, and he once aroused Royal merriment by referring to John Morley as 'that old-maidish Priscilla', though both of them must have known that he had 'anticipated the ceremony of marriage', to use a phrase of Rosebery.[1]

Although Campbell-Bannerman came to preside over the most brilliant administration that Britain had known since that of Lord Liverpool at the beginning of the previous century, its formation presented some difficulties since the Liberal Party had been acutely divided for a number of years: nevertheless such were the Prime Minister's powers of persuasion that he united all sections of it in his Government, and the only prominent Liberal who refused to join was Rosebery. As for himself, several of his colleagues took the view that he was not really capable of leading the House of Commons and that one of their number would do it much better, therefore it would be as well for him to go to the Lords: the Prime Minister did not share their apprehensions, and he resisted all efforts to persuade him to leave the Lower House.

It is said that when he was forming his administration he ran into some difficulty with the King. According to this story, before the prospective Prime Minister went to kiss hands Asquith warned him that the Sovereign would bring considerable pressure to bear upon him to appoint Dilke to the Foreign Office: Campbell-Bannerman scouted the idea, but what Asquith had envisaged did

[1] *Cf.* Lee, Sir Sidney: *King Edward VII, A Biography*, vol. II, pp. 442–443.

take place. Campbell-Bannerman told the King that Dilke was impossible in view of the celebrated case in which he had played so prominent a part, and that if his inclusion in the Ministry was the *sine qua non* of his own assumption of office then he must decline to form a Government: only then did the King give way.[1]

However this may be, the new Prime Minister was not destined to hold that office for long, for in April, 1908, he was compelled to resign owing to ill-health. The King was at Biarritz at the time, and he did not return home, but requested Asquith, whom he proposed to ask to form a government, to come out to him. This caused an outcry in some quarters, and *The Times* declared that the appointment of a Prime Minister on foreign soil was 'an inconvenient and dangerous departure from precedent'. Whether those who criticized King Edward for not coming home would have done so had they known that Asquith was not the least averse from a short holiday in the South of France is another matter. If there was any constitutional impropriety it was committed by Lloyd George. Before Asquith left London he naturally, in consultation with his colleagues, drew up the list of the Cabinet which he was going to submit to the Sovereign, and he was not a little amazed – as also was the King – to see it published in the *Daily Chronicle* before he had had time to obtain the Royal approval. When taxed with this disclosure Lloyd George, at whom the finger of suspicion was generally pointed, denied it, but there can be very little doubt who was really responsible.

Asquith, the fourth and last Prime Minister of the Edwardian era, is probably the most misjudged British Premier of modern times. He was born in 1852 at Morley in Yorkshire, and he was Head of the Government for more than eight years at a stretch, that is to say for a longer uninterrupted period than any man since the Earl of Liverpool in the early part of the nineteenth century, and he led the Liberal Party to victory at two successive General Elections. His Government carried some of the most controversial measures of modern times, such as the Third Home Rule Bill, the

[1] This story rests on the authority of the late, third, Viscount Elibank, who was Parliamentary Private Secretary to Sir Edward Grey from 1910 to 1914.

Disestablishment of the Welsh Church, National Health Insurance, the Parliament Act (for which his opponents never really forgave him), Old Age Pensions, and the creation of the Territorial Army; it also took up the challenge of Imperial Germany. Yet Asquith himself is in danger of going down to history as a weak man who did not know his own mind.

The reason for this quite unjust accusation is not, however, far to seek. On one occasion in the House of Commons when he was Prime Minister an Opposition Member tried to draw him out with an embarrassing question in respect of some quite trivial point of his future policy, and Asquith curtly replied, 'Wait and See.' It was a time when political passions were in any case roused, and the critics at once fastened on the phrase, which they were careful to take out of its context, and the Premier was in consequence irreverently termed 'Old Wait and See'. The mud stuck, and the innuendo was widely accepted as fact, with consequences to his reputation that are only too apparent today. Such is the legend; the story of Asquith's career shows how little it is substantiated by the facts.

He had probably the best mind of any Prime Minister of this century, and his son Raymond used to say that if he put a problem to his father the answer, considering the issue from all relevant points of view, came out as it were from a machine.

Asquith came from those Victorian middle-class surroundings which were for so long the basis of the Liberal Party, for he was the second son of a wool-spinner in none too easy circumstances, and since his father died when he was a boy of eight money was none too plentiful in his early years. He was educated at the City of London School and then at Balliol, of which college Jowett was Master. Asquith was one of his favourite pupils, and the older man prophesied a brilliant career for him. He was certainly one of Oxford's most devoted and illustrious sons, and he was for a time a Fellow of his college. What he was then he remained for the rest of his life, that is to say a scholar and a gentleman, with a somewhat academic approach to any problem with which he was called upon to deal. He was cool to the point of detachment; logical to the point of cynicism; and patient to the point of indifference. Such he was as an undergraduate, and such he was as Prime Minister. It was at once his strength and his weakness.

From Oxford to the Bar, and from the Bar to the House of Commons, was a natural transition. In 1886 Asquith was returned as Liberal Member for East Fife, and that constituency remained faithful to him until the Liberal *débâcle* at the end of the First World War. Through thick and thin he followed the fortunes of Gladstone, and in later days he was often referred to as the last of the Gladstonians. This loyalty brought its due reward, and when the Liberals returned to power in 1892 he was made Home Secretary. It was a great honour for a man of forty, who had never held office before, and who had only been in Parliament for six years, but Gladstone had learnt the lesson of Joseph Chamberlain, and was now ready to promote his young men.

Few of those who have heard Asquith in his prime will disagree with the statement that he was one of the greatest orators of the classical school, so that when the First World War came it was only natural that his speeches should rise to the heights that the occasion demanded. As a party politician he possessed, like Gladstone, the supreme merit of conveying the impression that the two-party system as it operated at Westminster corresponded with the fundamental division of humanity into wise men and fools – the Liberals, of course, being in the former category. The late Lord Salisbury used to say that Gladstone had the knack of making even his opponents almost feel that it was morally wrong to vote against him, and Asquith successfully employed the same technique. Yet these magnificent orations were made from the briefest of notes, and time after time his secretary, Bonham Carter, would be in terror that his chief would go on the platform with his speech unprepared, but his fears were never realized. As for the paucity of his notes, the story goes that once when he had spoken at some meeting long and eloquently on the Licensing Bill, a fervent female supporter came up to him with the request that he would let her have his notes as a memento of the occasion; Asquith readily agreed, and pulled out of his waistcoat pocket a small piece of paper on which were written three words – 'Too many pubs'.

Had Asquith died in the summer of 1914 succeeding generations would have placed him very high indeed, for no man who did not possess outstanding abilities could have controlled a team which contained such strong personalities as Lloyd George, Churchill, Haldane, Simon, Grey, and Rufus Isaacs. In effect, he displayed the greatest skill in co-ordinating a ministry which contained many of the most brilliant statesmen of the day, and he was undoubtedly at his best when presiding over his Liberal Cabinet, of which the members had by long experience become accustomed to work together as a team. When, however, the representatives of the Opposition took their seats in the Coalition administration the position became more confused and intrigues abounded. Yet Austen Chamberlain wrote of Asquith in December, 1916, 'He is a gentleman in the fullest sense of the word. Very pleasant to work with, very loyal to his colleagues, and with a great equanimity in good or evil fortune which is in itself a considerable asset in times like these.'[1]

Neither by temperament nor by habits was Asquith the sort of Prime Minister to tolerate an *éminence grise* of the type of J. S. Sandars, who had played that part to Balfour. Asquith was not lazy like Baldwin, and he was always at the helm, unlike Balfour. The influence exercised by Sandars was to no small extent due to his chief's poor health and frequent absence from London, but Asquith had no country residence at all during the early years of his premiership, and even when, not long before the First World War, he built The Wharf at Sutton Courtenay, that was within easy reach of Downing Street. He never went for a long holiday, save occasionally with the First Lord of the Admiralty on the *Enchantress*, when he was closely in touch with what was happening at home, and he never delegated authority: nor was he, like Churchill and Lloyd George, a man who thought aloud. He was very self-contained, and he strongly disliked talking politics at what to him seemed to be inopportune moments. He made up his mind by himself and announced his decisions to those whom they concerned; he did not come to them by discussion with his colleagues.

[1] *Cf.* Petrie, Sir Charles: *The Life and Letters of the Right Hon. Sir Austen Chamberlain*, vol. II, p. 55.

The differences between Asquith and Lloyd George were to prove even more fatal to the Liberal Party than those between Gladstone and Chamberlain in the previous century, and much has been written about them of late years. They were rather latent than patent during the Edwardian era, and they only came to a head in 1916, but their origin was of much earlier date, for it must be taken into account that Asquith was a Liberal Imperialist and Lloyd George was a pro-Boer at the time of the South African War. Asquith had long been doubtful concerning his colleague's discretion, and he became equally dubious about his honesty when Lloyd George gave the list of the prospective Cabinet to the *Daily Chronicle*.

In spite of this, Asquith was chivalry itself when the Marconi scandals took place in 1912–1913. Lloyd George was then Chancellor of the Exchequer, and it was alleged that he had been gambling in the shares of the Marconi Company as a result of his inside official information as a minister that it was about to receive an important Government contract. The Opposition was soon hot on his trail, and he was forced to admit that while he had had no dealings in the shares of the British Marconi Company he had in fact bought some of its American counterpart. On this the storm broke, and so violent was it that Lloyd George offered his resignation: not only, however, did Asquith refuse to accept it, but he vigorously defended his colleague in the House of Commons against all attacks. Had the Chancellor's resignation been accepted the Government, which was losing ground in the country, would have been strengthened, but it would have been the end of his political career. Thereafter Lloyd George conveniently forgot that it was the magnanimity of the Prime Minister which had saved him from disgrace; indeed, from that time onward his behaviour towards Asquith was far from being that of one in his position to a benefactor who had saved his career from shipwreck. Stories, which originated with the Chancellor of the Exchequer and his friends, were spread to the effect that Asquith was drinking heavily, and when, at the beginning of the First World War, the Prime Minister for some reason or another had at the last moment to depute Lloyd George to receive a Trades

Union deputation, care was taken to see that all London rang with the story that the real reason was that Asquith was too drunk.

Much of this is to anticipate, but it was a foretaste of what was to come after 1916, yet Lloyd George's hostility to his leader was intermittent: there were occasions when his rancour was unpardonable, and at other times he seemed willing that bygones should be bygones. He never seems to have realized that there are men whom the adroit use of a little flattery will not cause to forget an injustice. Even in the supreme crisis of 1916 it is doubtful whether his original intention was to displace Asquith as Prime Minister; he rather saw him as a sort of Merovingian King with himself as Mayor of the Palace. That he should ever have imagined this to be possible shows how little he understood Asquith.

In no respect was there a greater difference between Asquith and his successors at 10 Downing Street than in the size of what may be termed his personal staff, which, to quote Frank Owen's biography of Lloyd George,[1] 'consisted of his talented son-in-law, "Bongie",[2] and another secretary with a single typist'. There were other differences, too, from later practice. In those days Parliamentary Private Secetaries were very small fry indeed, and the one employed by the Prime Minister was no exception: his activities were of a routine nature in the House of Commons, and he rarely put in an appearance at Downing Street. Much of the work that would now be done by one in his capacity then fell to Bonham Carter's lot. On the other hand, he had during his earlier years with Asquith the co-operation of one of the greatest Chief Whips in history, the Master of Elibank, and that was of the utmost value to him in his dealings with the rank and file of the Liberal Party. Bonham Carter was particularly happy in his relations with the Irish Nationalists upon whose support, after the first General Election of 1910, the fate of the Liberal Government was so largely dependent. Their leader 'was that commanding Parliamentary figure, John Redmond, ruling the bulk of his party with

[1] P. 404.
[2] The late Sir Maurice Bonham Carter, who in due course married Asquith's daughter, Violet.

an eagle eye and a rod of iron. . . . Fierce-faced William O'Brien led a little group, independent of the Redmondites, and a veritable thorn in their sides.'[1] It often required all Bonham Carter's tact and ability to keep the Redmondites and the O'Brienites in line behind his chief's administration.

To pass from the leaders to the led. Of the Conservative Party record during the Edwardian era the less said the better. In a long-forgotten book entitled *Tory Democracy* the late Lord Henry Bentinck had some interesting observations to make on the subject. After pointing out that 'the people gave its confidence (with a three years' break) from 1886 to 1900 with a remarkable constancy to the Tory party, because the party gave sufficient evidence of its honesty in the cause of the commonweal'.

It was not until the death of Lord Salisbury that its popularity began to wane. Under his successor its policy suffered a change. It gradually lost its national character, and fell under the influence of sectional interests. The confidence of the working man was alienated, and turned into suspicion, first of the influence of the Church in education, then of the South African and afterwards of the British capitalist. The Tory party lost the confidence of the people on the day when it laid itself open to the suspicion that it was engaged in a capitalist conspiracy, and it will not regain it until it clears itself of that suspicion. And that is the beginning and end of the matter.

It would be kinder, perhaps, to draw a veil over the party's career from 1906 to the outbreak of the War;[2] but this much must be said, that it alternated from stupidity to factiousness, and from factiousness to stupidity. Whether Mr Lloyd George's Budget was rejected from pure panic, or in the interests of Tariff Reform, is now of no importance, and whether it was wise to hand the party over bound hand and foot to the goodwill and pleasure of Sir Edward Carson, need not now be argued; but this much is clear, that there was nothing either Tory or democratic in a policy which for party purposes strained the Constitution, and for the sake of a faction disputed the sovereignty of the Imperial Parliament, and threatened the very existence of democracy itself.

[1] Murray, Lieut-Col. the Hon. Arthur: *Master and Brother*, pp. 23–24.
[2] *I.e.* the First World War.

> There seem to be occasions in the history of the Conserva-
> tive Party when, as Disraeli remarked, its leaders preserve the
> institutions of the country as they do their pheasants, merely in
> order to destroy them.

These are hard words, but they contain a great deal of truth; it
is, however, necessary to go back a little further than did Lord
Henry to get at the root of the trouble as it manifested itself during
the Edwardian era.

During the closing decades of the nineteenth century the Liberal
Party under the influence of Gladstone, himself in origin a Tory
of the Canning school, began to shake itself free of Whig control,
and the Whig magnates thereupon began to secede to the Conservatives. Unhappily for the domestic peace of the British Isles, this
development coincided with one of the recurring crises in Irish
affairs, and as the aforesaid Whig magnates were acred up to the
eyes with Irish land they swung their new-found Conservative
friends into opposition to Irish national aspirations. The negotiations between Lord Carnarvon and Parnell during the first Salisbury administration show what might have happened had wiser
counsels prevailed.[1] It is, indeed, difficult to resist the conclusion
that some agreed form of self-government should have been
given to Ireland by the Tories in the eighties of last century.
Joseph Chamberlain may have been sincere in his opposition to
Home Rule, but that was not the case with the Whigs; they were
thinking in terms of the estates with which William of Orange had
rewarded their ancestors two hundred years earlier.

Lord Henry Bentinck was right in his belief that the Whig
influence, which was definitely sectional, did not begin to be
dominant until after Lord Salisbury's death, though even before
that it had been sufficiently strong to embitter permanently the
relations between England and Ireland. Thereafter it was disastrous, and the Conservative Party became increasingly Whiggish
in its approach to every problem that presented itself, with the not
unnatural result that it lost three General Elections in succession.

As for Ireland, her representatives in the House of Commons,

---

[1] *Cf.* Young, Kenneth: *Arthur James Balfour*, pp. 93–94.

as the price of Home Rule which they never got until it was too late, were compelled to stultify themselves by voting for Liberal measures in which they did not really believe, until their long-suffering constituents turned to Sinn Fein in despair. Indeed, it would be impossible to exaggerate the evils on both sides of the Irish Sea which have arisen because the heirs of the Cavaliers adopted the policy of the Roundheads. It would, however, be wrong to hold the Conservative Party wholly responsible for the Anglo-Irish estrangement of modern times, for the Crown must bear its share of the blame. Had Queen Victoria paid as much attention to Ireland as she paid to Scotland – above all, had she created another Balmoral there – some, at any rate, of the troubles of the last hundred years might have been avoided: as it was, during her whole reign she spent less than five weeks in Ireland, while her visits to Scotland covered nearly seven years. Her son endeavoured to make amends, but his reign was so short, and the situation had so badly deteriorated, that there was little he could do.

The England of 1901 was an aristocratic community, and this fact was reflected in the attitude of both the Conservative and Liberal Parties. There was, in effect, a governing class divided into two parties, and for this there had not yet been substituted two party machines each with its own class basis, as was to be the case later in the century. This governing class unfortunately reproduced all the worst characteristics of high French society before the Revolution, for it believed that it could quite easily have the best of both worlds; that it could draw all the practical advantages which come from settled habit and custom, such as an extreme reverence for the law of property; and that it could at the same time feel 'advanced', being firm in the conviction that the challenges to all conventional morality could be trusted to remain inside the covers of the appropriate books. It was a governing class which too readily spared itself effort. Most of its members were content to be morally and intellectually passengers, and many of them disloyal passengers at that, while clear to read was the text from their already neglected Old Testament, 'Yet a little sleep, a little slumber, a little folding of the hands to sleep: so shall thy poverty come as one that travelleth, and thy want as an armed man.'

The first sign that the old order was coming to an end was the Conservative *débâcle* at the General Election of 1906, and, curiously enough, one of the few people who realized what was impending was Balfour, for as early as January 17th of that year he wrote to Austen Chamberlain:

> I have been much preoccupied since Saturday's declaration about your seat and others in the Birmingham district, for it is quite obvious – at least so it seems to me – that we are dealing with forces not called into being by any of the subjects about which Parties have been recently squabbling, but rather due to a general movement of which we see the more violent manifestations in Continental politics; and I cannot help fearing, therefore, that the new Labour issue may carry away seats in the Midlands which, under other circumstances, would have been practically safe. But I trust I am wholly wrong.
>
> I am profoundly interested in this new development, which will end, I think, in the break-up of the Liberal Party, and, perhaps, in other things even more important.[1]

In some instances it was those physically or mentally most remote from what was taking place who seem to have been possessed of the greatest vision, for Sir Wilfrid Laurier, then Prime Minister of Canada, wrote to Professor Hewins, 'The recent elections have undoubtedly opened a new era in the history of England. The England of the past may survive partially yet for a few years, but it is a democratic England which now takes its place. The Labour element will count henceforth as a very important factor, and it is difficult to foresee exactly to what extent, but certainly to a very large extent, it will control legislation.'[2] If this statement was in some respects to prove an exaggeration, subsequent events have shown that there was much truth in it, and although the turning-points in the lives of nations are not so clearly defined as some authorities would have us believe, it is difficult to resist the con-

---

[1] Petrie, Sir Charles: *Life and Letters of the Right Hon. Sir Austen Chamberlain*, vol. I, p. 176.

[2] Hewins, W. A. S.: *The Apologia of an Imperialist*, vol. I, p. 159.

clusion that the year 1906 represents a very definite landmark in the annals of Great Britain. It was then that the nineteenth century really ended, though its ghost was to walk until 1914; social and economic rather than political problems became the more important; while abroad the *status quo*, which had existed relatively intact for nearly two generations, began to give evidence of its approaching collapse. The writing was on the wall, even if it was noticed by comparatively few.

The dust raised during these years by the combatants in the political arena was so considerable that it was by no means easy to see what was going on. Apart altogether from the Conservative attitude towards Ireland, both parties were to some extent untrue to their traditions, while loudly proclaiming their devotion to them. The Liberals, driven to the Left by the loss of the Whigs in 1886, increasingly sponsored Socialistic measures which would have horrified their former leaders, though fate had willed it that this policy should ultimately benefit not them, but the nascent Labour Party. The Conservatives, on the other hand, seemed to have lost the impetus which they had received by the accession of Joseph Chamberlain and his Liberal Unionists, and also to have forgotten what Disraeli had taught them in the matter of social reform. It was, in effect, an era of many political paradoxes, not the least of which was the fact that while it culminated in a catastrophe, that catastrophe was not the one which had been generally anticipated. English eyes were for the most part turned to the West, in the direction of Ireland, rather than to the East, in the summer of 1914.

In the picture as painted by Balfour and Laurier the Liberals had no very definite place, for as they became more markedly democratic the City and the financial interests which had previously supported them tended to find a new political home in the now urbanized and commercial Conservative Party. It was at this time, almost in the hour of triumph after the General Election of 1906, that the Liberal Party began to show signs of disruption and weakness. Their predominantly middle-class support was one cause of their failure to recognize the rising economic claims of the workers, with the result that those Radicals who had formerly supported them, however reluctantly, were turning in the direction of the new Independent Labour Party. Nevertheless, the final breach was slow in coming, and as late as the last triumph of the Liberals, in 1906, their relations with Labour were comparatively friendly. For the fact that this friendship did not continue the blame has been placed upon Asquith:

> Had Sir Henry Campbell-Bannerman lived it is very possible that a concordat might have been achieved, but his successor, Asquith, was quite incapable of appreciating the change of outlook which was familiarizing the mass of the workers in Trade Unions with Socialist aspirations.[1]

At the same time it cannot be denied that the Liberal Government of 1906 effected a great deal. It gave South Africa self-government; it pleased the Trade Unions by emancipating them from the liabilities imposed by the Taff Vale decision; and it provoked a contest with the Lords over the land charges in the Budget of 1909. Old Age Pensions were first allowed out of State funds, workmen's compensation was extended, national health insurance and unemployment insurance were introduced, and trade boards were set up to fix minimum wages in sweated industries. Finally, after the prolonged dispute with the Lords and two General Elections in 1910, the Parliament Act restricted the veto of the Peers and altogether abolished their right to interfere in financial legislation.

To pass to the appearance of Labour upon the political scene, where its activities were in due course to be as revolutionary as those of the internal combustion engine in another sphere. The British Labour Party did not take its present name until 1906, when it first appeared as a substantial party in the House of Commons, having won thirty seats. It had been founded six years earlier, as the Labour Representation Committee, and it was the direct descendant of Keir Hardie's Independent Labour Party which had come into existence in 1893. The I.L.P., out of which the Labour Party grew, was the immediate outcome of the spread of the New Unionism, ushered in by the great London strikes of

[1] The Right Hon. Sir Henry Slesser in *The British Party System*, p. 82.

gas-workers and dockers in 1889. The New Unionism brought large numbers of less-skilled workers into the Trade Union movement and led to big changes in Trade Union policy; while the Reform Acts of 1884 and 1885 were also favourable to the growth of the working-class movement because they extended the franchise to many of the less-skilled. These workers, and the new leaders who represented them, wanted improved conditions and greater security: the slogans of the new Unionists and of the I.L.P. were the legal eight hours day, the legal minimum wage, and the Right to Work. The I.L.P. further gave its allegiance to Socialism, which had previously been represented in Great Britain by the Marxist Social Democratic Federation, but the new Socialism for which it stood was evolutionary and undogmatic, and its immediate concern was social reform. Its leaders were much influenced by the Fabian Society: *Fabian Essays* had been published under Bernard Shaw's editorship as long ago as 1889, and Sidney Webb and his associates were busily engaged in producing tracts full of information about the distribution of wealth.

Under Keir Hardie's guidance the I.L.P. set out to persuade the Trade Unions to support independent working-class political action, but this was by no means the innovation that might be supposed, for the miners had been acting in this way ever since the Reform Act of 1867 had enfranchised a section of the workers in the towns. What was new was that whereas in the past the Trade Unionists who were returned to the House of Commons had attached themselves to the Liberals, they were now urged to cease this practice: seven years of intensive propaganda partly achieved its purpose, and the Labour Representation Committee was born.

At first its growth was slow, but the Taff Vale Judgment of 1901, which in effect made strikes almost impossible by threatening the Unions with actions for damages caused by them to employers, brought many more Unions in, and greatly increased the political keenness of all. Somewhat paradoxically Labour joined with the Liberals in opposition to Tariff Reform, and it won nearly all its thirty seats in 1906 with Liberal support. It was able to secure the passage of the Trade Dispute Act of 1906, and it also succeeded in putting on the statute book the first Act authorizing the feeding of children at school. On the other hand it received a severe blow by the Osborne Judgment of 1909 which declared all political action by Trade Unions to be unlawful, and thus knocked away the financial foundations of the Labour Party. In these circumstances it was forced on the defensive in the two General Elections of 1910, and all it was able to do was to defend the seats it already held, and contest a very few others. It just about held its own, and its apparently increased strength was due to the fact that the Miners' Federation, whose representatives in the House of Commons had sat as Liberals up to 1909, had joined it in that year.

Few would now deny that the Labour Party came into being to deal with abuses which should never have been allowed to arise, though it is not everyone who will agree with Lord Henry Bentinck in his assertion that Charles I 'should have been a member of a Labour government'. That many of the abuses were the direct result of the unhappy events of 1688 will now hardly be denied, and when power passed into the hands of the middle classes after 1832 they showed themselves in the main to be as indifferent to the sufferings of the poor as the Whig oligarchs had been in the previous century. In fine, there were no 'jobs for the boys' in Socialist circles in the Edwardian era, but there was much genuine idealism about the Independent Labour Party and the Fabian Society, while there was precious little about a Conservatism dominated by Big Business and Whig Irish landlords, or a Liberalism in the grip of the men of the Marconi scandal.

CHAPTER II

London Life

THERE can be little doubt that for the well-to-do, and for no inconsiderable part of the middle class, the acme of material comfort and well-being was achieved during the reign of King Edward VII. The opening years of the present century specially favoured the *rentier* and the successful professional and business man; a moderate fortune could be accumulated without undue effort, and Income Tax was assessed at little more than a shilling in the pound. Travel was cheap and easy, and house rents were on a reasonable scale. Nor was this all, for overseas investments were between two and three thousand million pounds, and they brought into Great Britain an unearned increment of several hundred million sterling a year.

London was still in the main the London of the Victorian era, and the central scene of a now vanished age. Piccadilly remained a line of dignified mansions and clubs from Gloucester House at the corner of Park Lane to Devonshire House at the corner of Berkeley Street. At the beginning of the reign motor-cars were rarely seen, hansom cabs and open or closed carriages being still the recognized means of transport, the coachmen in top-boots and the footmen in livery, with a long coat in winter.

Ladies riding in Rotten Row used side-saddles, though their habits no longer came below their ankles, and they were usually followed by a mounted groom. Numbers of people rode there every morning between nine o'clock and one, while in the summer particularly after church on Sunday, under the trees along the Ladies' Mile or on the grass opposite Stanhope Gate, much of London fashion was to be met. There were tan riding-tracks along

Constitution Hill and Birdcage Walk, by which a few Members of Parliament still rode down to Westminster, and as late as the First World War at least one judge arrived at the Law Courts on horseback each morning. Unmarried girls in society seldom walked out without a maid, and were always taken to dances by chaperons. Ladies wore long skirts brushing the ground, tightly laced corsets, and, in the evening, eighteen-button gloves reaching to their armpits, and carried fans. Top-hats and frock-coats, particularly when the Court was in residence, were the ordinary dress of gentlemen of leisure, of whom there were plenty on four or five hundred pounds a year, who spent much of their time shooting, hunting, and fishing on their richer friends' estates, or lunching and dining with them in London.

The great mansions such as Devonshire, Lansdowne, Montagu, Grosvenor, Dorchester, Stafford, and Spencer Houses, all now destroyed or turned into clubs or public offices, were inhabited by their owners. It is true that there were a few millionaires from the United States and South Africa, but although there was plenty of comfort and some luxury, there was little ostentation. The majority of people probably lived within their incomes, even if they did not save as much as in Victorian times, for in spite of the South African War and Sir William Harcourt's death duties, the Income Tax, as we have seen, remained round about the moderate figure of from 6d. to 1s. in the pound, while super- or surtax was unknown. A house in St James's Place could be rented for two hundred pounds a year, and a staff to run it – cook, parlourmaid, and housemaid – cost sixty-four. In effect, for very many people life was a pleasant and easy round, and even the small *rentier* could live at his ease.[1]

This scene was reflected in the world of the stage which mirrored the national life in a way that it had not done since the Restoration. An evening at a West End theatre was a social event. Patrons of the pit and gallery did not put on evening dress, but they looked for this courtesy from the stalls and dress circle: even the lighter entertainments called for a stiff collar, white waistcoat, and tails. The proprietors of Daly's, the Gaiety, the

[1] *Cf.* Mersey, Viscount: *A Picture of Life, 1872-1940*, pp. 183-184.

Prince of Wales's, the Adelphi, and the Lyric, where most of the musical comedies were staged, frowned upon the free-and-easy manners of the variety houses. 'No Smoking in the Auditorium' was an accepted rule and characterized the West End theatre as opposed to the West End music-hall. Sir Arthur Pinero, indeed, went so far as to attribute the decline of Edwardian musical comedy, and the rise of go-as-you-please revue, to female influence, the argument being that once it became clear that women did not object to tobacco their male friends tended to take tickets for revue where a cigarette or a pipe was permissible, rather than for an entertainment where the 'No Smoking' rule persisted.

It was the age of the actor-manager, and he was by no means always drawn from the ranks of such master-showmen as Tree and Alexander, for a few hundred pounds saved out of salaries, supplemented by cash advances from non-professional admirers, sufficed to launch many a player into management, and not a little theatrical history was determined by the fact.

Among the great names was that of Charles Hawtrey. It is not easy to describe his appeal to a generation that has never seen him act, but perhaps the secret of it was that he could gauge to a nicety how to time a phrase, and the moments during which a chuckle could profitably be prolonged; there was also the charm of his husky voice and the assumption of an almost childlike innocence. Hawtrey's early career had been varied. 'It would be an exaggeration to say Charles was educated at Eton. What we do know is that at fourteen he was making a book on the Derby, and cleared £2. 10. 0., thanks to a hunch that the outsider, Doncaster, would win.'[1] It won at 45 to 1, but Eton soon had had enough of Hawtrey, and he passed on to Rugby, whence he went on the stage. He began to make his name in the eighties, but his luck really came when he purchased all rights in *The Private Secretary* and put it on at the Globe: he made about £100,000 out of the play, but lost it all on the turf. Others of his successes were *A Message from Mars* and, later, *Ambrose Applejohn's Adventures*. For a time he had Miss Compton, aunt of Fay Compton and Sir Compton Mackenzie, as his leading lady, and in *Robin Goodfellow*

[1] Short, Ernest: *Sixty Years of Theatre*, p. 185.

in particular she had some wonderful lines: at one point in that play she reached home after a rough Channel crossing and heralded her arrival with the words, 'Is lunch ready? I'm dreadfully hungry. I never eat anything crossing the Channel. Quite the reverse.'

Then there was Cyril Maude, who spanned several theatrical generations, for he was born in 1862 and lived until 1951. He entered into management at the Haymarket in 1896, in association with Frederick Harrison, and he was there for ten years. Maude, both off and on the stage, was one of the most charming men possible, being excellent company, and he was always prepared to place his vast experience of the stage at the disposal of the young. He possessed a very great asset in his wife, Winifred Emery, who was the ideal leading lady. The revivals of old English comedies, with her in the costume parts she knew so well how to play gracefully, can justly be described as historic, while her husband as old Hardcastle, Bob Acres, and Sir Peter Teazle was in the great tradition. In 1906 the Maudes moved to the Playhouse, where they remained until the outbreak of the First World War.

Irving was a Victorian rather than an Edwardian, and he died in 1905: he was, it must be admitted, a most unattractive character in private life whatever his merits as an actor. His wife, from whom he was separated, whenever possible occupied the stage-box in order to embarrass him, and the first thing he did on entering the theatre was to pull the curtain aside to see if she was in the house. In the end he gave instructions that she was not to be allowed into the theatre, and in this instance at any rate the sympathies of all who had ever met Lady Irving were with her husband.

As for Gerald du Maurier, he was in a class by himself: his outstanding characteristic was his uncanny sense of what an audience would find effective in a theatre, and this not only as an actor but also as a producer. Yet no one has started a stage career with fewer manifest gifts, for he had none of the good looks of the traditional juvenile 'lead' and he had no special vocal powers, but, as the late Ernest Short well put it, 'his only obvious asset was that he knew how a gentleman should behave in a club or a drawing-room'. He described himself as a dinner-jacket comedian. No small part of du Maurier's success as an actor was due to the fact that he could always put an audience at its ease, and this gift is as rare on the stage as it is in the lecture-hall or upon the political platform: in effect, the principle which underlay all his stage work may be summed up in the words 'Don't force it', and this fitted the sentiment of Barrie's plays most happily, for it would have been so easy to topple them over into sentimentality by over-acting.

The series of Barrie rôles was only part of the debt which the Edwardian theatre owed to Gerald du Maurier, for when he appeared as Raffles in 1906 he gave London its first crook play. The pace of the production startled the audiences first into attention and then into admiration. Du Maurier's acting seemed casual, yet it created a sense of tension which was in the highest degree exciting, and he worked up to an emotional climax, in itself the more thrilling because the method was then unfamiliar to playgoers. *Raffles* ran for a year and was followed by *Brewster's Millions*, which had 321 performances in its opening run; the example set in London proved infectious in the provinces, and there was a time when touring companies to play it could not be organized quickly enough. The plot was concerned with a harassed legatee, who was left a large fortune by one uncle on condition that within six months he spent a smaller fortune left by another: frantically du Maurier spent his money, but with equal momentum it poured in. So successful was his stage career that in 1910, at the age of twenty-eight, he was able to join forces with Frank Curzon at Wyndham's on a contract which gave him a salary of £3,000 a year and 25 per cent of any profits.

In the theatre, as in so much else, the Edwardian age was one of transition. Just as the journalist after the turn of the century exploited the public interest in topics which aroused debate, so dramatists awoke to the fact that the same technique could be successfully applied to the stage. Among a section of the theatre-going world a reaction set in against the drawing-room plays of Pinero, Jones, and Wilde, and of this move in the direction of 'plays with a purpose' the protagonist was Bernard Shaw. Of course there was nothing really new about all this, for when Shaw wrote *Heartbreak House* he was only using a genre with which

Aeschylus and Euripides were familiar: in Elizabethan drama Thomas Dekker's *The Honest Whore* was a study of fallen women akin to *Mrs Warren's Profession*, and reflected a similar tolerance.

What was new in these British plays of ideas was that ideas of any sort had been markedly absent from the British stage during the greater part of the nineteenth century. The emphasis had been laid rather on the entertainment value, and the talent of the dramatist was considered secondary to that of the actor or actress: even in the palmy days of Pinero and Jones the primary aim of the man of the theatre was entertainment, and ideas were associated with some telling dramatic conflict. The writers of intellectual comedy, on the contrary, wanted people to think as well as to laugh. This point is very well illustrated in Shaw's *Major Barbara* when Andrew Undershaft is discussing with his wife and son the question of the boy's career.

LADY BRITOMART UNDERSHAFT (*uneasily*). What do you think he had better do, Andrew?

UNDERSHAFT. Oh, just what he wants to do. He know nothing; and he thinks he knows everything. That points clearly to a political career. Get him a private secretaryship to someone who can get him an Under Secretaryship; and then leave him alone. He will find his natural and proper place in the end on the Treasury bench.

Or again:

UNDERSHAFT. What does govern England, pray?

STEPHEN. Character, father, character.

UNDERSHAFT. Whose character? Yours or mine?

STEPHEN. Neither yours nor mine, father, but the best elements in the English national character.

UNDERSHAFT. Stephen, I've your profession for you. You're a born journalist. I'll start you with a high-toned weekly review. There!

The fourteen years before the First World War also saw the production of a number of plays which were based on studies of life in the North of England, and were associated with what is often called the Manchester School. They owed much to Miss Horniman, and noteworthy examples were produced at the Gaiety Theatre in Manchester whence they made their way to the West End of London. One of Miss Horniman's discoveries was Stanley Houghton, who was much under the influence of the contemporary Irish stage,[1] and he persuaded her to try out similar folk drama with a Lancashire setting.

Hindle Wakes was his first experiment of this nature. It was concerned with a young mill-hand, Fanny Hawthorn, who spent an illicit weekend with a mill-owner's son, and found herself pregnant as a result. The Puritan mill-owner threatened to cut his son off with the proverbial shilling unless he made 'an honest woman' of the girl by marrying her, but Fanny had other ideas.

ALAN. Then you didn't ever really love me?

FANNY. Love you? Good heavens, of course not. Why on earth should I love you? You were just someone to have a bit of fun with.

ALAN (*shocked*). Fanny! Is that all you cared for me?

FANNY. How much more did you care for me?

ALAN. But it's not the same. I'm a man.

FANNY. You're a man, and I was your little fancy. Well, I'm a woman, and you were my little fancy.

ALAN. But do you mean that you didn't care any more for me than a fellow cares for any girl he happens to pick up?

FANNY. Yes. Are you shocked?

ALAN. It's a bit thick. It is really.

Galsworthy treated a similar subject in *The Eldest Son*, though with deeper insight and richer irony. The historical importance of such plays lies in the fact that however trite their themes today, in the opening years of the century they came as a complete surprise to the average English audience.

In quite a different sphere the Edwardian era witnessed the rise of the immortal George Robey. He had the advantage for a West End audience of having been born a Cockney, although the greater part of his boyhood had been spent in Birmingham. His father was a civil engineer, and for a time Robey had been an under-

[1] *Cf. infra*, pp. 166–168.

graduate at Jesus College, Cambridge, but some skill as a mando-
lin player led to concert engagements even in those early days, and
by 1891 he had appeared on the stage of the London Aquarium
in the rôle of assistant to a spook mesmerist. Robey's job was to
accept hypnotization and not raise any objection when pins and
needles were driven into him: having been mesmerized he sang
a Gaiety song, 'A little peach in an orchard grew', and thus learnt
to face an audience. The manager of the Oxford Music Hall in
Tottenham Court Road chanced to hear Robey and gave him the
chance of an extra turn at a matinée: Robey took it, dressed as a
curate, and sang 'You can tell her by the pimple, simple pimple
on her nose'.

A twelve months' contract followed and thereafter success soon
came, but it was hard work: he might have a brougham of his
own, with a dresser as well as the coachman on the box, but he
had to do four houses a night. The first turn would be at the
Metropolitan in Edgware Road, then one at Collins's at Islington,
by 10.30 he would be at the Oxford, and as the clock struck 11.0
he would put in an appearance at the Palladium. With the passage
of the years there came an assurance which those who have seen
Robey in his great days are never likely to forget: a lift of the
hand, the single word 'Desist', and he could silence even the men
and women in the huge promenade which surrounded the whole
ground-floor at the Oxford, after which he would make his song
and patter plain to the last boy or girl at the back of the gallery.
Unforgettable, too, was the lift of the Robey eyebrows, with an
expression of pained surprise, and the words 'I mean-ter-say!'

Famous as he was during the Edwardian era, the height of
Robey's career was surely reached in the First World War, when
he made the transition from Variety to Revue. The production of
The Bing Boys in April, 1916, was one of the great events in British
theatrical history, and Robey showed of what he was capable when
he sang with Violet Loraine that duet which will ever echo in the
ears of all who heard it:

> If I were the only girl in the world
> And you were the only boy,
> Nothing else would matter in the world today,

We could go on loving in the same old way.
  A Garden of Eden just made for two,
    With nothing to mar our joy;
I would say such wonderful things to you,
There would be such wonderful things to do,
If I were the only girl in the world
And you were the only boy.

Any account of the Edwardian stage, however brief, must contain some mention of George Edwardes, who was, in one capacity or another, one of its outstanding figures. An Irishman, he had originally been intended for the Army, but while he was still at his crammers a Dublin manager, Michael Gunn, who had business connections with D'Oyly Carte, asked George to superintend a company touring in *The Lady of Lyons*, and from that to the Savoy itself proved but a short step. He was a fabulous figure, and this greatly added to his reputation. In appearance he was a tall, big-built, good-looking Irishman, with a pair of markedly straight eyebrows over two very blue eyes. Horse-racing, chess, and poker were his hobbies, and from time to time success on the turf would save a tottering theatrical venture, while it was no unusual thing for him to win or lose £500 at poker in a single night. His general knowledge was of the scantiest, and when it was suggested to him that the hoax of the cobbler Koepenick would form excellent material for a comic-opera plot George would have none of it, saying, 'I think this fellow, Kubelik, has had advertisement enough.' Nor was this all, for he had little ear for music and very little insight into the problems of libretto-writing. On the other hand, in his methods of management anything less like the autocratic rule of W. S. Gilbert cannot be imagined. It is recorded that on one famous occasion George cabled to the United States for a leading lady, and then forgot all about her until she presented her card at Daly's with the intimation that she was ready to perform. Edwardes was in no way abashed, and remarked, 'It will be all right on the night, my dear'; and so it was. His tame authors and musicians were mobilized to provide whatever was necessary, and Marie Tempest, the actress in question, duly made her entrance.

The real contribution that George Edwardes made to the English theatre was his early realization of the fact that the days of burlesque were numbered. The well of possible puns was running dry, and the store of potential themes capable of furnishing burlesque material was diminishing. George was under no illusions that if musical shows were not only to continue, but also to attract the women who were becoming an increasingly important element in the audience, a new technique was required. This proved to be the musical comedy, which was characteristic of what Herbert Farjeon summed up as 'spanking days', when

> Hats were hats of startling size,
> And waists were waists and thighs were thighs!

So much for the theatre, which represented an important aspect of London life in Edwardian days: the West End clubs also constituted an influential factor which the social historian of the period cannot afford to ignore. One would have imagined that the class from which they drew their membership has never been so affluent as at that time, but its fortunes seem to have been subject to more vicissitudes than is generally supposed. If the Carlton be taken as typical, it would seem that the number of bankruptcies was extraordinarily high by modern standards. A typical year was 1895 when six members, of whom half were peers, were compelled to resign for that reason, and figures remained fairly constant during the last decade of the nineteenth century. For lack of data, it is impossible to compare these figures with those of any earlier period, but they seem high for an era of such prosperity as the country had never previously known; and they would seem to show that not everybody, even in the upper classes, in that so-called age of privilege, found life easy. For some equally inexplicable reason, the number of bankruptcies would seem to have dropped during King Edward's reign. It may be added that the custom seems to have been to reinstate a bankrupt member once he had obtained his discharge, though a good deal naturally depended upon the individual in question.

The West End clubs appear to have changed but little during the first decade of the present century, though they were probably more select, and their members were certainly better behaved, than had been the case in an earlier age. They were also used by those who belonged to them primarily as meeting-places, not as eating-places – particularly at lunchtime – as has now become the custom: members came to them to discuss the problems of the day. The normal member was either in the country or in London: if he was out of London he did not use the club; if he was in London he probably spent a large portion of his time there. Nor were wives yet serious competitors for the clubman's leisure hours. The Edwardian male would go down to his club for a few hours to idle away the time while his wife remained at home engaged either in looking after the children and servants, or in sewing a fine seam.

The great controversy of the era in Pall Mall and St James's Street centred round smoking – if it was to be permitted and in what rooms. These years also witnessed a considerable development of women's clubs, though several of the older ones had already been in existence for some time. As a rule, the prices in women's clubs tended to be higher than in their male equivalents, and in 1907 Major Arthur Griffiths wrote, 'Breakfast for eighteen-pence will compare favourably perhaps, but the set charges for luncheon at two shillings or half-a-crown may seem expensive to economical men, content with a cut off a cold joint for eight-pence; but ladies possibly require more at this essentially feminine meal. Good living is not by any means despised or unattainable in ladies' clubs, and their cellars are said to be as well supplied and as largely patronized as those of any clubs in London.'[1] The Empress asked fifteen guineas by way of annual subscription, which was the same as the Carlton.

The same author is also responsible for the surely apocryphal story of the man who called at a women's club and asked for a certain member: she was duly 'paged', but without success, and the visitor was about to go sorrowfully away when a very attractive damsel came up to him and said, 'You want Mrs So-and-So, do you? She is not here, I know. Won't I do as well?'[2]

One new club that came into existence in these years was the

---

[1] *Clubs and Clubmen*, pp. 155–156.
[2] *Ibid.*, p. 155.

1900. From the beginning it was a typically English institution, for its name gave no clue to its constitution or its activities: it was not founded in 1900, and it has never had 1,900 members. In fact its origin dates from 1905, when a number of Conservative Members of the 1900 Parliament who were not standing again at the impending General Election, but were desirous of preserving the ties of friendship formed with many of their fellow Members, resolved to form a club and meet and dine together periodically. Soon, however, its scope was enlarged to include Conservative candidates and 'such other persons as the Committee think suitable by reason of their services to the Conservative cause'.

From the beginning the outstanding characteristics of the 1900 Club were informality and independence. The club had premises of its own in Pickering Place, just off St James's Street, and on various evenings of the week Conservative Front Benchers would attend there to exchange views with the members. The secretary was Thomas Comyn-Platt, to whom the successful inception of the club was largely due. In the Tariff Reform and Free Trade controversy, as well as in the dissensions leading up to Balfour's resignation of the Conservative leadership in 1911, the 1900 Club played a prominent part, and the majority of its members were critical of the party machine, which, in consequence, viewed it with no friendly eye.

Its meetings were highly confidential, and verbosity was sternly discouraged: it was said that the ideal member was he who remembered Sir William Harcourt's advice to a young speaker, namely to think of his first sentence and his last, and to bring the two as close together as possible. Nevertheless this happy state of affairs was not always reached, and there is a legend to the effect that a speaker was holding forth at inordinate length on one occasion when Balfour was present. A member left the room during the discourse, and returned some ten minutes later. 'Hasn't he finished yet?' he inquired of Balfour. 'Oh yes,' came the reply, 'some time ago, but he hasn't sat down.' Another story of Balfour at the 1900 Club is that he asked some new and pompous M.P. how he liked the House of Commons, and then went on, 'My dear fellow, there is no reason whatever to be frightened. In that placȩ all you have to do is to speak as long as you like and as often as you like. You will rapidly acquire that contempt for your audience which every bore always has.'

In the spring of 1907 the 1900 Club made history by giving a dinner at the Albert Hall to the Colonial Premiers, and some idea of its scope can be gathered from the fact that among the refreshments for the sixteen hundred diners there were ordered:

Beef for soup (lbs)	4,500	Champagne, bottles	1,400
Whole salmon	200	Hock, bottles	1,500
Quails	2,500	Liqueur brandy, bottles	300
Asparagus (sticks)	25,000	Chartreuse, bottles	300
Fresh strawberries (lbs)	600	Crême de menthe, bottles	500
	Whisky, bottles 300		

There were five hundred cooks and waiters, and the total cost was four thousand pounds.

This meal was exceptional, and was one of the largest dinners ever held in London up to that time, but it was an era of heavy eating. For instance, when the Lord Mayor of Liverpool[1] in 1902 gave a dinner in honour of Lord Rosebery the menu was:

Caviar   *Anchois*

Tortue Claire

Saumon, Sauce Médoc   *Filet de Sole à l' Adelphi*

Poulet, Reine Demidoff   *Asperge en Branches au Beurre*

Quartier d' Agneau

Filet de Boeuf Hollandaise

Granit au Kümmel

Canard Sauvage   *Bécasses*   *Russian Salad*

Pouding Impérial   *Macedoine au Fruits*   *Méringue au Creme*

Pouding Glacé à la Chantilly

Dessert

[1] The late Sir Charles Petrie.

Private dinner parties of eighteen or twenty people were the rule rather than the exception, and the small dinner was unknown. Tablecloths had not yet been discarded, and luxurious table decorations, in which smilax played a conspicuous part, were still in vogue. Men wore black waistcoats with their tail-coats unless they were going to a dance, on which occasion gloves also were indispensable. The dinner-jacket was as yet rare, and was somewhat contemptuously referred to as a 'bum-freezer'. The older men never took kindly to them, and Tommy Case, the President of Corpus Christi College, Oxford, of whom more anon, replied to an undergraduate who asked him to come in a dinner-jacket to a reception at which women, including the wife of the Warden of Wadham, were to be present, 'Sir, I have never exposed that portion of my anatomy to any lady save Mrs Case, and I do not propose to make an exception in favour of the wife of the Warden of Wadham. I will come in a tail-coat.'

King Edward VII had been on the throne for some years before there was any general relaxation of the customs which had obtained during the later decades of his mother's reign, and when change came it began in the highest ranks of society – the customs of the middle classes were hardly affected when the First World War broke out. Social relationships were subject to a rigid code of etiquette. All women who had any social pretensions had 'At Home' days to which they strictly adhered. When a man paid a call he took his hat, stick, and gloves into the drawing-room, for to do otherwise was for him to lay himself open to the charge of behaving as if he were at a hotel. Attendance at a dinner or a dance necessitated a formal call soon afterwards. Informality of any sort was frowned on – behaviour was either correct or it was not, and it is difficult to resist the conclusion that there are many advantages in having a definite code in such matters.

To return, however, to the West End clubs. The later Victorian period had in very truth been their golden age in more senses than one, but if the Carlton is any guide it would appear that there was a slight falling-off during the opening years of the present century – perhaps the influence of the motor-car was already beginning to make itself felt. However this may be, at the last meeting of the committee in the Queen's reign it was reported that the balance at the bank amounted to £21,488 8s 9d, and there were eighty servants whose weekly board was 12s 6d each. During the previous week 156 dinners and 274 luncheons had been served, though in considering this figure it must be remembered that the month was January, when a good many members would not be in London; in a normal summer week about 200 dinners and 400 luncheons were the average. Furthermore, the number of those wishing to join the club showed no sign of diminution. Candidates who were elected at the turn of the century had been on the waiting-list for seventeen or eighteen years, and it was accepted by the committee that men who put their names down in 1901 might have to wait twenty or thirty years.

Without going into details it would appear that the membership position was not so good at the end of the King's reign as it had been at the beginning, so even if the First World War had not taken place it might in due course have become difficult. On the other hand, the balance at the bank was almost the same, there were only two more servants, and the cost of their weekly board was unchanged; what, however, does seem to have changed was the taste of the members, for a memorandum of the Wine Committee, dated March 6th, 1913, states that 'the consumption of Vintage Ports has of late been steadily increasing'.[1]

It used to be said in those days that no one who had attained middle age was sure of election at any club, and to illustrate this the story was told of a man who had been blackballed for one of the more famous. He was walking dejectedly down St James's Street, feeling that the world held no future for him, when he met a friend to whom he related his sad story. 'I don't see what you have to worry about,' said the friend, 'hundreds of men get elected to clubs every year because nobody knows anything about them; so cheer up, old man, for clearly somebody knew something about you.'

It has been affirmed that the history of the West End clubs is the history of London manners since the Restoration, and many a habit which had fallen into desuetude elsewhere still survived in

---

[1] *Cf.* Petrie, Sir Charles: *The Carlton Club*, pp. 142 and 160–161.

them during the Edwardian period. It was, for instance, not un-known for members to be seen sitting about club-houses in their hats, though the twenty-sixth Earl of Crawford, who died in 1913, is said to have been one of the last clubmen to have a meal in a coffee-room in a top-hat. The influence of the Public Schools was also to be noticed in the taboos which had been evolved, and newly elected members of some clubs were warned that they would be well advised not to sit in the window of the smoking-room until they had been elected for at least two years, and then only if they were wearing a silk hat. At the Carlton one row of tables along the wall was called Brook Street, 'because no one knew the people who lived there'.

However this may be, some very odd people were elected to clubs. A member one day walked into by no means the least famous of them, and although he had not been there for some time his arrival did not evoke any special comment beyond such casual remarks as, 'We haven't seen you lately.' In fact, the mem-ber in question had been in a mental home, from which he had just succeeded in escaping. He walked into the coffee-room, ordered his lunch in a normal way, and while he was waiting for it he called for a bowl of ice; when this was placed before him he proceeded to pile the pieces upon the convex top of his bald head, from which they kept on rolling down on to his own and neigh-bouring tables. Meanwhile he alternately glared and shouted at the servants, whom he frightened to such an extent that when he demanded a carving knife to eat his oysters he had to fetch it him-self as no one dared to approach him.

By this time the secretary had got in touch with Scotland Yard, but the police inspector who came in answer to the summons de-clared that he was unable to take any action as the member was in effect in his own house, since the club was to all intents and pur-poses his private residence. Upon this a hasty conference took place between the secretary and such members of the club commit-tee as were in the building, and as a result of their deliberations a couple of magistrates and two doctors who were in the club were besought to sign an order for removal to an asylum, but they hesitated to take the responsibility. In the meantime the lunatic was master of the situation; he now had the coffee-room to himself. and he ranged up and down it, brandishing the carving knife, while the terrified servants stared at him from what they hoped was a safe distance. The end was anticlimax, for the madman suddenly walked out into the street, where he at once fell into the clutches of a keeper who had come in search of him.

Another club possessed a tamer and more inoffensive lunatic whose craze was to walk perpetually up and down stairs. The moment he came in of a morning and had put away his hat and umbrella, he started for the top floor, ascending with a set, purposeful air, as though he had important business in the card-room, billiard-room, or upper smoking-room which he had completely forgotten when he arrived; then he would strike his forehead with the absent-minded despair of a short memory, turn on his heel, and quickly run down the stairs which he had just mounted. This procedure was continued almost interminably. In due course a lift was introduced into the club; this was at first a sore trial to the inveterate climber, who viewed it with profound distrust until, with increasing infirmity, he discovered its value, after which he became a positive nuisance to his fellow members by his excessive use of it.

Then there was – and unfortunately still is – the type of member who, when sober, could be a very charming fellow, but when he had drink in him became truculent and violent. One of this sort was a certain earl who had to resign from the Carlton for having struck a fellow member down with a chair in the hall, but he was also a member of the Thames Yacht Club, and one evening there after he had been drinking heavily he was descending the staircase when he encountered a new member in the process of ascending it. The second man made every endeavour to avoid his lordship, and the staircase was a broad one; but the peer was swaying from side to side to such an extent that this proved impossible, and a collision took place. On this his lordship enquired roughly whether the other man knew who he was. The reply came to the effect that the man who was ascending the stairs was a new member; that it was the first time he had been in the club since his election; and that he knew no one there except his proposer and seconder. 'Then you b——y well remember me the next time we meet,' bellowed the nobleman, and hit the second man under the jaw with such force that he went down the whole flight of stairs. The inevitable happened; his lordship had to resign from the Thames Yacht Club as he had done from the Carlton; and he died some years afterwards without a club at all.

Edwardian travel was still very much an upper and upper-middle-class affair: for the mass of the population holidays with pay was a matter of the future. An exception were domestic servants, who received a fortnight's holiday with salary, but after that were entitled to board wages if their employer did not require their immediate services. It was, incidentally, generally estimated that the keep of a horse and a domestic servant was about the same, namely a pound a week. In these circumstances Bank Holidays really meant something, and the seaside resorts were thronged on such occasions: absenteeism, in the modern sense, was rare, for there was a good deal of unemployment, and an employee who took time off would soon find himself out of work, which meant that he and his family would soon starve, a state of affairs which was also likely to be the sequel of a strike.

For those who could afford it the feature of the age was the 'cure'. No history has yet been written of the spa life of Europe, which had its origin in the reign of Louis XIV and to all intents and purposes died with the outbreak of the First World War. Its origins are obscure, but there can be little doubt that its demise was due to the ingenuity of the members of the medical profession who came to realize that it was much more profitable to put their patients on a diet at home under their immediate supervision rather than to send them abroad to some watering-place where they would have to split the fee with a foreign physician. The example was to no small extent set by the Sovereign, of whom the Duke of Windsor has written:

> King Edward would meanwhile repair to his favourite water-ing-place, Marienbad, in Bohemia, for his annual cure. There in the company of friends he would submit to a Spartan régime: drinking the waters, eating only boiled food, and walk-ing off the effects of a year's fine living. Much reduced in girth,

he would rejoin my grandmother at Balmoral, where, succumbing to the irresistible genius of his French chef, he would in about two weeks undo all the drastic and beneficial effects of the cure.[1]

The King regarded his trip to Marienbad as relaxation, and he resented any interference on the score of official business. One year, however, Sir Edward Grey urged upon him the advisability of a meeting with the German Emperor, who was very desirous of seeing him, and King Edward reluctantly agreed, only insisting that it should be as informal as possible. It took place at a wayside station in Bavaria, but when the British Royal train approached, the King, much to his annoyance, observed that not only were there what seemed to him to be an excessive number of troops present, but that his nephew was on the platform wearing the full-dress uniform of the Royals of which he was honorary colonel. As King Edward descended from his carriage his delighted suite heard the following exchange, 'Willie, you've got the wrong trousers on.' 'But, uncle, they're the ones grandma sent me.' 'Possibly, but we've changed the width of the stripe since then.' For the rest of the time that the two monarchs were together, so eye-witnesses have averred, the Kaiser was clearly discomposed, which may well have been the object of the original observation.[2]

These Royal visits to Marienbad were not without their lighter moments. One year the King went to see a play called *Die Hölle*,[3] which from the name he took to be a melodrama, and having nothing else to do he thought it would amuse him to go and see it. When he arrived, however, he discovered that it was a dull and rather vulgar music-hall performance, its name being due to the fact that the caste came from a low place of entertainment in Vienna of the name of Die Hölle. After the first act King Edward was so bored that he walked out, and in due course the British Press made great play with the incident; it was said that the King had gone to an improper performance, and had left in disgust

[1] *A King's Story*, p. 53.
[2] This story rests on the authority of the late (third) Lord O'Hagan, who was a Lord-in-Waiting to King Edward VII.
[3] 'The Underworld.'

to show his disapproval. Letters arrived from England thanking him for making so firm a stand in the cause of morality, among them one from the Bishop of Ripon, Dr William Boyd-Carpenter, in which he expressed the satisfaction of the whole Church at the Royal protest against an obscene musical comedy. When asked what reply should be sent, the King said, 'Tell the Bishop the exact truth. I have no wish to pose as a protector of morals, especially abroad.'

Another episode concerned Maud Allan. Among the King's friends at Marienbad was Mrs Hall Walker, and she introduced him to Maud Allan, at that time an unknown dancer who had not as yet appeared in London: the King not unnaturally expressed a wish to see her dance, but the prospect of this alarmed Ponsonby who was in attendance on him. 'I had been told', he writes, 'that she danced more or less naked, and I was afraid that the English Press might get hold of this and make up some wild story. I therefore went to Mrs Walker, and said that I had heard that Miss Maud Allan danced with only two oyster-shells and a five-franc piece, and questioned whether it was quite wise for the King to see her.' Mrs Hall Walker reassured him, and the performance duly took place. 'The dance was very exceptional,' Ponsonby continues, 'and I must say that Miss Maud Allan was really wonderful. Her dance as Salome with the head of John the Baptist was really most dramatic, and, although I cannot say she wore many clothes, there was nothing the least indecent about her performance.' The fact that she had danced before King Edward was later used as an argument with the London County Council to allow her to perform in the theatres under their jurisdiction.[1]

What purpose these 'cures' at Continental watering-places served so far as those who took them was concerned is a moot point. The régime, at least at Marienbad, was strict for those accustomed to the delights of upper-class life in the earlier years of the century. The first waters, and very nasty they were – the connoisseurs declared that those at Carlsbad were even more unpleasant – had to be taken at eight, the second at twelve, and the third at six: as the springs were a mile apart this ensured that every-

[1] *Recollections of Three Reigns*, p. 242.

one walked three miles a day, as any form of vehicular transport was frowned upon by the doctors. The morning was spent in undergoing various forms of treatment, mostly repulsive, in which the application of mud played no inconsiderable part. The afternoon was devoted to golf or driving, and by ten o'clock bed was very definitely indicated. The menu at all meals was of the plainest for those taking the 'cure', which generally lasted three weeks.

The Marienbad golf club was a notable social centre, and it was run by a committee consisting of Prince Trauttmansdorff as President; the Abbot of Tepl, whose monastery owned Marienbad; the Burgomaster; two aldermen; and two hotel-keepers. If the control was thus in local hands, the players were cosmopolitan in the extreme, ranging from Lloyd George and T. P. O'Connor to the most dubious of Russian princes and Polish counts. In consequence there was more than one amusing contretemps on the links. One day, for instance, a Russian nobleman appeared with a mashie which had prongs like a hayfork, and claimed that with it anyone could easily play a ball in long grass as the prongs went through the grass like a comb: unfortunately for his theories, however, on this occasion he had impaled his ball on one of the prongs, and the question arose whether he should drop the ball with the penalty of one stroke or just shake it off and go on playing. A crowd collected, and the point was argued in all the leading languages of Europe: finally it was settled with the disqualification of the Russian for using an illegal club.

These cosmopolitan gatherings at Marienbad and other continental spas served a political as well as a social purpose, for they enabled the statesmen of Europe to meet and exchange views in an atmosphere of calm and relaxation. In three weeks quite a lot of business could be done, and that in the most unostentatious manner. It is true that today the world's leaders are continually meeting one another, but it is not quite the same thing; they come together with the maximum amount of publicity, in circumstances of considerable tension, and for two or three days at most, which is very different from the leisurely sojourning which characterized spa life in the days before the First World War.

The impressions of foreigners are always of interest, especially when they are of the eminence of that great Russian balletomane, Alexandre Benois, who visited London with his wife in 1899. They found that 'the entire way of life seemed to have remained the same as it had been in the days of Beaconsfield and Gladstone; manners, morals, and customs seemed to be those of David Copperfield's time; and London still seemed to us to breathe an air of wit and perfect taste that belonged to a former age'. It is somewhat surprising that they should have been so complimentary, for they put up at a revoltingly dirty boarding-house in Montagu Place, Bloomsbury.

What impressed the Russians most was 'the filth in the lavatory which was situated just under the attic and lacked plumbing, and the badness of the food, which chiefly consisted of problematical soups and something reminiscent of shoe-soles instead of roast'. However, they overcame the latter of these drawbacks by having their meal at a public-house, where 'for a very low price we were served with an immense slice of roast beef with boiled potatoes, and a very tasty gooseberry or rhubarb pie'. They also found it amusing to eat in a real English way, sitting on a high stool with the plate on a narrow tin counter.

One impression of London at the turn of the century could only have been made on a foreigner:

At that time the English were famed for being the least warlike of all nations. Although the better half of the world was owned by England, although she had acquired it not only through the cunning and perfidy of her diplomats but also by force when necessary, the general opinion on the Continent was that her army was almost non-existent in comparison with those of other nations. This superficial judgment was based on the fact that England obstinately rejected conscription, which had been introduced in all other countries, and that hardly a soldier or an officer was to be met with in the streets of an English town in uniform.

Yet on the other hand a military ceremony takes place daily on the Horse Guards Parade which seems to prove the existence of a veritable cult for military affairs. The 'Changing of the Guard' at Buckingham Place is performed with a near religious zeal and an impeccable precision, which leave no doubt of the conviction of the participants that they are fulfilling a sacred duty, no less significant than the state religion expressed in services of the Anglican Church.

'Life stands still in England on Sundays', Benois commented, so on the last of them that he was in London he took a ride on the top of a bus from the Strand to Hampton Court. He was tempted to undertake the adventure by 'the inviting smile of the conductor', and he certainly had no reason to regret his decision, for 'one picture followed another, and they formed a most interesting and typical entity'. His bus was held up by a Salvation Army procession, and he was intrigued by some young men who held long poles to the upper windows with purses for collections attached to them. From Richmond Bridge 'one of the most beautiful views in England opens out: a picture immersed in green with the shining river in the centre'. In Bushey Park 'masses of people dressed in their Sunday best were promenading' under the chestnut trees, while 'peace and propriety reigned everywhere'. The internal combustion engine was soon to change all that.[1]

Among the various evolutions in the capital which had their origin in Edwardian days none proved to be more far-reaching in its consequences than that of which the centre was Fleet Street, and which will always be associated with the name of Alfred Harmsworth, better known as Lord Northcliffe, whose mantle in more recent times fell upon Lord Beaverbrook. On May 4th, 1896, there appeared the first number of the *Daily Mail* – the Popular Press was born, and journalism was never to be the same again. Northcliffe's policy was to give the public what it wanted, or what he induced it to think that it wanted, and to present the news in such a way that it could be taken in at a glance. The *Daily Mail* cost a halfpenny, so there was no class of reader who could not afford it, but in 1907 Northcliffe spread his wings more widely and acquired *The Times*. The political influence of the Press, however, was of relatively slow growth, and it is to be noted that at the General Election of 1906, although most of the newspapers were supporting the Conservative Party, it suffered the greatest defeat

[1] Benois, Alexandre: *Memoirs*, vol. II, pp. 174–180.

in its history: apparently Northcliffe could persuade his readers to grow sweet peas, but not to vote for Tariff Reform.

It is difficult to resist the conclusion that although the power of the Press was building up during the early years of the present century it did not reach its apogee until the First World War. By that time Northcliffe had become possessed of an influence such as no newspaper proprietor has ever exercised before or since, for with *The Times* and the *Daily Mail* both under his control he could spread his views with equal effect among the classes and the masses, and in his heyday he was responsible for half the circulation of the London Press. It must also be remembered that the newspapers of those days had virtually no competition to face: the power of the pulpit and the platform, which had been considerable up to Victorian times, was rapidly waning, and wireless, as a means of disseminating news, had not yet come into existence.[1]

There were also quite a large number of newspapers from which to choose, and the metropolis in that respect resembled modern Paris rather than the London of today. The *Daily Express* was a newcomer, for it was established in 1900 by Chas. Pearson and Co. and, like the *Daily Mail*, was originally sold at a halfpenny, but it did not make the same rapid headway. Indeed, for several years its only asset was its editor, R. D. Blumenfeld, than whom there has never been a greater journalist, or, it may be added, a kinder-hearted man. Week after week he had to go down to the House of Commons to collect from the paper's guarantors enough money to pay the staff, but he struggled on, and the *Daily Express* survived. His reward was the arrival of Lord Beaverbrook, then Max Aitken, in England, for even those who ever since that time have been most disposed to criticize Beaverbrook will hardly deny that with Winston Churchill he was one of the most remarkable men that Britain at home or overseas produced during the present century. Beaverbrook came over to England from Canada in 1908 on what may be termed a reconnoitring expedition, and he returned two years later – scarcely more than thirty and a millionaire – with the intention of settling down, as well as of entering

[1] *Cf.* Blake, R.: *The Unknown Prime Minister*, p. 294.

politics as a protagonist of imperial unity and Tariff Reform. In 1914 he acquired control of the *Daily Express*, and from that date its success was assured by the day-to-day collaboration of Blumenfeld and himself.

Apart from *The Times* there were three serious dailies of Conservative principles, namely the *Standard,* the *Morning Post,* and the *Daily Telegraph.* The days of the first of these was already numbered, but the *Morning Post* was at its most influential in the Edwardian era. It was pre-eminently the organ of Society, whose deeds it faithfully chronicled, and that was the heyday of Society. As a not unnatural corollary it was widely read by domestic servants, both male and female, and this fact was reflected in its advertisement columns, which were full of notices of 'situations vacant'; so much so, in fact, that the story went that an employer once said to her butler, 'Would you like to see a paper?' and handed him the *Morning Post*, only, however, to be met with the reply, 'No, thank you, my lady: I am perfectly happy in my present post.'

Most significant where the future was concerned was the appearance of the illustrated daily, and by the date of the King's death the *Daily Graphic,* the *Daily Mirror,* and the *Daily Sketch* were already in existence.

London was not yet reduced to a mere two evening papers, but had the choice of half a dozen, among which one of the liveliest and best written was the *Globe*. It was owned by a certain Sir William Madge, who, owing to his parsimonious treatment of his contributors, was generally known in Fleet Street as 'Manure Madge'. He paid his leader-writers at space rates, and it was his habit to write himself the opening sentences of each leader, the relevant deduction then being made from the leader-writer's cheque. He met his match in one member of the staff, allegedly P. G. Wodehouse, who indicated on the proof that Madge's lines were to be printed in italics, and then continued, 'This represents the point of view of the ordinary stupid, unthinking Englishman.'

The evening papers, it may be added, had a microscopic circulation, and at the height of its influence the *Westminster Gazette* –

'the sea-green incorruptible' – never had an assured circulation of more than twenty thousand copies.

The Edwardian Press naturally reflected Edwardian social habits, and that accounts for the pre-eminence of the serious weeklies at that time. They were originally published on a Saturday morning, and were read over the week-end by those who had either received them by post (there were Sunday deliveries of letters in those days) or had bought them on their way home from their offices on Saturday afternoon. The Sunday newspaper was unknown in any respectable household, and in an age when the Victorian sabbath was still observed there was plenty of time to peruse a weekly from cover to cover before Monday morning. In these circumstances it is little wonder that men like Lord Robert Cecil, later third Marquess of Salisbury and Prime Minister, thought it an honour to contribute to the *Saturday Review*.

Above all, there was the *Pink'un*, which sailed closer to the wind than any periodical of today, but which purveyed what George Robey used to call 'good, clean, wholesome fun'. It might be bawdy; but it was never suggestive, possibly because, as Douglas Jerrold put it, 'the *Pink'un* was written by men for men, not by boys for women'.[1]

[1] *Georgian Adventure*, p. 93.

CHAPTER III

The Provinces

·◉·

I N 1909 it was estimated that nine out of ten families in the
larger centres of population had migrated there from the
countryside within three generations, but those who had settled
in London found very different conditions from those who made
their homes in the provincial cities. Their house rent was immeas-
urably higher, for the mean weekly price of two rooms in the
capital was six shillings, while in the provinces it was little more
than half that amount; for four rooms the variation was between
nine shillings in the one and five shillings in the other. The working-class flat was in the main a thing of the future, although it
was much in evidence on the Continent; but the English had not
yet taken to it, and were still struggling to maintain in the urban
aggregation to which they had migrated some semblance of a
home. This desire explains the enormous acreage of chimney-
pots and tumbled cottages which was revealed in what has been
termed 'a kind of smoky grandeur' which met the eyes of the
Edwardian visitor as he was borne along the railway embank-
ments of South and East London. Much light is thrown upon the
lives of the weekly wage-earners in the industrial districts by
their family budgets. Classified according to the net receipts, they
revealed an ever-growing proportion devoted to the essentials of
bodily nutriment, until, at the bottom, where the income was
permanently below the 'living wage', there was practically no
margin left when the demand for food had been satisfied. 'For the
incomes below thirty shillings, two-thirds of the total income is
spent on food,' a Board of Trade investigator has left on record,
'while in the case of the incomes of forty shillings and above,

about fifty-seven per cent is spent on food.' Amongst the poorest classes of the population actually one-fifth of the total expenditure on food was spent on bread and flour, while tea, in the lowest income groups, called for ninepence farthing a week and sugar for eightpence.

Official statistics can be misleading, but for the conditions prevailing in the industrial North in the Edwardian era there is Lady Bell's penetrating study of Middlesbrough. It then possessed a population of slightly more than a hundred thousand, and it had grown up almost overnight in the nineteenth century to meet the demands of the Iron Trade. Its inhabitants came from the countryside, from neighbouring townships, and from Ireland and Scotland, and round the furnaces which they tended there rapidly grew up mazes of little two-storied cottages. It was essentially a proletarian city with its grey streets and few public buildings, all set in a background of drabness. Lady Bell wrote her book to reveal what the Iron Trade, which people outside 'know but by name, perhaps, as a huge measuring gauge of the national prosperity, is in reality, when translated into terms of human beings'.[1]

She shows us a population in many respects more fortunate than was often the case elsewhere, for by contemporary standards wages were high and hours were short, while life in Middlesbrough, though exacting and laborious, was possibly more exhilarating than the long hours spent in the humidity of a cotton factory or even than the perpetual scribbling of a clerk in an ill-lighted office. It was a population continually wrestling with the iron upon which its subsistence depended; tearing it out of the ironstone, directing rivers of molten metal into their proper channels, and bending the forces of heat to the will of man. 'The path the iron worker daily treads at the edge of the sandy platform, that narrow path that lies between running streams of fire on the one hand and a sheer drop on the other, is but an emblem of the Road of Life along which he must walk. If he should stumble, either actually or metaphorically, as he goes, he has but a small margin in which to recover himself.'

[1] All quotations are from Lady Bell's Book, *At the Works*.

At the same time Lady Bell had no illusions about the working-classes of Middlesbrough, and in her book she draws attention to a number of their shortcomings, such as the enormous disproportion of attendance at public-houses and at places of religious worship; the universal prevalence of betting and gambling; the thoughtlessness and wastefulness which often produced economic collapse; the ignorance of child-rearing and the laws of health; and the darker side of the artificial restriction of families. She shows her readers boys and girls of fourteen or younger being turned loose to pick their way through the most difficult period of life, just at the age when the boys and girls of another class are most completely surrounded with careful and humane influences. The married woman of the working classes, 'handicapped as she is by physical conditions and drawbacks, with but just bodily strength enough to encounter the life described', may be defended against the fluent criticism of 'her more prosperous sisters – whose duties are divided among several people, and even then not always accomplished with success'.

In the light of more recent experience it is interesting to note that Lady Bell found that the standard of longevity had fallen from that prevalent among agricultural workers, and that men who were formerly too old at sixty had now become too old ten years earlier, 'but we cease to be surprised when we realize how apt the conditions are to tell upon the health even of the strongest, and how many of the men engaged in it are spent by the time they are fifty. To say that this happens to half of them is probably a favourable estimate.' With regard to the women, Lady Bell has no use for the argument often put forward in her day to the effect that a beneficent Providence had made the working classes insensible to conditions which their betters would have found intolerable. 'It is not only bringing children into the world,' she says, 'that affects the health of the working woman. It is an entire delusion to believe that they are, as a rule, stronger, hardier, healthier, than the well-to-do. Their life is a continuous toil. They rarely go outside the doors of their houses, except for Saturday marketing and Sunday evening exercise. Recreation, the stimulus of changed garments, rest during the day, or the other minor comforts which other classes find so necessary are not for them. They are mostly convinced that it is wrong to sit down and read a book at any hour of the day. Their interests, not unnaturally, turn towards the stimulus of drinking, and of betting and gambling – two elements which at least can give colour in a life set in grey.'

There is no reason to suppose that during the first decade of the present century working-class life in Middlesbrough was any more 'set in grey' than in any other industrial centre: everywhere it was drab, especially by comparison with what its practitioners saw when they 'looked back through the smoky tunnel of the last three generations to the green fields of their ancestors[1]'. In these circumstances nothing in the nature of excitement came amiss. 'Has there been a row?' asked a reporter of a neighbour at a gathering summoned at Westminster by the suffragettes or the leaders of the unemployed. 'No,' came the cheerful reply, 'but we still 'ave 'opes.' Yet the social reformers of the day were looking ahead, and among them was C. F. G. Masterman:

> No one can question the revolution which has overtaken the industrial centres in the last two generations of their growth. Reading the records of the 'hungry forties' in the life of the Northern cities is like passing through a series of evil dreams. Cellars have vanished into homes, wages have risen, hours of labour diminished, temperance and thrift increased, manners improved. The new civilization of the Crowd has become possible, with some capacity of endurance, instead of (as before) an offence which was rank and smelling to heaven. But this life having been created and fixed in its development, the curious observer is immediately confronted with the inquiry: what of its future? Are the main lines set as at the present, and later development confined to variations in length and direction along these lines?
>
> In such a case progress will mean a further repetition of the type; two cotton factories where there is now one; five thousand small, grey-capped men where there are now three; perhaps, in some remote millennium, fourteen days of boisterous delight at Blackpool where now are only seven. A race can thus be discerned in the future, small, wiry, incredibly nimble

---

[1] The late (first) Viscount Dunrossil.

in splicing thread or adjusting machinery, earning high wages in the factories, slowly advancing (one may justly hope) in intelligence and sobriety, and the qualities which go to make the good citizen. These may at the last limit their hours of labour everywhere to the ideal of an eight hours day; everywhere raise their remuneration to a satisfactory minimum wage; everywhere find provision for insecurity, unemployment, old age. The 'Crowd' is then complete. The City civilization is established. Progress pauses – exhausted, satisfied. Man is made.[1]

The sea-ports were changing too, and none more than Liverpool.[2] It was still the second port of the empire, and its inhabitants rightly felt themselves to be citizens of no mean city. The Mersey was thronged with ships of every tonnage and of all nations, and the great Atlantic liners were one of the local sights. Visitors were always taken for a ride on the now defunct Overhead Railway to see the docks, and the activity to be observed along the riverside always made Liverpool electors, Tories as most of them were, a little sceptical about Joseph Chamberlain's new national remedy of Tariff Reform. The shadow of Southampton had not yet fallen across the Merseyside. Some notable buildings were put up at this time, especially the new Adelphi Hotel and the Royal Liver Building. It was of the latter that the first Lord Mersey, better known as Mr Justice Bigham, observed, in reply to a stranger who asked him what it was, 'I don't know; probably new chambers for F. E. Smith.' The foundation stone of the Anglican cathedral was also laid during this period.

Of course, the Liverpool of those days was very different from what it was later to become. There was no Mersey Tunnel until some years after the First World War, and when motor-cars began to make their appearance in any quantity the ferry-boats across the river became uncomfortably crowded, especially on Saturday nights when people had been visiting friends in the Wirral Peninsula or had been for a run in North Wales: if one missed the last boat from Birkenhead there was nothing for it but to leave the

[1] *The Condition of England*, p. 115.
[2] For an account of Victorian Liverpool *cf.* the author's *The Victorians*, ch. iii, *passim*.

car there for the night or to return home by way of Warrington, where was to be found the first bridge across the Mersey. Within the city itself means of locomotion had recently been greatly improved, for about the beginning of the century the conversion of the tramway system from horse to electric traction was carried out, and by the end of 1902 the whole of the tramways had been electrified.

Much of what was soon to be built over was then open fields: Mossley Hill church was on the edge of the country, while Allerton and Childwall were definitely rural. Memories, too, were still fresh of a very different Liverpool from the progressive and well-ordered city of Edwardian days. The older generation could remember the great fire that destroyed the Landing Stage, and recollected what their elders had told them of the cholera epidemic, when grass grew between the cobbles in Castle Street. The links with the past were numerous and strong, and even those in middle age could recall when there were no buildings between Princes Avenue and Parliament Street; fresh in their minds, too, were the crowds that in their youth used to flock to the public hangings outside Walton Jail, and on these occasions domestic servants always expected time off duty to see the execution.

Yet the life of Edwardian Liverpool was changing, and as elsewhere the prime factor in the change was the motor-car. North Wales, now the playground of South Lancashire, may have been unspoilt, but, save for a few places like Llandudno, it was very remote: it was still the Wales of Borrow. It must, however, be confessed that the Welsh hotels at that time left a great deal to be desired, and in the visitors' book of one of them a disgruntled guest wrote:

> If ever you go to Dolgelly,
>   Don't stay at the Royal Hotel;
> For there's nothing to put in your belly,
>   And no one to answer the bell.

There was, incidentally, little unity in the Wales of those days, for the great division between church and chapel affected every social relationship. To be a Nonconformist implied the profession of

Liberalism and a belief in the infallibility of Lloyd George, while Churchmen were always Tories who considered him as an emanation of the infernal regions. The Conservative standpoint was well expressed in some jingling lines which were very popular about the time of the first General Election of 1910:

> Lloyd George no doubt,
>> When his day is out,
> Will ride in a flaming chariot.
>> He will sit in state
> On a red-hot plate
>> 'Twixt Satan and Judas Iscariot.
> Ananias that day
>> To Satan will say,
> My claim for precedence now fails:
>> So move me up higher,
> Away from the fire,
>> To make room for that liar from Wales.

Within a few years a change came over the scene, and what had necessitated a week-end's holiday became accessible in a few hours' run on a Sunday afternoon. All this led to an inevitable relaxation of established habits, and the outbreak of the First World War found Liverpool society with a very different outlook from that which had characterized it at the death of Queen Victoria. The opening of the new Adelphi Hotel was another factor operating in the same direction. Its teas became fashionable, and thus was initiated the custom of entertaining away from home, which had previously been unknown. The more old-fashioned denounced it as a sink of iniquity where young men drank more than was good for them, but then the same thing had been said of the 'Bear's Paw': at any rate the old bonds were gradually being relaxed, and men and maidens were repairing in increasing numbers to the Adelphi to eat and dance. The coming of the cinema had also much to do with establishing a more rational relationship between the sexes.

The passage of time has caused many misconceptions to arise with regard to the social conditions of the past, and no illusion is more persistent, especially in the South of England, than that in the provinces the Sunday of sixty years ago was a day of gloom and misery. In reality, nothing could be further from the truth, though it was very different from what it has since become. Games were not usually played in public or in private, and no one would take his carriage out on a Sunday. Church-going was universal, and after church those with any social pretensions took a turn along Princes Avenue, while in the afternoon the young men used to call upon those of whom they had recently been the guests at dinner or a dance. In effect, Sunday was a day of rest, and as such it met a definite need, for if the business-man of those days did not work any harder than now he worked longer hours: the head of a firm was at his office by nine, and he rarely left it until five-thirty, while he never took Saturday morning off as a habit. There was no compulsory early closing, the shops did not shut before eight, and the mass of the population worked a full six-day week, so a little rest on Sunday by no means came amiss.

For those who went to church there was ample provision in the Liverpool of those days, and all denominations were well served in this respect. The Presbyterian Church of England excelled in the person of Dr Watson, the great 'Ian Maclaren'. Every Sunday morning Sefton Park Presbyterian Church was crowded to the doors – so much so that even pew-holders had to be in their places a quarter of an hour before the service began, and there was a majesty about the church officer that would not have disgraced a Lord Chamberlain. Dr Watson was also a popular social figure, being an accomplished after-dinner speaker, and he was everywhere a welcome guest. In those days it was the custom for the Lord Mayor to visit in state during his year of office the place of worship which he normally attended, and on one occasion at Sefton Park Church an unexpected incident occurred. Doubtless the explanation was that Dr Watson was preoccupied with his coming sermon, for in the bidding prayer he omitted several categories and electrified the congregation by praying for the 'Lord Mayor, Aldermen, and Councillors of this city, and others who have lost the kindly light of reason'.

In the Anglican Church there were Archdeacon Madden – whose only son was to die a hero's death on the German wire at

Givenchy in March, 1915 – at St Luke's and Canon Harford at Mossley Hill, as well as Canon Lancelot, the Principal of Liverpool College. There was also the Bishop, Dr Chavasse, who was universally respected. The diocese was not in those days an easy one, and his predecessor had not rendered it any less difficult, but Dr Chavasse steered his way between the High Churchmen and the followers of Wise with marked success, and he was as greatly beloved outside as inside the ranks of his own communion. There had, it must be confessed, been a good deal of sectarian bitterness in the concluding years of the nineteenth century, and this was liable to raise its head whenever the Irish Question became acute, but it was confined to certain elements, and it was on its decline during the Edwardian era. There were many Jews in Liverpool, but there was no anti-Semitic feeling, and no one would have dreamed of objecting to men like Alderman Louis Cohen on the score of their race or religion.

Politics in Liverpool were lively in the extreme – as, indeed, they had been since the days of Canning, Brougham, and Huskisson – and nearly every ward was contested each succeeding November, for in those days the municipal elections were held on the first of that month, while when a General Election took place nobody appeared to talk of anything else. The issues in the municipal fights were often trivial enough – one is said to have turned on the position of a coffee-stall – but the rivalry to which they gave rise testified to the interest taken by the electors in the administration of their city. There was no sign of apathy in any quarter.

Of the local M.P.s, F. E. Smith, elected for Walton in 1906, was easily the most outstanding. Those who only knew him in later days as a Cabinet Minister can have no idea what a tower of strength he proved to be to the Tories in the North in the years that followed his return to the House of Commons in the hour of disaster for his party. After two decades of almost continuous office the Conservative Party was dumb-founded by its overthrow, and especially was this the case in Lancashire. That county had been traditionally Tory since Jacobite times, and now it had proved false to its old allegiance. Preston was gone, Balfour was defeated in Manchester, and even Lord Derby's son and heir had lost his seat, while no less than four of Liverpool's nine divisions were represented by Liberals or a Nationalist. It seemed the end of all things. Then there appeared this youthful-looking David who displayed not the least fear of the formidable Goliath, and before long the initiative in Lancashire was back in Conservative hands. His superb insolence almost took the breath away, and in particular he had a manner with hecklers which soon silenced the most determined opposition. When a man shouted out, 'The Tories want to tax my food,' he instantly replied, 'No, Sir: there is no proposal to put a duty on thistles.' At the first General Election of 1910 he was addressing a meeting in a theatre at Llandudno, and there were not fifty Conservatives in the house: one man, obviously put up by the Liberals, asked if the Tories proposed to tax music. 'What sort of music?' retorted F.E. 'Instrumental or vocal?' Thinking to score heavily the heckler replied, 'Vocal.' 'No,' was the immediate response, 'that is raw material. Under Mr Chamberlain's pledge it comes in free.' It was all very much in the tradition of Bolingbroke, Canning, and Disraeli, and in many ways F.E. belonged to the eighteenth century than to the twentieth, which was at once his strength and his weakness.

In later life he made many enemies among those who did not know the kindness of heart which lay behind an arrogance of manner, and his attitude towards the Irish Treaty alienated many of his earlier associates. In Liverpool he had none but friends, for his basic kindliness was too well known for it to be otherwise. His hand was always held out to those whom life had treated hardly, and he helped many a lame dog over a stile. He made more than one serious mistake in the course of his career, but no one could ever accuse F. E. Smith of being either a hypocrite or false to his friends.

One of the most popular of the local M.P.s was Sir John Harmood-Banner, the 'Banner of Everton', as he was generally known. His cheery face and substantial figure were always an encouragement to his supporters. Sir Robert Houston, on the other hand, was a good deal of a mystery, and many people were puzzled to account for the fact that he was regularly returned for West Toxteth while he rarely set foot in the constituency. He even held the seat in 1906, though since his time it has rarely returned a Conservative. His opponents used to declare that the explanation was to be found in bribery, which may well have been the case, but all the same they never brought a petition against his return. The present Lord Birkenhead, in his biography of his father, describes Houston as 'a shipping magnate of ruthless character and questionable methods, a bearded pirate, the type of shipowner described by Kipling in *The Mary Gloster*',[1] and the matter may well rest at that.

Another unattractive, though extremely formidable, Liverpool figure of those days was Sir Archibald Salvidge, the chairman of the Liverpool Working Men's Conservative Association. Although a brewer by trade, he would not appear to have made brewing pay, for his financial position was always delicate, and on at least one occasion the hat had to be taken round to relieve his embarrassments. This was done by F.E., who raised five thousand pounds for the impoverished publican, though Salvidge expected to receive twice that amount: of this sum Lord Derby, Alderman Cohen, and Messrs Cain contributed a thousand each, and the rest came from friends in London. Salvidge was possessed of a hectoring, not to say bullying, manner, and it must be admitted that he often carried his point. Twice at least, however, he was thwarted: the first time was when he tried to browbeat Lord Woolton on the latter's first arrival in Liverpool, and the second was when he ventured to cross swords with Lord Beaverbrook, in which contest he very definitely had the worst of it. Lord Beaverbrook has aptly referred to Salvidge as 'Lord Derby's Sancho Panza'.

Derby himself is not easy to assess in spite of the fact that he has been the subject of a first-rate biography by Randolph Churchill, but not even the barest account of Liverpool in the early years of the present century could pretend to be complete without some reference to him. The influence of the Stanley family in the Merseyside seaport had long been one of the outstanding features of Lancashire life, and it had never been seriously challenged

[1] *F.E.*, p. 71.
[2] For his earlier career *cf.* Petrie, Sir Charles: *The Victorians*, pp. 94–96.

either by the neighbouring Earls of Lathom or Sefton, or by the Marquess of Salisbury who was a considerable ground landlord, especially in the Childwall area. To understand the hold which the seventeenth Earl of Derby had upon South Lancashire in general, and Liverpool in particular, in the Edwardian era it is necessary to go back several centuries, for in essence it was a case of feudalism protracted into modern times, and nowhere would it have been possible to find its like.

The first Stanley of whom there is any authentic record seems to have been Adam de Stanley who was living in the reign of Stephen, and from that day to this the family has always been of great importance in Lancashire, and very often in national politics as well. In fact there is no family in the kingdom which can show a longer record of public service, and its members have at one time or another been distinguished as statesmen, sportsmen, and scholars. No less than nine of the predecessors of the present Earl of Derby have been Knights of the Garter, while nearly all have been Lords-Lieutenant of Lancashire. From very early times the Stanleys have been a great force in the south of the country, and on occasion they have been described as 'of Liverpool', so close is their connection with that city. The sixteenth and seventeenth Earls of Derby were Lord Mayors of Liverpool, and many members of the family have at one time or another represented the city in the House of Commons. In the Middle Ages the Stanleys had a residence in Liverpool called the Tower which they received the permission of Henry IV to fortify; this, incidentally, was matched by the castle, which stood where the statue of Queen Victoria now is, and which belonged to the rival family of Molyneux, now Earls of Sefton.

In 1385 the Stanleys acquired by marriage their present residence of Knowsley Hall, seven miles from Liverpool: successive Earls have added to the building, not always to its advantage, but its present owner is engaged in pulling some of it down, partly in order to make it more habitable and partly to improve its appearance. In addition to being large landowners in Lancashire the Stanleys in the later Middle Ages acquired the Isle of Man, and from 1405 to 1736 the head of the family was 'Lord of Man', where he exercised a semi-independent jurisdiction: how effective that jurisdiction could be is shown in the opening chapters of Scott's *Peveril of the Peak*. The Stanley rule in the island came to an end in 1736 when the tenth Earl of Derby died without a son, and Man passed to the Duke of Atholl, whose grandmother had been a daughter of the seventh earl.

During the Wars of the Roses the Stanleys were no more consistent in their allegiance than most of their contemporaries, and they had done very well for themselves, as may be gauged by the fact that the head of the family was Constable of England during the reign of Richard III. Then came the invasion of Henry Tudor, and Stanley duly appeared in arms on the side of Richard. The two armies met on the field of Bosworth, and at an opportune moment the Stanleys changed sides, attacking the Royal army in the flank. This decided the issue, and Richard was killed in the attempt to rally his forces; the battered crown which had fallen from the dead monarch's helmet was found in a hawthorn bush, and was set by Thomas Stanley on the head of the victorious Tudor, who was at once acclaimed as Henry VII. For this extremely dubious behaviour Thomas Stanley was in due course created Earl of Derby, but the circumstances of his elevation to the peerage have been remembered against his descendants down to the present day whenever they have appeared to 'hedge' on any political issue. Nevertheless, unworthy as may have been the motives which originally induced the Stanleys to support the Tudors, they remained steadfastly loyal to the new dynasty, otherwise they would assuredly have lost their property and their heads. The third earl, who died in 1572, was so celebrated for his magnificence and liberality that Camden wrote, 'with Edward Earl of Derby's death, the glory of hospitality seemed to fall asleep'. The next earl was sent by Elizabeth I as ambassador to France and to Spain, and was also Lord High Steward.

When the Stuarts succeeded the Tudors on the throne they had no more devoted servants than the House of Stanley, as was proved by two dramatic incidents when war broke out between Charles I and the Parliament.

Among the possessions of the family at that time was Lathom

House, near Ormskirk, and while the seventh Earl of Derby was away fighting for the King, his wife was in residence at Lathom with their children. In due course the place was besieged by the Roundheads, and although its defences were weak the Countess of Derby refused to surrender. For three months in the spring of 1644 she defied with three hundred men a besieging force ten times as strong, and when all seemed lost the Parliamentarian commander, a Colonel Rigby, gave her one last chance to surrender Lathom House and everything in it. 'Tell that insolent rebel,' was her reply, 'he shall neither have persons, goods, nor house. When our strength and provisions are spent we shall find a fire more merciful than Rigby; and then, if the providence of God prevent it not, my goods and house shall burn in his sight; and myself, children, and soldiers, rather than fall into his hands, will seal our religion and loyalty in the same flame.' Fortunately such a sacrifice proved unnecessary, for when the garrison was at its last gasp it was relieved by the arrival of Prince Rupert.

When the Royal cause went down the Stanleys went down with it, for Lord Derby was among the prisoners captured by Cromwell in his victory over Charles II at Worcester in 1651. He was too staunch a Royalist to be given any mercy, so he was beheaded outside the *Man and Scythe* inn at Bolton. So deep an impression did this event make upon his successors that the late Earl of Derby, who died as recently as 1948, though he frequently visited Bolton, could never be persuaded to pass the place where his predecessor had met his death.

With the coming of the eighteenth century the hereditary tastes of the Stanleys seem to have undergone some modification. It was not so much that the twelfth earl neglected the duties of his position, for he was Lord-Lieutenant of Lancashire for fifty-eight years, but he was more interested in sport than in politics, so in 1780 he founded the race which bears his name, and thus commenced that interest in the turf which has been perpetuated by his successors in the title. Curiously enough, the Derby has only been won by a Stanley on four occasions in its whole history: the first of them was by the founder of the race himself in 1787 with Sir Peter Teazle, and the other three were in 1924, 1933, and 1942, when the late Lord Derby won with Sansovino, Hyperion, and Watling Street respectively.

The first wife of the twelfth earl died early in their married life, and the widower, as a contemporary put it, 'contracted an alliance which drew upon him the attention of the whole country. He led to the altar Miss Elizabeth Farren, a fascinating actress, and at that time perhaps the chief attraction of Drury Lane.' Marriages between the peerage and the stage were not so common in those days as they have since become, and so there was a good deal of raising of eyebrows in certain quarters, but this particular marriage turned out a great success, and the former Miss Farren proved an excellent Countess of Derby.

The middle years of the nineteenth century saw the House of Stanley rise to even greater heights in the person of the fourteenth earl, who lived between 1799 and 1869, and who was three times Prime Minister as well as being one of the foremost classical scholars of the day. Lytton wrote rather disparagingly of him as 'frank, haughty, and rash, the Rupert of debate', but Disraeli, who served under him for many years, was much kinder when he paid a special tribute to his capacity for labour and his mastery of detail, which were never sufficiently appreciated because the world was astonished by the celerity with which he dispatched public affairs': he finally summed up his old chief's contributions to the country's good in the words, 'He abolished slavery, he educated Ireland, and he reformed Parliament.' The character and career of the fourteenth Earl of Derby was typical of the versatility which has distinguished so many members of his family. Great statesman he might be, but he was also a scholar, a sportsman, and a great landed proprietor, and he was just as happy in his library, in the gardens and coverts of Knowsley, at Newmarket or Epsom, as he was in Parliament or in Downing Street. His life also marked a great span in British politics, for in his youth he was member of an administration whose head had held office under the Younger Pitt, while in his old age he presided over a government in which one minister was to be Premier when Sir Winston Churchill first took his seat in the House of Commons.

There was even a moment about this time when it looked as if the Stanley family might rise higher still, for the son of 'the Rupert of Debate', himself to be twice Foreign Secretary, was mentioned as a possible King of Greece. When Disraeli heard of the suggestion he wrote, 'It is a dazzling adventure for the House of Stanley, but they are not an imaginative race, and, I fancy, they will prefer Knowsley to the Parthenon, and Lancashire to the Attic plain.' Disraeli was right in his forecast, and the vacant Greek throne went to the present Duke of Edinburgh's grandfather, then Prince George of Denmark.

This digression into the history of the Stanleys is not as irrelevant to an account of Edwardian Liverpool as may at first sight appear, for it is a background which must be appreciated if the unique position of the seventeenth Earl of Derby is to be understood. There is nothing remarkable in the fact that the Stanleys should have been predominant in Lancashire in past centuries when, save for a town or two, the country was wholly rural, and sparsely populated at that, but it was remarkable that they should have retained their influence after it had become one of the most highly industrialized areas in the world. The explanation lies in their accumulated prestige down the ages.

The seventeenth earl succeeded to the title in 1908: his father had a long record of public service behind him both at home and overseas, but he was a good deal of an introvert, and he was never the outstanding figure either in Lancashire or in the political world at large that his son became. To the latter the munificence of his ancestors had certainly descended, as one incident abundantly proves. He became godfather to Field-Marshal Haig's son, and shortly afterwards Haig was found writing to his wife: 'Lord Derby gave me the enclosed to you for his godson. I believe it is £100 which he wants you to invest for the young man. I told Derby that I felt ashamed at his giving such a large present: I personally would have preferred a spoon or cup or something small, but he said it was his rule to give £100 to every one of his godsons – so I accepted it with grateful thanks.' When Derby's second son, Oliver, who might have become Prime Minister instead of Eden but for his untimely death, was M.P. for Westmorland he paid the whole of his expenses, and all the local Conservative agent had to do was to apply to Knowsley whenever any money was required. He could well afford, it may be noted, to be munificent at this rate. 'The gross rent roll of the Derby estates at this time, before expenditure on maintenance, amounted to little short of three hundred thousand pounds a year. Some two-thirds of this was re-invested in improvements, but he received, from his landed properties alone, a net taxable income of around one hundred thousand pounds a year, at a time when the standard rate of Income Tax was one shilling in the pound.'[1]

In appearance and manner Derby was the bluff, John Bull Englishman of tradition, but he was known to his enemies as 'the smiling Judas'. Lord Beaverbrook summed him up very well:

> Derby was a tiresome speaker, but a good letter-writer, often in his own hand. Popular and holding the affectionate respect of the public, he was never a heavyweight contender in Cabinet Councils. Supported by his Town Properties and his Broad Acres and the Hereditary Virtue of his House, he was the Champion in Lancashire Party organizations. He took infinite trouble to please the Press, and reaped his reward in high praise from Government and Opposition newspapers. . . . Always threatening resignation, he never signed off. Derby was the godfather of Haig's child, yet of him Haig wrote 'like the feather pillow (he) bears the mark of the last person who sat on him'.[2]

If Derby often appeared to poor advantage on the national stage, he was at his best where Lancashire, and in particular Liverpool, was concerned. He was in very truth their patron, and his reward was the popularity he enjoyed in his own county. He had many opponents but few real enemies, though in retrospect it is possible to criticize him on the score that he was inclined to rely too much on F.E. and Salvidge.

Edwardian Liverpool was not without a *cause célèbre*, and this occurred in 1905. In the previous year a new Licensing Act had introduced a method of reducing licences, of which the number on Merseyside was excessive, by compensating those whose licences

[1] Churchill, Randolph S.: *Lord Derby*, p. 95.
[2] *Men and Power*, *1917–18*, p. XVI.

were extinguished out of a levy on those who retained theirs. After the Act had been in operation for some months the *Liverpool Daily Post*, then under the editorship of Sir Edward Russell, came out with an article accusing the Conservative majority on the Bench of having packed the committee charged with the operation of the Act in such a way as to hinder the effective prosecution of its objects, and in particular of having levied an insufficent sum to carry out their duties properly. The Conservative members of the committee thereupon accused Sir Edward of criminal libel, largely at the instigation of one Frodsham, who was among the complainant justices and was also a partner in the firm of solicitors which was instructing the plaintiffs. Of this Sir Edward's grandson has well remarked, 'The advice which his firm gave their partner could not have been more misguided. Whatever prospect there might have been of winning an action for libel against the *Daily Post*, there was little likelihood of being able to persuade a Liverpool jury to convict its editor of such a crime, for he was held in the highest esteem and greatly loved.'[1]

There was an imposing array of counsel on both sides, and Rufus Isaacs, later the first Marquess of Reading, led for the defence. From the beginning, and more especially as soon as he realized that the judge was against him, he concentrated upon Sir Edward's personal character. Sir Charles Petrie, Leader of the Conservative Party in Liverpool, who had been none too happy about the procedure adopted by his fellow plaintiffs, came under cross-examination,

I think you have known Sir Edward Russell for a number of years?

Yes.

And you look upon him as an honourable man whose word you would accept?

Yes, I always esteemed Sir Edward.

And you accept the statement, whatever the value of it may be, that he had no desire to impute to you any personal motive or any corruption or dishonesty?

Yes, no personal motive.

[1] Russell of Liverpool, Lord: *That Reminds Me*, pp. 18–19.

Fortified with such testimony from the plaintiffs Isaacs went to work with a will, and in later years Hewart was to say, 'Perhaps he had never done anything better in all his career at the Bar.' In his final speech Isaacs told the jury that it was a shameful thing to have set in motion what he called 'the cumbrous machinery of criminal law' in this case. To have brought 'a man who has passed forty-five years of his life in an honourable position in your city into the category of the criminal accused of a crime and who, if his were being tried in the ordinary court, under ordinary procedure as a criminal, would be taking his place in the criminal court surrounded by the adjuncts and accessories of such a court. It deprives a man of the ordinary position that a citizen would like to take, that he has never been accused of committing a criminal offence.'

The result, in spite of the judge's summing-up, was a foregone conclusion, for the jury were out for a mere eighteen minutes before returning with a verdict of 'Not Guilty'. There were cheers from every part of the court, and on coming out of St George's Hall the defendant was carried shoulder-high through cheering crowds to his waiting carriage; nor was this all, for the eight prosecuting justices had to pay the costs of the prosecution. It is hardly necessary to add that this case caused, at any rate temporarily, much division and controversy in Liverpool social circles.

All this while expansion of the city's boundaries was very definitely the policy of the Corporation, and there had been a big move forward in this respect in 1895, though at the cost of conceding differential rating for fifteen years: as a result Walton, Wavertree, and the remaining portion of Toxteth Park were incorporated, which increased the population from 504,000 to 642,000.

The new reign witnessed a good deal of manoeuvring for position between Liverpool and her neighbours. In 1900 some inhabitants of Garston petitioned for incorporation as a borough in the same way as Bootle had successfully done thirty years earlier; but Liverpool was prepared this time. It opposed the petition on the ground that the proposed borough would interfere with the future expansion of the city, and two years later Garston came in: Fazakerly was added in 1904. After the Edwardian period, but before the First World War, the districts of Allerton, Much and Little Woolton, and Childwall were included. These steps were taken, not because the districts in question were already urbanized, but because they were likely to become so in the future, and the Corporation, at that time probably the most far-sighted Local Authority in the kingdom, wished to be able to plan their development.

Those responsible for Liverpool's destinies were in a definitely expansionist mood, and this led to a memorable head-on collision with Bootle. Any extension of the docks must necessarily take place in that direction, while the coastal strip north of Bootle was becoming every day increasingly attractive for the more expensive type of suburban development, so that a good deal of rateable value was accumulating there, and upon this the Finance Committee was casting covetous eyes. Their predecessors had rather supinely allowed Bootle to be incorporated in 1869, but an attempt had been made in 1895 to repair the damage by a proposal for a voluntary amalgamation between the two authorities: Bootle, however, would have none of this, and its position had recently been strengthened by its elevation to the status of a County Borough under the Local Government Act of 1888.

There the matter rested until 1902, when the question was reopened by a proposal to annex the townships of Litherland, Orrell, and Ford. So far as Liverpool was concerned it was clearly now or never; if Bootle were given the right to expand its continued existence could no longer be questioned, so Liverpool put forward a counter-proposal for the annexation of Bootle itself, as well as the three townships and Fazakerley. There then ensued what can only be described as some pretty smart electioneering of which the outstanding characteristic was a competition in offers of differential rating: on balance Liverpool offered slightly better terms, but except in Fazakerley, where these were accepted, the Local Authorities in the townships preferred to come in with Bootle, whose opposition continued to be adamant.

The next step was in 1903 when the Local Government Board, of which Walter Long was then President, held an enquiry, at which both parties put their cards on the table – one had almost written at which no holds were barred. The Liverpool case was a strong one: tangible advantages would be secured by Bootle in the event of amalgamation, particularly in such matters as secondary education, while the development of transport there was to some extent being held up until the two Authorities had agreed upon the tramway routes. 'The strongest part of Liverpool's case was the most general: the essential continuity of Liverpool and Bootle, and their common dependence on the port and the docks. This general argument was weakened but by no means destroyed by the counter argument that the port and docks themselves – the sphere where unity was most essential – were already under the unified administration of the Mersey Docks and Harbour Board.'[1] On the other hand there was the opposition of the Local Authorities affected, though this was to some extent offset by the activities of what may perhaps be termed Liverpool 'Fifth Columnists' in their areas. Finally, however, the Local Government Board was convinced, and Liverpool obtained its Provisional Order.

Nevertheless Bootle refused to accept defeat, and carried the dispute to the House of Commons, where the Provisional Order was quashed on the general principle that Parliament would not consent to the coercion of small Local Authorities into amalgamation, particularly where the smaller Authority, as in the case of Bootle, had the status of a County Borough. It may be noted that the dispute by no means took place in an atmosphere of academic calm, for, especially in Bootle, a good deal of heat was generated. On the day when Parliament finally rejected the Order three telegrams were sent to Bootle from London: the first ran, 'Thank God we have won'; the second, 'Bill rejected, put flags up'; and the third, 'Bootle has won a glorious victory, and Liverpool is beaten.' It would be foolish to imagine that the enthusiasm thus engendered represented the unanimous opinion of the citizens of Bootle, but it was sufficiently vocal to justify the *Liverpool Courier* in heading its column describing these events as 'Inde-

[1] White, Brian D.: *A History of the Corporation of Liverpool, 1835–1914*. The Mersey Docks and Harbour Board had been established in 1857 in spite of the strenuous opposition of the Liverpool Corporation.

pendence Day in Bootle'.[1] What never seems to have occurred to anyone was to hold a plebiscite of those affected.

Nothing, however, can obscure the fact that during the Edwardian period Merseyside was increasingly becoming a single community. It is true that the tunnel was still some distance in the future, and that crossing the river by ferry left a good deal to be desired, but in 1886 the Mersey Railway had come into existence, and the results of this were not long in making themselves felt. On the Cheshire side, in addition to the town of Birkenhead, the dormitory satellite of Wallasey was growing fast, and it was itself to become a borough in 1910, while the transformation of the more distant villages of Heswall and Hoylake into suburbs of Liverpool had already begun. In effect, there was a rapidly increasing number of people whose lives were spent partly on one side and partly on the other side of the river. The Council did not wholly favour this state of affairs, for it passed a resolution requiring its employees, from the Town Clerk downwards, to reside within the city boundaries.

The whole development has been well summed up by a recent writer, and his remarks throw no inconsiderable light upon the outlook of Merseyside in the opening years of the present century:

> The most striking feature this story is the very strong separatist tendency and will to independence in all the suburban areas. Except to a limited extent in the case of Birkenhead, there is no evidence in the record that this was due to any special faults and failures on the part of the Liverpool Corporation. There is in fact a good deal of evidence that much of this separation was due to financial reasons of a not easily defensible character – that the suburban population wished to avoid paying its share towards the inevitably high cost of the social services in an area with so much poverty as Liverpool, and that the exodus to the suburbs was in fact in one of its aspects a flight from civic responsibility.
>
> On the other hand, the stubborn and positive attitude of Bootle cannot be explained entirely in these terms. It seems also clear that the subjective aspects of community life could be more readily developed and preserved, even where the objec-

[1] July 7th, 1903.

tive basis was reduced to a minimum, in a smaller area such as Bootle, than in an area of the large size which Liverpool had now attained. If this is so the situation clearly demands both large and small authorities, and the argument for a federation or two-tier system is thereby strengthened. In the light of this it could reasonably be maintained that the policy of direct absorption pursued by the Liverpool Corporation after 1880 was almost as harmful as their previous neglect of the problem; not only because it reduced the willingness of the smaller authorities to enter a federation, but because in the long run it tended to lower the level of civic consciousness in Liverpool itself. The problem, however, has everywhere proved difficult, and the mistakes in connection with it are hardly discreditable.

Contrary to what is often asserted, the Edwardian era was not by any means one of purely material progress, and if proof of this be required it is to be found in the building of Liverpool cathedral. The bishopric had been founded in pursuance of an Act of Parliament of 1878, and the first occupant of the see was John Charles Ryle, who had had a distinguished career at Christ Church, Oxford. He was a man of commanding presence, Evangelical in his views, and he did not take kindly to opposition, which meant that he was not the easiest of ecclesiastics with whom to deal: on the other hand he had many difficulties with which to contend and he mentioned that 'of the four sees which Lord Cross's Act had called into existence, not one started under such heavy disadvantages as Liverpool, its population being twice as large as that of Newcastle or Wakefield, and a third larger than Southwell, each of which contained nearly double the number of benefices'. Ryle was on several occasions urged to take in hand the question of a cathedral, but rightly or wrongly he preferred to devote his energies to providing for overcrowded districts, where many more clergy and churches were urgently needed.

In 1900 Dr Ryle was succeeded as bishop by Dr Chavasse, of whom mention has already been made. His views on the need for a cathedral, as well as on many other subjects, differed fundamentally from those of his predecessor, and he at once suggested

---

[1] White, Brian D.: *A History of the Corporation of Liverpool, 1835–1914*, p. 176.

that a small committee be appointed to formulate a proposal. Civic patriotism was nowhere lacking in the Liverpool of those days, and one of the most prominent citizens, namely Sir William Forwood, accepted the chairmanship in circumstances that reflected the highest credit upon him: provided that the question of a site and the appointment of a general committee was deferred until the promises of financial help gave reasonable expectation of success he promised to give up all other work, and for six weeks to devote himself to canvassing for the Building Fund. So successful were his efforts that before long a sum of £325,000 was paid or promised, and included in this figure were £25,000 contributed by the representatives of the Earle and Langton families towards the erection of the Lady Chapel: the other old Liverpool families, it may be added, were equally generous.

The next step was the selection of a site, and in due course the committee decided on St James's Mount as being both central and commanding, a decision with which no one would wish to quarrel. Parliamentary sanction was, however, necessary, and by the Liverpool Cathedral Act, 1902, the cathedral committee acquired the whole of St James's Mount and Gardens and St James's Walk, a space of 1,020 feet in length, and 248 feet in its greatest breadth. The winning design was that of Gilbert Scott, a young man of only twenty-one, who was accordingly appointed architect, and on July 19th, 1904, the foundation stone was laid by King Edward VII: the Edwardian age had, however, ended before the cathedral came into use with the consecration of the Lady Chapel.

Academically, as well as ecclesiastically, these years were notable ones in the history of Liverpool, for in 1903 the Privy Council granted a full Charter for an independent Liverpool University. The university was already attracting a number of remarkable men, foremost of whom was Sir Charles Sherrington, who had come to Merseyside in 1895 on appointment as Holt Professor of Physiology. 'In Liverpool Sherrington reached the peak of his research contributions to the analysis of the motor behaviour of the organism. It was here that he worked on the mechanism of reflex action, on reciprocal innervation, on decerebrate rigidity, and on cortical localization. Here also he published his only book on the physiology of the nervous system.'[1] Sherrington as a physiologist did honour to the young university by holding one of its Chairs, while as a philosopher and a poet he did much for the humanities in Liverpool as a whole.

It is not suggested that Liverpool was unique among the cities of Great Britain in its progressive activities during the Edwardian era, rather was it typical – that is why they have been recounted at some length: the countryside might be dying, but the great cities were flourishing. London might be the capital of the kingdom, but its influence was not as great as it was later to become. Two World Wars have resulted in a concentration of authority in Government hands that would have seemed impossible to the vast majority of Edwardians, and the Government is situated in London. Sixty years ago in cities like Liverpool what went on in the capital aroused little interest, and no great prominence was given to it in the local Press: national newspapers were in their infancy, while the London ones did not reach Liverpool much before noon, and in any case they were not widely read. All this explains the creative municipal life in the provinces in the opening years of the century.

[1] Cohen of Birkenhead, Lord: *Sherrington*, p. 9.

CHAPTER IV

The Countryside

————◦◉◦————

WHEN King Edward VII succeeded his mother the countryside in the main, and particularly in the South of England, presented a sorry spectacle, for apart from certain favoured neighbourhoods, and the specialized population which served the needs of the country-houses, it was hastening to decay. No one stayed there who could possibly find employment elsewhere, and all the young people with energy and initiative forsook the life of the villages and fields for that of the towns. The peasantry was unique in Europe in its complete divorce from the land, and it found no attraction in the cheerless toil of an agricultural labourer upon what was a scanty wage. In consequence the villages increasingly tended to be left to old women and children, while the ancient skilled occupations were becoming lost arts.[1]

The written evidence to this effect is overwhelming, quite apart from the memory of those still alive. 'There is no social life at all,' wrote a Somerset clergyman. 'A village which once fed, clothed, policed, and regulated itself cannot now dig its own wells or build its own barns. Still less can it act its own dramas, build its own church; or organize its own work and play. It is pathetically helpless in everything.' He saw no prospect of this decay being halted. 'As things go on now,' was his forecast, 'we shall have empty fields, except for a few shepherds and herdsmen, in all the green of England. Nomadic herds will sweep over the country, sowing, shearing, grass-cutting, reaping, and binding with machines: a system which does not make for health, peace, discipline, noble-

_____
[1] *Cf.* Masterman, C. F. G.: *The Condition of England*, p. 160.

ness of life. . . . England is bleeding at the arteries, and it is her reddest blood which is flowing away.'[1]

In rural Essex the situation was no better, for an observer in that county found the land becoming one 'vast wilderness' and a 'retreat for foxes and conies', while the houses were tumbling into decay, no new ones were being built, and apathy was settling down like a grey cloud upon the whole population. 'The sturdy sons of the village,' he laments, 'have fled, they have left behind the old men, the lame, the mentally deficient, the vicious, the born tired.' Farm buildings and cottages were rapidly going to pieces, and there was a steady increase in the agricultural returns of 'land laid down to grass', but which he considered 'would be better described "as land which has laid itself down to twitch and thistle"'. This particular critic would appear to have been something of a Little Englander, since he had no use for 'those glowing patriots who, in their anxiety to build up an Empire, have been grabbing at continents and lost their own land'.[2] Though what exactly they should have done about it he does not condescend to inform his readers.

From Wiltshire there comes the same catalogue of woes, and in that county an observer reported that it was a common saying, 'As long as a man stays on the land he can't call his soul his own.' This critic deplores the passing of the old village gentry, who both understood and sympathized with the labourer, while the larger farmers, who had replaced them, like the middle class in the towns, hated and despised those beneath them.[3] In such a society it was hardly surprising that news of even the most stirring events should filter down into the countryside like the noise of something far away, and the General Election of 1900, the South African War, and the death of the Queen did scarcely more than ripple the surface of these deep waters; of far more importance was the untimely summer rain which ruined the harvest, eviction from a cottage, the illness of a wife, or the calamity of advancing age, for there was as yet no Old Age Pension.

[1] Marson, C. L.: *The Commonwealth.*
[2] Quoted by Masterman, C. F. G.: *The Condition of England*, p. 161.
[3] Pedder, D. C.: *Where Men Decay.*

Even for the farmer life was monotonous, though not as monotonous as twenty years earlier, before the coming of the bicycle, when Richard Jefferies could write that 'the farmer in his isolated homestead was more cut off from the world than the settler at the present time in the backwoods or on the prairies'.[1] Amusements there were none, other than could be had at the ale-house or by riding into the market-town to the inn there. Almost down to the Queen's death a spell of drinking was the staple diversion for many an otherwise respectable farmer. It was not unusual for some well-to-do one of the old school to ride off on his nag and not to be heard of for a week, till he was discovered at a distant roadside inn, where he had spent the interval in straightforward drinking.

There were several reasons for the sorry state of the countryside, and at the beginning of the twentieth century the immediate cause was the agricultural slump in the seventies of its predecessor. The mechanical inventions, and particularly the improvement in the means of communication and transport, gave powerful assistance to the process which had been going on since the end of the eighteenth century, and led to a further transfer of population from the villages to the towns, so that by 1901 no less than 77 per cent of the inhabitants of the United Kingdom were resident in urban districts. While the towns and their suburbs showed a rapid increase at each decennial census, the purely agricultural areas, including the whole of Ireland except the north-eastern corner, were almost stationary or actually retrogressive. The opening up of new countries beyond the seas, and the development of oceanic and railway transport, combined to bring into England those supplies of cheap foreign food and raw materials which were as valuable to the manufacturers as they were detrimental to the agricultural interest. The acreage under wheat and other grain crops declined steadily, and, as we have seen, the labourers left the land to seek employment in the mills and factories. National prosperity, as measured by manufacturing production and the statistics of imports and exports, was at a higher level than ever before in 1873, when Great Britain was called

[1] *Round About a Great Estate.*

upon to make good the destruction of capital caused by the Franco-German War; but in the years that followed a succession of bad harvests told heavily on agriculture, and prices were further depressed by the extension of wheat-growing in the United States, which was now pouring grain into England.

There was no permanent recovery in the rural economy after this. In 1874 the area under wheat in the United Kingdom was in the neighbourhood of four million acres, but by the Queen's death it had fallen by considerably more than half; other arable crops also declined, though not to the same extent. At the same time the average freight per quarter of wheat by ship from New York to Liverpool fell from 5s 6d in 1871 to 10d in 1901,[1] so that the imports of wheat per head of the population doubled and those of meat quadrupled between 1870 and the end of the century. In effect, although the general wealth and productive activity continued to grow, the agricultural interest had no share in this expansion, and it is to be noted that the value of land as assessed for Income Tax was eleven millions lower in 1899 than it had been thirty years earlier.

The real cause for the decay of rural England, which was a long process, must be sought much further back, and it is to be found in the Enclosures, a piece of the grossest injustice which had been admirably summed up in the lines:

> The law locks up the man or woman,
> Who steals the goose from off the common;
> But lets the greater villain loose,
> Who steals the common off the goose.

Ever since the fall of the Stuarts the rich had been getting richer and the poor had been getting poorer, and by the beginning of the twentieth century the process was complete. While the monarchy was still an effective force there had been a strong yeoman and peasant class with property of its own. It is difficult to say how many people thus possessed the land upon which they lived, but it has been estimated that half the nation was in this happy position.[2] The holdings varied from a hundred to two hundred acres,

---

[1] *United States Statistical Abstract*, 1902.
[2] *Cf.* Belloc, H.: *Charles the First*, p. 24; also Jerrold, D.: *England*, pp. 65–66.

down to those of the cottager with his four or five. Some of these small-holders had to pay dues to the squire, but as long as they did so they could not be dispossessed. As early as 1714 this state of affairs was already becoming a memory, and 'the physical presence of the poor (except of those trained and adorned for domestic serfdom) grew distasteful to the rich man, whose ancestors had eaten and made merry at the long board of the Elizabethan manor.'[1]

The eighteenth century carried a very long way the revolution by which the rich became masters of the land, but the Enclosure Acts were only the logical results of the victory of the vested interests over the nation, as represented by the monarchy, in the Civil War and at the Revolution. In earlier days the rich had been checked by the Prerogative Courts such as the Star Chamber and the Council for the North,[2] but now the same people made the laws as Members of Parliament and administered them as Justices of the Peace. It thus became impossible for the poor to obtain justice at all when they came into conflict with those who governed the country, and this explains why Jacobitism drew so much of its strength from what are now called the working classes.[3]

Not until Charles I had been in his grave for twenty years did Parliament pass a General Enclosure Act which facilitated the passing of private bills, and not until the final collapse of monarchy under George III did the process acquire its final swiftness and momentum. Between 1760 and 1797 there were no less than 1,539 private Enclosure Acts by which the estates of the gentry were nicely 'rounded off', while the yeomen became tenant farmers, liable to rack-renting and eviction. In many cases the commons were enclosed without adequate compensation to those who had the right of pasturage on them, and so were deprived of the means of keeping a cow or goose, or of cutting turf for fuel. Some received no allotment because they could not prove their claims, while others sold their allotments and so became mere tenants, to

[1] John, E.: *King Charles I*, p. 70.
[2] These were far from being the organs of oppression the Whig historian would have us believe; *cf.* Reid, R. R.: *The King's Council for the North, passim.*
[3] *Cf.* Bates, C. J.: *History of Northumberland*, pp. 265–266: 'The attachment of the working classes to the Stuart cause was much deeper than might now be supposed.'

be turned out at the whim of their landlord. In effect, the process was tragically mismanaged, with the cruellest injustice to the poor, for it was conducted by the larger landowners, with their hired lawyers, whose chances of future employment rested on the reputation they could win among the landowning gentry.

Goldsmith well described these happenings when he wrote:

> Those healthful sports that grac'd the peaceful scene,
> Liv'd in each look, and brighten'd all the green;
> These, far departing, seek a kinder shore,
> And rural mirth and manners are no more.

Or again:

> Ye friends to truth, ye statesmen, who survey
> The rich man's joys increase, the poor's decay,
> 'Tis yours to judge, how wide the limits stand,
> Between a splendid and a happy land.

Dr Hunt bore eloquent testimony to the widespread effect of these changes. 'Nor could the small farmer either keep his place. . . . If his holding was unaffected by enclosure, the loss of domestic industries rendered him less able to pay his rent; if it was to be enclosed, he found himself with a diminished income at the very time when he most needed money; if he managed to keep his land for a while, he was ruined by some violent fluctuation in the price of corn. Sooner or later he sank into the labouring class.'[1] That was exactly what was intended, and well might that stout Tory, the late Lord Henry Bentinck, write during the course of the First World War, 'Our modern progress is in reality nothing but a progress of recapture by the people of what was once their own.'[2]

Most unfortunately for the wretched people concerned the Enclosures were coincident with the decay not only of domestic spinning, but also of the other industries which had been carried on in the villages from time immemorial, for with the growth of the big estate came the practice of having farming implements, harness, and household utensils made and mended in the towns rather than by local labour. In this way the peasantry, deprived at the same time of their ancient rights of commonage and of the

---

[1] *The Political History of England*, vol. X, p. 275.
[2] *Tory Democracy*, p. 5.

possibility of adding to their incomes by carrying on some industry at home, became entirely dependent on agricultural wages at a time when these were not sufficient to provide a livelihood; consequently they were either forced into the factories in the towns, or came on the rates.

The distress caused by the Enclosure Acts was widespread. For example, the villages of Wiston and Foston, in Leicestershire, before enclosure each contained about thirty-five houses; in Wiston every house disappeared except that of the squire, while Foston was reduced to the parsonage and a couple of herdsmen's cottages.[1] All over the country in 1901, not least in the south-west, were to be witnessed the traces of this tragic revolution in shrunken hamlets and desolate lanes once bordered by the cottages of a proud and independent peasantry. The Rev. Richard Warren gave valuable evidence of this as a result of a walking-tour which he took in 1799. Near Cheddar he got into conversation with a friendly labourer:

> 'Ah, Sir,' said my new acquaintance, 'time was when these commons enabled the poor man to support his family, and bring up his children. Here he could turn out his cow and pony, feed his flock of geese, and keep his pig. But the Enclosures have deprived him of these advantages. The labourer has now only his 14d per day to keep himself, his wife, and perhaps five or six children, when bread is 3d per pound, and wheat 13s per bushel. The consequence is, the parish must now assist him. Poor-rates increase to a terrible height. The farmer grumbles, and grows hard-hearted. The labourer, knowing that others must maintain his family, becomes careless, or idle, or a spend-thrift, whilst his wife and children are obliged to struggle with want, or to apply to a surly overseer for a scanty allowance.'

Mr Warner gave it as his own opinion that the Enclosures were a benefit to the landlord, the large farmer, and the clergy, 'but these advantages are purchased by so large a proportion of individual evil, that it becomes a question of morals as well as policy, a

---

[1] Cf. Howlett, J. L.: *Enquiry into the Influence which Enclosure has had on Population*, p. 10.

question as difficult as it is important, whether that system ought to be generally adopted.'[1]

The views of W. H. Hudson in the spring of 1903 are not without interest:

> Why are we lacking in that which others undoubtedly have, a something to complete the round of homely happiness in our little rural centres; how is it that we do not properly encourage the things which, albeit childlike, are essential, which sweetly recreate? It is not merely the selfishness of those who are well placed and prefer to live for themselves, or who have light but care not to shed it on those who are not of their class. Selfishness is common enough everywhere, in men of all races. It is not selfishness, nor the growth of towns or decay of agriculture, nor any of the causes usually given for the dullness, the greyness of village life. The chief cause, I take it, is that gulf, or barrier, which exists between men and women in different classes in our country, or a considerable portion of it – the caste feeling which is becoming increasingly rigid in the rural world, if my own observation, extending over a period of twenty-five years, is not all wrong.[2]

For two generations, that is to say during the Victorian period, the desolation of the countryside was materially aided by the supersession of the road by the railways. For many years after the coming of 'the iron horse' the highways sank into a deep somnolence, from which it appeared that they would never reawaken, and in some places they even became grass-grown from little use; in due course the bicycle made its appearance, and that brought a little life back to them, but places without a railway-station were still very cut off from the outside world in the early years of King Edward VII. The only sound that would disturb the nocturnal slumbers of a citizen of Shaftesbury, in Dorset, to take a typical example, would be the faltering footsteps of a late reveller, or the hooves of a horse when his master rode in to fetch the doctor to some urgent case at an outlying farm or cottage. Yet all over the British Isles the situation had been very dif-

[1] Warner, R.: *A Walk Through some of the Western Counties of England*, pp. 49–52.
[2] *Afoot in England*.

ferent within living memory, for in the reign of George IV over three hundred coaches used to pass Hyde Park daily. Now as late as 1908 a traveller could write of Somerset, 'Driving on, after a time we dropped down from a breezy eminence to a low-lying, level, drowsy land of deep green meadows watered by sluggish streams, wherein for miles we met only a farmer's waggon crawling slowly along, the meeting of which but served to accentuate the general loneliness of the prospect, a prospect that stretched far away into a mysterious distance of misty blue. Densely populated as England is, gridironed all over with railways, yet there are districts in it the very abode of loneliness, where the centuries come and go with little outward change, and the country looks much the same as it did in the days of the Stuarts, or even before their time.'[1]

With the road there fell into desuetude that other old institution, the inn, for the day had passed when the innkeeper of a town was only less important than the squire, and often served as its mayor.

The Crooked Billet Hotel and Posting-house on the Bushmead road had been severed from society by the Crumpletin Railway. It had indeed been cut off in the prime of life: for Joe Cherriper, the velvet-collared doeskin-gloved Jehu of the fast Regulator Coach, had backed his opinion of the preference of the public for horse transit over steam, by laying out several hundreds of pounds of his accumulated fees upon the premises, just as the surveyors were setting out the line.

'A rally might be andy enough for good and eavy marchandise,' Joe said, 'but as to gents ever travellin by sich contraband means, that was utterly and entirely out of the question. Never would appen so long as there was a well-appointed coach like the Regulator to be ad.' So Joe laid on the green paint and the white paint, and furbished up the sign until it glittered resplendent in the rays of the mid-day sun. But greater prophets than Joe have been mistaken.

One fine summer's afternoon a snorting steam-engine came puffing and panting through the country upon a private road of its own, drawing after it the accumulated rank, beauty

[1] Hissey, J. J.: *An English Holiday with Car and Camera*, pp. 79–80.

and fashion of a wide district to open the railway, which presently sucked up all the trade and traffic of the country. The Crooked Billet fell from a first-class way-side house at which eight coaches changed horses twice a day into a very seedy, unfrequented place. . . . Still it was visited with occasional glimpses of its former greatness in the way of meets of the hounds, when the stables were filled, and the long-deserted rooms rang with the revelry of visitors.[1]

If the country-inn of Victorian and early Edwardian days had few guests apart from the isolated party on a driving-tour, a form of amusement which had quite a number of devotees in the eighties, those who did come were rarely in a hurry, and were only too ready to express their opinion of the treatment they had received; so in consequence the visitors' book was very far from being the soulless affair it is today.

Some of the entries are far from flattering, and it is difficult to understand why the landlord should have allowed the comments in question to remain in the book. Such are:

> I came here for change and rest,
> The landlord took the change,
> And the waiter took the rest.

and

> The Crown is painted on the board
>   This inn hangs out as sign.
> And only monarchs could afford
>   To stay here or to dine.

The same sentiment was expressed in the visitors' book of a Scottish hotel:

> Mine host of mine inn is a very small man,
>   For a soldier he'd need to be larger,
> But if war should break out, he'll do what he can;
>   He'd make a magnificent charger.

One visitor who had been satisfied with neither the fare, nor the charges, nor the accommodation, when asked by the landlord to 'write something' in the book wrote, 'Quoth the raven . . . !' Yet the earliest recorded entry was of a flattering description,

---

[1] Surtees, R. S.: *Ask Mamma*, ch. LI.

and it was made by the Imperial ambassador in the year 1129 when staying at the *Fountain* at Canterbury – 'The inns in England are the best in Europe; those in Canterbury are the best in England; and the *Fountain*, wherein I am now lodged as handsomely as if I were in the King's Palace, the best in Canterbury.'[1] Before visitors' books came into fashion it was the custom for wits to scratch their comments on the window-panes, and an example of this is the couplet which Swift scratched with a diamond on the window of his room at the *Three Crosses*, an old inn which formerly stood at Willoughby on the Holyhead road:

> There are three crosses at your door;
> Hang up your wife, and you'll count four.

Upon reading this the landlord is said to have changed his sign to the *Four Crosses*, and, however this may be, it was certainly known as such in the coaching days.

The Edwardian period witnessed the rapid development of the motor-car and consequently the re-birth of the road: indeed, this was in no small measure due to the example of the King himself, for he was one of the earliest motorists in Great Britain. His first trip in a motor-car took place two years before his accession when Mr Scott-Montagu, M.P., afterwards the second Lord Montagu of Beaulieu, drove him in a 12 h.p. Daimler at Highcliffe whilst he was staying with the Cavendish-Bentincks. In those days motoring was regarded as a very low affair, and quite unworthy of Royal patronage, but by March, 1902, the King was the possessor of several cars, and he had made a long motor tour in France. Considerable pressure was put on him to use a 'motor-coach' at his Coronation, and he was by no means unwilling to assist the nascent British motor industry in this way, but when it was pointed out to him that such a vehicle would have to be without noticeable vibration, noise, vapour, or smell the King reluctantly decided that the proposal was unworkable, and it was consequently abandoned.[2]

All the same he continued to be a great patron of motoring, and garages were constructed at Windsor, Sandringham, and Buck-

---

[1] *Cf.* Burke, Thomas: *The English Inn*, p. 30.
[2] *Cf. The Autocar*, December 9th, 1901.

ingham Palace: his own first choice of cars was a Daimler and a Mercedes, and he understood something about their engines. In 1905 King Edward became the Patron of the Automobile Exhibition at the Crystal Palace, and two years later, of its successor at Olympia; while in 1907 he added the title of Royal to the Automobile Club, and in 1909 – with rare prescience – to the Aero Club. Nor was he an anonymous motorist, for his cars were always known by the fact that they alone in the kingdom bore no number-plate.[1] It may be noted that this proclivity did not meet with his mother's approval, and Queen Victoria was not attracted by a photograph of her eldest son in an open motor, wearing a tall hat which had been shaken or blown over his nose. 'I hope', she told the Master of the Horse, 'you will never allow any of those horrible machines to be used in my stables. I am told that they smell exceedingly nasty, and are very shaky and disagreeable conveyances altogether.'[2]

There was a good deal of truth in the old Queen's comments, for in its earlier days motoring was much more of an adventure than might now be supposed, and not always a very pleasant adventure. In the first place the motors themselves were far from comfortable, and the jolting which their passengers received was more like the motion required to churn milk into cheese than anything else, for the roads were indescribably bad. Then, again, body-building was in its infancy, and in some makes the driver's seat was over the engine, which did not make for basic coolness on a long run. Nor was even this all, for the motorist was liable to be assailed with cries of 'stink-pots' or greeted with the odd stone, and one of the species was welcomed by an old lady at Pitlochry on his arrival there with the words, 'None o' your stinking paraffin lamps for me.'

Progress was also very slow, partly due to repeated breakdowns and partly to frequent punctures, for all roads were liberally besprinkled with nails from horses' shoes. Mr J. H. Turner, for many years agent to the sixth Duke of Portland, has left on record particulars of what must have been one of the earliest runs in

[1] *Cf.* Lee, Sir Sidney: *King Edward VII, A Biography*, vol. II, pp. 396–397.
[2] *Cf.* Portland, Duke of: *Men, Women, and Things*, p. 316.

Scotland, namely from Paisley to Langwell in Caithness, a distance of just under three hundred miles, which he and three companions covered in three days in September, 1901.

The car used was a 10 h.p. Arrol-Johnston of the dogcart type, with tiller steering, large diameter wooden wheels with solid tyres, seated for four, and, we are told open to 'a' the airts the wind could blow'. On the steepest hills the party averaged eight miles an hour, and from Helmsdale to Langwell they did the twelve miles in an hour. Heads were shaken over their rashness, and the inn-keeper at Helmsdale, in a manner reminiscent of the old man in *Excelsior*, begged Mr Turner not to take his car over the Ord of Caithness, for if he did he would 'live to regret it'. From the time the party left Paisley until it reached Langwell not another motor vehicle of any description was seen, though this was perhaps not very surprising in view of the fact that it is doubtful if there were more than a hundred cars in Scotland at the time; on the other hand, in that same autumn of 1901 there were from twelve to fourteen taxis plying the streets of Edinburgh.[1]

Even as late as 1909 the journey from Oxford to Shaftesbury took a single day, and it was not always easy to get petrol. One motorist in Somerset in these early times on asking for it at an inn met with the reply, 'Petrol! I don't know what it is; I never heard the name before.' On another occasion, however, in the same county, a young woman in an equally remote place at once came forward and produced what was required: when surprise was expressed at it being so readily forthcoming in such an out-of-the-way district she replied, 'You may well call it out-of-the-way; it's awfully dull here, there's nothing doing, nothing to do, and no life about the place. You see I've lived in London all my life, and am used to the town; I don't feel as how I shall ever get used to the country, but I've got married, and have to live with it; my husband is away all day, and I feel terribly lonely at times. It is a relief to have even a stranger to talk to. The greatest excitement we have is when a motor-car passes by; it makes it a bit cheerful like for the moment. We started selling petrol not so much for the profit of the thing, as because it gives me something to do when my man's away, and it gives me someone to pass the time of day with.'

The motorist of those days may have been subject to inconveniences which his modern successor can hardly imagine, but he saw the last of an England that was soon to be a thing of the past, namely the England of Trollope and Whyte-Melville. An early motoring centre, for example, was *Pople's New London Hotel* in Exeter, now hardly even a memory in that city. In spite of its name it was formerly a famous coaching house, and is mentioned with the *Old London Hotel* in Paterson's *Roads* and other pre-railway guides. However, by the time that the motorist came to use it the courtyard had been roofed over and converted into a spacious lounge. As early as 1907 the landlord could tell a visiting motorist, 'In the old days sixty coaches used to pull up at this house every weekday, and no less than four hundred horses were stabled here. Now, in the summer-time, the large majority of our visitors arrive by motor-car.'

Old customs, as well as old buildings, survived, and at Berrow in Somerset there was still to be heard on the appropriate Sunday a long exhortation against the wickedness of duelling. This was due to a lady who lived in the neighbourhood, and whose lover was killed in a duel there; upon her death a clause was found in her will stipulating that the rent of a certain meadow 'should be for ever devoted to the payment of a minister for annually delivering a sermon in Berrow church on the crime of duelling', and certainly during the reign of King Edward VII the fee was paid and the sermon preached. In Leicester the visitor attending one of the churches could still hear from the pulpit a long discourse upon 'the glorious and ever-memorable victory' over the Spanish Armada, for in 1640 one Thomas Haynes, a citizen of London, died, and left in his will twenty shillings a year for a sermon to be preached annually in Leicester in reference to the Spanish defeat.

During one of his peregrinations in the West of England in the opening years of the present century Mr Hissey came across the following item in a local newspaper:

Mr. Phillimore, charity commissioner, has been conducting an inquiry into the charities of the parish of Ilsington, South Devon. In respect to a sum of £360 left by one Ann Hale, it was stated that the interest of the money had to be paid to six of the oldest poor people who were able to repeat the catechism openly in the parish church at Ilsington. Mr. Phillimore: "Is that done now? Because the custom would be rather picturesque." The Vicar: "Picturesque, but not altogether edifying. It is an extraordinary and unique thing, and I do not think that there is a similar charity in the country. The custom of having it every two or three years has sprung up lately. The colloquial way of making application to me is, 'Please, sir, is it my turn to say my prayers this year?' It used to be competitive originally, but the practice has been dropped. Each person saying the catechism gets 22s. or 23s.". Mr. Phillimore: "That is worth saying the catechism for, and I think the custom ought to be maintained."[1]

Life proceeded at a more leisurely pace in Edwardian England than has more recently been the case, and at Ecton, in Northamptonshire, a notice was to be found in a cottage window to the effect that 'letters for Mr ...., Surgeon, may be left here on Tuesdays and Fridays'. On a villager being asked how the inhabitants got along without a resident doctor, he replied, 'Get along: we gets along right enough. We never want a doctor until us be dying, and then a doctor bain't much good!' This recalls the contemporary, but possibly apocryphal, story of the staff officer who rode over to the lines of the 9th Lancers on Salisbury Plain in the middle of the hunting season in quest of the Adjutant, only to find a notice on the door of that gentleman's office saying that 'the Adjutant will attend at this office on alternate Fridays'. It was not stated which those Fridays were.

In one respect the motorist of the first decade of the century shakes hands across the years with his successor of the seventh, and that is where the signposting of the English road is concerned. In 1908 Mr Hissey wrote that 'at present, signposts are apt to be too local in their information, frequently only pointing the way to places near at hand and of small importance'. His words ring

[1] *An English Holiday with Car and Camera*, p. 154.

equally true today, for although the situation is improving there is much to be done before it is ideal, as more than one local authority would do well to realize.

With regard to the food with which the motorist was likely to find himself regaled, it was a good deal less varied than it would be today, and an entry in the diary of the late Lord Mersey, under date of 1907, throws some light both upon this and other aspects of the Edwardian countryside:

> At the end of July I was sent by the Board of Trade on a confidential enquiry to ascertain the position between Railways and Traders in the West of England as to rates, services and freights. This took me to a number of provincial centres. It was odd to find that fresh fruit and vegetables sent from Normandy to London via Southampton came at a cheaper rate than similar produce from Hampshire. I visited some thirty towns, and interviewed about two hundred people. The inns, except at Blandford, Ludlow, and Launceston, were very poor, and I think I must have eaten most of the tomato soup, roast lamb, and plum tart in England, and tasted some of the worst claret in existence. At Shrewsbury two old farmers took their boots off in the only public sitting-room, and then read Dryden aloud to each other.[1]

Four years earlier W. H. Hudson had much the same experience in the same part of the country, on this occasion at Shepton Mallet:

> I had to go for my lunch to one of the big public-houses, called hotels; but whether it called itself a cow, or horse, or stag, or angel, or a blue or green something, I cannot remember. They gave me what they called a beefsteak pie – a tough crust and under it some blackish cubes carved out of the muscle of an antediluvian ox – and for this delicious fare and a glass of stout I paid three shillings and oddpence.[2]

The countryside during the Edwardian period was dominated, as neither before nor since, by the country-houses, which had not yet become 'stately homes', for their owners lived in, not on,

[1] *Picture of Life, 1872–1940*, p. 221.
[2] *Afoot in England.*

them. They had their critics, and it will be remembered that Sherlock Holmes on one occasion referred scathingly to the 'butlers, footmen, maid-servants, and the usual overfed, underworked staff of a large English country-house'.[1] They varied, of course, in size, and they varied in respect of the type of parties that were given in them, but it can safely be said that the amount of entertaining done reached its peak during these years. The coming of the motor-car and the improvement in the railway services made it easy to fill them, while their owners were in no way pinched in the pocket, for when King Edward came to the throne Income Tax was a mere shilling in the pound, there was no surtax, and the effect of the Death Duties imposed in the previous decade had hardly been felt: servants were plentiful and cheap, though whether they were as efficient as they appear in retrospect is open to question.

That these large country-houses and the parties that went on in them brought a good deal of money into the impoverished countryside cannot be denied, but it is doubtful if they brought much else. Society at all levels was still rather rough, and the sense of humour was everywhere pretty crude; nor were the young ladies of the day as modest in their behaviour as they doubtless like to make out to their Elizabethan grand-daughters. Apple-pie beds and pillows covered with flour were the general rule, and the young man who stayed in a country-house had need to be on perpetual guard against these and similar booby-traps. A particularly irritating custom in every sense of the word was to sew a mustard-leaf in the crutch of a man's dinner trousers which made its presence increasingly felt as the evening progressed: a thin sprinkling of sodium, which explodes on contact with water, on the bottom of a chamber-pot also never ceased to provoke merriment. Yet when there is taken into account the ragging that went on in the Services, the Universities, and the Public Schools these week-end diversions appear relatively innocuous, if not very edifying.

From time to time these country-house parties could be made to serve diplomatic purposes, and one such instance occurred only

[1] *Wisteria Lodge.*

a few days before the old Queen died. The scene was Chatsworth, where a large party of about fifty was assembled for amateur theatricals, and under cover of this Baron von Eckardstein was invited to meet Joseph Chamberlain in order to discuss Anglo-German relations. What ensued has been admirably described by Mr Julian Amery:

> Among the guests at Chatsworth were two young people much in love. On the very night of the Baron's talk with Chamberlain, they arranged to meet in *her* room when the company was retired. But Chatsworth, as Dr. Johnson once remarked, is "a very fine house"; and the young man, fearing to mistake another room for his lady's, asked her to leave a sign to show which was her door. On the spur of the moment she promised to drop a large sandwich on the floor outside. Now Eckardstein was a voracious eater, accustomed to devour a whole cold chicken before retiring. That evening, however, the prolonged discussion of foreign affairs had intercepted his hopes of lighter refreshment. Hungry and morose he was retiring to bed, when, as he walked along the passage to his room, he saw a sandwich lying on the floor. Making sure he was alone, he pounced upon this dusty prey. In an instant it was devoured; and the course of true love was made less smooth than ever.[1]

Foremost among the country-house sets were 'The Souls', of which membership was confined to a charmed circle of 'personages distinguished for their beauty, breeding, delicacy, and discrimination of mind', as the *St James's Gazette* afterwards described them, and the female members included some of the most beautiful and intelligent women in the high society of the day. They held dinners in London, or gathered at some country-house for the week-end, to discuss literature and the arts, to play charades, and to write poetry or plays, which latter they acted on the lawns. They were, it may be added, 'serenely aware ... of their superiority to the common herd and the mundane activities of the day'.[2] It is said that their nickname was originally given to them by Lord Charles Beresford at a dinner party at Lord Brownlow's house in

---

[1] *Life of Joseph Chamberlain*, vol. IV, p. 143.
[2] Mosley, L.: Curzon, *The End of an Epoch*, p. 44.

the early summer of 1888 when he said, 'You all sit and talk about each other's souls – I shall call you "The Souls".'

Whether their morals were any better than those of their less intellectual contemporaries is open to doubt, and this is not diminished by the presence in their midst of Harry Cust, who was perhaps the most notorious lecher of the day. He was a Conservative Member of Parliament, first for Stamford and then for Bermondsey, for a number of years, and he was for a time editor of the *Pall Mall Gazette*, but the pursuit of women was his preoccupation. On one occasion a titled lady who was a member of 'The Souls' found that she was with child by him, and as her husband had been abroad for eighteen months her position was somewhat embarrassing. However, no less a person than Arthur Balfour came to the rescue and took counsel's opinion, with the result that matters were smoothed over and the baby, a girl, was accepted as part of the noble and injured husband's family. 'Such contretemps were not uncommon among the group whose intercourse was by no means purely intellectual.'[1] It was indeed a wise child who knew his own father in that world.

Largely owing to these country-houses and the parties that took place in them the Edwardians have acquired a bad reputation on the score of their morals, though to what extent this was justified is not easy to say. 'I don't know how the old man got away with it,' a grandson of King Edward VII recently remarked, but the answer is that he always behaved with the utmost dignity and circumspection in public, and that was typical of his age. There might be all sorts of 'goings-on' at these big country-house parties, and the *Morning Post* would publish a complete list of those who were present, but only the initiated had any idea who was likely to be found in bed with whom. The present era is one of exhibitionism, and a reputation for vice is an asset to a young man or a young woman in certain circles, but in Edwardian days the opposite was the case, and it is difficult to resist the conclusion that the real sin was to be found out. Which attitude is preferable can only be a matter of opinion.

In this connection the Lord Cadogan, who was Lord-

[1] Young, K.: *Arthur James Balfour*, p. 145.

Lieutenant of Ireland, used to tell a story of a man who was travelling to that country, and arrived at Euston just in time to catch the Irish Mail, which left at 9.0 p.m. He was bundled by the porter into the nearest first-class carriage, which he found empty except for an extremely attractive young lady. They became very friendly during the course of the journey, and by the time they reached Holyhead she had granted him the last favours. Before they parted on the boat she said, 'I don't know your name, and you don't know mine; but I trust that if we ever meet again you will not recognize me.' At Kingstown the woman went off to the South, and the man to the North to stay with friends. A few days later he received a letter saying that his great-uncle, who lived in the South, was dying. This great-uncle, who was old and rich, had for many years been estranged from the family, and had recently married a young wife whom none of them had seen.

The great-nephew, who was heir-presumptive, set off at once, but on his arrival found that the old man was already dead; in his bedroom was his widow – the young woman of the train. The succession to the title and property could not be determined until the statutory ten months had elapsed, but shortly before this occurred the lady gave birth to a son, who thus cut his father out of everything.

The outward segregation of the sexes, and the taboo on all that related to their mutual relations, both a legacy of Victorianism, was a rigid convention, though we now know that from Royalty and the Cabinet downwards there was very considerable laxity in the private lives of those who were generally regarded as pillars of society; yet if a woman of the middle class went in a hansom alone with a man who was neither her husband nor old enough to be her grandfather her reputation was irretrievably lost. The ruling convention was directed against unmarried men and women ever being alone together unless they were engaged, and not always then. If an engagement was broken off the girl suffered in consequence, while divorce – like cancer – was never mentioned in polite society. As a result, in the upper and upper middle class the young men were driven to somewhat sordid intrigues in other quarters, and youths in their late teens were apt to rank among their fellows according to their alleged triumphs over what were generally termed 'skivvies' or shop-girls, and it is doubtful if such connections were really good for either party.

However this may be, it was avicide and vulpicide, rather than fornication, which in the main brought together the members of an Edwardian house-party. The amount of game slaughtered was quite fantastic, and this was due partly to the improvement in fire-arms and partly to that of the raising of birds. It was in very truth the heyday of the 'crack shot', and among the foremost of those who qualified for this appellation were the Prince of Wales (later King George V), Lords Ripon, Walsingham, Forester, and Huntingfield, and Mr Rimington Wilson. Some of these 'crack shots' were in reality trained marksmen and little else: with perfectly drilled loaders, who knew their every characteristic, and with the constant practice provided by the firing of more than thirty thousand cartridges a year, they killed their birds to admiration, but when the drive was over they were a little inclined to lose interest in the proceedings until called upon to shoot again.

Some idea of the bags before the First World War can be obtained from a pheasant-shoot at Hall Barn, Beaconsfield, the residence of Lord Burnham, on December 18th, 1913, when seven guns accounted for 3,937 birds. Among the party was King George V, and in reply to a question Lord Burnham's agent testified to the accuracy of that monarch's shooting. 'I will tell you what I saw myself,' he said. 'After lunch they were in Dorney Bottom. The birds were coming over very fast and very high. I watched the King and kept count. He brought down thirty-nine birds with thirty-nine consecutive cartridges, and only with the fortieth did he miss.'[1] On another occasion at the same place he fired 1,760 cartridges from his guns in a single day.

King George V, it is to be noted, always used hammer guns, and when he was only shooting with two this lost a fraction of time while his loader was cocking them: when three guns were employed this did not matter as a third man cocked them. His father, though very fond of shooting, was never in the same class as his son.

[1] Cf. Gore, John: *King George V, A Personal Memoir*, p. 230.

It would be interesting to know how long obsolete fire-arms continued to be used – probably much longer than is generally supposed; there was certainly an old man who used to shoot rabbits in the park at Ashridge with a muzzle-loading gun with remarkable accuracy just before the Second World War. Another devotee of tradition was Sir Stephen Gaselee, one-time Librarian of the Foreign Office, who had a small property, with some admirable partridge-shooting, in Cambridgeshire, and as he objected to smokeless powder those who shot with him said that after a few minutes the scene of their activities came to resemble an eighteenth-century battlefield. There was one outstanding difference between those days and the present, for it would have been considered the height of bad form to have sold the game shot: it had to be distributed to all and sundry, and this after a big shoot was a task in itself.

If the Edwardian era marked the apogee of covert-shooting it found hunting past its zenith. The late Lord Willoughby de Broke in his Introduction to *The Sport of Our Ancestors*[1] asked the question in respect of the three generations of the nineteenth century, 'Which of them had the best of it – the grandfather who was born about 1810, the father who was born about 1840, or the son who was born about 1870?' He answered by a decision in favour of the grandfather, and since the section of the community with which he was dealing was the country gentleman his choice can hardly be seriously disputed. With those who began life in the sixties and seventies, and who were in the full vigour of middle age when the old Queen died, it was somewhat different:

> Their greatest treasure is the link they can preserve with that picturesque country life of which their grandfathers could tell them. Some of them, for instance, had the rare privilege of taking their first lessons in driving four horses from the men of old time who had driven the mail coaches. . . . As boys and girls they had a glimpse of the placid country society of the undiluted mid-Victorian type, before its character was destroyed by the multiplication of quick trains up to London, automobiles, kodaks, telephones, and weekend parties.

[1] Published in 1921.

The atmosphere of Eton and Oxford was much the same as it had been in the time of their fathers, particularly the Eton of Dr. Hornby. There was a very slight draught, almost imperceptible, when Dr. Warre of revered memory succeeded Dr. Hornby, the effect of which can only be appreciated by those who were at Eton when the change took place. The nature of the change was the substitution of a certain flavour of the orderly room for the dignified, flexible, countryhouse compromise that prevailed when Hornby was headmaster. At Oxford the Bullingdon, fox-hunting, steeple-chasing set was still flourishing. Those who went to Oxford at any time, say, between 1885 and 1895, found it to be exactly the place their fathers had described.[1]

It is true that the Edwardian hunting-man enjoyed advantages unknown to his father and grandfather in that he could without undue inconvenience go out with packs very far afield: his grandfather would have had to hack all night along a turnpike-road, and even his father would have been doomed to spend hours sitting up in an ordinary railway carriage, whereas he could enjoy a relatively luxurious journey in a sleeping compartment. At least one enthusiast used to attend every Saturday meet of the Galway Blazers by the simple expedient of catching first the Irish Mail from Euston on Friday evening and then the connection from Dublin to the West on the following morning. In effect, by the time that King Edward VII came to the throne the railway, without any assistance from the motor-car, had enabled the M.P. to hunt anywhere within a reasonable distance of London after a night at Westminster, and it had opened to the undergraduates of Oxford the pastures of Warwickshire and Buckinghamshire as alternatives to the groves of Waterperry and the thickets of Bagley Wood.

All the same the glory had departed – or was departing, for social and political unrest was beginning to pervade the hitherto quiet life of the countryside, so that perhaps the greatest asset of the Edwardian foxhunter was the memory of the exploits of his youth, and such remarks as, 'We are having rather a thin time

---

[1] P. 17. Lord Willoughby de Broke made his first attempt at coaching in London under the tuition of Charles Ward, who had driven the Exeter *Telegraph*.

now, old chap, but we have had a bit of the old, and thank goodness! no one can take it away from us,' best expressed his outlook.

Down practically to the end of the nineteenth century town was town and country was country, but thereafter they began to become confused, until today it is difficult to say where the one begins and the other ends. This is in no small measure due to the improvement in the means of communication, and the development began to make itself felt first in the neighbourhood of the capital, partly because the country immediately surrounding London is on the whole more attractive than that surrounding most of the great provincial cities, and partly because it was easier to get there; until the coming of the motor-car North Wales, for example, was far more remote for the citizen of Liverpool or Manchester than was Sussex for the Londoner. In this way there came into existence that 'stockbroker country', which is neither urban nor rural, and even before King Edward VII was in his grave it was a safe opening to a conversation with an unknown woman at any City function to ask her how far from Guildford she was living.

That shrewd observer of human nature, the late Dr McNair Wilson, has a good deal that is of interest to say about Edwardian Northumberland, where he practised for some time. At first, as a Glaswegian, he felt very much like a fish out of water, for the whole social structure was quite unfamiliar to him. In Glasgow there had only been two classes, the rich and the poor, but in Northumberland he found four, namely the squires, the yeomen farmers, the farm workers, and the clergy, and the distinctions between them were very finely drawn. The squires lunched and dined with other squires, lunched but did not dine with the big farmers, but neither lunched nor dined with anybody else, except, of course, the parson. It took Dr Wilson some time to sort it all out, but in due course one of the more communicative of the squires enlightened him. 'It's like the Army. A colonel's a colonel, and a sergeant-major's a sergeant-major. Everybody knows exactly what is expected of him, and you can't change it.' He was right, for in a curious kind of way the ghost of the Feudal System had them all in its grip. It was rank rather than class that determined a man's place in the social hierarchy, for a farmer might make a fortune without securing a single invitation to dinner, but if he bought one of the 'places', and so became a squire, his position as squire was immediately accorded to him.

Northumberland was Radical in its political allegiance, but this fact seems to have had little bearing on its social outlook. Sir Edward Grey, then Foreign Secretary, was Member of Parliament for the constituency in which Dr Wilson was living, and one night he addressed a meeting in a village hall on the subject of Lloyd George's land taxes; during the course of his remarks he declared that the idea that the ownership of land ought to confer any kind of political right was absurd. 'Landed families,' he went oh, 'in opposing this reform are trying to assert such rights. I hope that you will give them no support.' He sat down, and an old farmer rose to move the vote of thanks. 'We are proud of Sir Edward,' he declared, 'not because he is Foreign Minister of this country, nor because his word is heard with respect in every foreign country, but, first and foremost, because he belongs to one of our oldest landlord families.' Dr McNair Wilson glanced round, but 'nobody, not even Sir Edward himself, seemed to be in the least amused or surprised.'[1]

[1] *Doctor's Progress*, p. 101.

CHAPTER V

Oxford and Cambridge

————•◉•————

THE Edwardian era at Oxford and Cambridge was essentially a period of transition, though this fact was not so obvious to contemporaries as it has become in retrospect. Within living memory – that is to say until 1858 – the two universities had been governed by the Elizabethan statutes of 1570 and the Laudian statutes of 1636, and even when reform came their susceptibilities had been treated very tenderly, for the colleges were allowed to draw up their own statutes subject to the approval of the Commissioners appointed by Parliament, though at Oxford only Exeter, Lincoln, and Corpus Christi availed themselves of the privilege, the others leaving it to the Commissioners to draw up ordinances for them. In 1877 there was another Universities Act of which the main object was to increase the teaching facilities at both, to encourage research, and to diminish the number of clerical and 'idle' fellowships. The new leaven, however, worked slowly, and, as we have seen, to the average undergraduate neither university seemed to have changed much from what it had been in his father's time.

At Oxford the outstanding figure when the Queen died, though he was very shortly to follow her to the grave, was the Bishop, William Stubbs. Those were the days when a purely Anglo-Saxon background was still accepted for English history, and of this theory Stubbs and Freeman were the great protagonists – so much so, in fact, that the irreverent coined the verses:

> Ladling out the butter,
>   From alternate tubs:
> Stubbs butters Freeman,
>   And Freeman butters Stubbs.

His approach could be disconcerting. He was accustomed to walk from Oxford to Cuddesdon in the afternoon, and on his way he passed a cramming establishment then kept by Dr Grundy, the ancient historian. Grundy asked him to come in to tea whenever he felt inclined, and on the first occasion that he availed himself of the offer he was accompanied by his chaplain, a very shy man of the name of Holmes. It happened that Mrs Grundy was young at the time, and had been brought up in a family where live bishops were unknown, so she was naturally a little frightened of him. She opened the conversation with some remark about the weather, to which the Bishop replied with a wave of the hand in the direction of the chaplain, and the crushing observation, 'I always refer questions about the weather to my chaplain, Mr Holmes.' It was difficult to tell who was the more embarrassed, Mrs Grundy or Holmes. In actual fact the Bishop had the reputation of being a great humorist, but those who knew him best were inclined to think that men in his position could acquire such a reputation somewhat easily.[1]

Not that Grundy himself was remarkable for his sense of humour. In middle life he decided to conduct a personal investigation of the tactics of the battle of Marathon, and in particular to decide on the momentum with which the Athenian hoplites reached the Persian lines. Accordingly he put on the appropriate armour and charged down the hill, only to arrive breathless at the spot where the Persians would have been drawn up. From this he deduced that the Athenian advance must have lost all its momentum, for it never seems to have occurred to him that a young Greek hoplite might be in better condition than a middle-aged Oxford don, whose only exercise was playing croquet.

The Oxford of the first decade of the present century was remarkable for outstanding personalities, and very high among them must be placed Thomas Case, the President of Corpus Christi. In addition to being a very successful Head of a House he was no inconsiderable wit, and some of his sallies deserve to be rescued from oblivion. Two undergraduates were one day following him up the High, and one of them was heard to remark

[1] *Cf.* Grundy, G. B.: *Forty-five Years at Oxford*, pp. 91–92.

to the other, 'Look at that old boy's trousers: they're far too long for him.' Case turned round, 'Yes,' he observed, 'my trousers are like young puppies – they want strapping.' On another occasion, probably after a Bump Supper or a College Smoker, the chaplain's oak had been screwed up, and when that worthy, the Rev. Charles Plummer, went to take chapel the following morning he was unable to get out of his rooms. Looking from his window he saw the President walking in the Fellows' Garden, and called out in the high falsetto for which he was famous, 'Mr President, Mr President, I'm screwed.' To which came the instantaneous reply, 'Sleep it off, Mr Plummer; sleep it off.' In the interests of historical truth it must be stated that this particular story is also told of Case's immediate predecessor at Corpus, Thomas Fowler, who, incidentally, spoke with a strong Lincolnshire accent, so mischievous undergraduates were wont, when they breakfasted with him, to get the sugar basin to the far end of the table from him in order to hear him say, 'Will you pass the shogger, please?' Of Case's humanity one instance will suffice. During the First World War there were cadets in part of the college, and one morning it was reported that one of them had had a girl in his rooms all right. The Dean at the time was the aforesaid Grundy,[1] in whose veins the milk of human kindness did not flow very freely, and he urged Case to report the matter to the military authorities, but the President refused. 'He's a decent young man,' he said, and added, with a twinkle in his eye, 'After all, we were young ourselves once.'

Herbert Warren, of Magdalen, was another outstanding figure of those days, and he was assisted in his self-imposed task of creating modern Magdalen by the disrepute into which some of her rivals had temporarily fallen. For instance, on November 16th, 1911, the Earl of Derby is found writing to King George V in reply to a request that Lord Stanley should go to the same college as the Prince of Wales:

There appear to be three in the running – Christ Church, New, and Magdalen. New College I should not like as according to

---

[1] His only, and exceedingly dubious, claim to fame is that he was head of the caucus which kept Asquith out of the Chancellorship.

the Archbishop of York[1] there is much trouble there, and his is a judgment I would implicitly rely on. Christ Church is a large college apparently where all the *nouveaux riches* go, and where the sole object seems to be to spend money and prove themselves men instead of being what they are – boys. Magdalen would appear to have none of these disadvantages, and if Your Majesty choose this college I can only most humbly say I should be very content.

King George was at this time in the Red Sea on his way to India, and he replied to the effect that 'although I do not propose to settle anything until my return home, I should think that Magdalen College without a doubt is the one I shall choose as it appears to have all the advantages and none of the disadvantages of the other two'.[2] It would not seem to have occurred to either parent to ask the opinion of their respective offspring. What was the nature of the 'much trouble' at New College does not transpire, but Mr Randolph Churchill suggests that the Archbishop may have 'heard of the incendiary activities two years before of Mr Alfred Duff Cooper and his friends'.

The cloud under which Christ Church was resting was to no small extent of its own making. In 1892 the ninth Duke of Marlborough had come of age, and there were great festivities at Blenheim to which a number of undergraduates were invited. The Christ Church authorities refused their men permission to go, and those who defied the ban were 'sent down'. Action so petty inevitably gave the college a bad name of which it did not entirely rid itself until after the First World War. Warren saw the opportunity of putting Magdalen in its place in the eyes of the world, and he took it.

The Duke of Windsor has placed his views of Warren on record:

The President was a man of learning; it was therefore disillusioning to discover that the thing he appeared to value most in the world was his connexion with a certain baronet, a fact he managed to insert into every conversation. It was generally

---

[1] Cosmo Gordon Lang: the 'Old Lang Swine' of the abdication crisis.
[2] *Cf.* Churchill, Randolph S.: *Lord Derby*, *'King of Lancashire'*, pp. 156–158.

suspected that he was obsessed with the idea of filling Magdalen with titled undergraduates; hence, whenever he beamed upon me, I was never quite certain whether it was with a teacher's benevolence or from a collector's secret satisfaction with a coveted trophy.[1]

Whether Warren was quite so much of a snob as has been alleged is open to doubt, but the stories depicting him in that light are legion. Perhaps the best is the one which purports to give an account of the interview between him and the late Prince Chichibu of Japan when the latter came into residence at Magdalen. After various matters had been discussed Warren asked the Prince what his name meant in his own language, and was told 'the Son of God'. At this the President beamed, and remarked, 'You will find that we have the sons of many other distinguished men at this College.' Probably a good many of these snob stories had originally been told about Oscar Browning by generations of Cambridge men, or about Mahaffy at Trinity College, Dublin.

Another Head of a House of whom many anecdotes were told was the Warden of New College, Spooner, but most, if not all, of the 'spoonerisms' attributed to him – certainly the bawdy ones – were not his. Of the respectable slips, 'I suppose you came by the town drain', and 'Two rags and a bug' are probably the best.

In spite of the reforms of the previous century there was still a certain amount of slackness among the senior members of the University, as may be gathered from the fact that a recent Professor of Ancient History had delivered his statutory number of eight lectures all in one week of each term, and for the rest of the year had resided in London. The old life fellows were by no means extinct, and few of them had ever done any tuition for their college. To give Curzon his due he exerted himself to put matters upon a more satisfactory footing from the moment that he was elected Chancellor after Goschen and over Rosebery, though it would be an exaggeration to say that he was ever popular, for he was apt to treat the Dons in the same way as he had treated his subordinates in the Indian Civil Service – and anywhere else for that matter. Anyhow Warren, who was his Vice-Chancellor at one

[1] *A King's Story*, p. 98.

time, wrote 'that he loved Oxford there can be no doubt. Whether loved or not in return, he should certainly be highly esteemed by her.'[1]

He was not the first, but the third, Edwardian Chancellor, for Salisbury was still in office when the Queen died, and his thirty-five years' tenure of the post only came to an end with his own death in 1903. Though always ready to go into action when necessary he had followed the old tradition as Chancellor, and for the most part had been a figurehead and an absentee: here, as in other spheres, he proved himself a pungent critic rather than a reformer, and although he made some scathing remarks about 'idle Fellows' who had won their position by writing Greek Iambics, he did nothing about them.

His successor proved to be the first Viscount Goschen, who was already over seventy at the time of his election, which was in reality an agreed compromise. In national politics he was a Liberal Unionist who had become very much of a Conservative, while academically he was a 'moderate'. The Liberals, headed by men like Professor Pelham, accepted him as the best Conservative – from their point-of-view – that they could get, while although the Conservatives would have preferred Curzon he was away in India, so they were prepared to take Goschen, more particularly since on account of his age his tenure of the Chancellorship was not likely to be prolonged. Yet even so Goschen was not accepted without question, for the tradition had long been that the Chancellor should be a member of one of the old governing families of the kingdom, and Goschen hardly fulfilled this qualification; so Dr Henderson, the Warden of Wadham, approached the Marquess of Lansdowne, then Foreign Secretary, but he refused to allow his candidature to go forward. Lord Rosebery proved at first more amenable, but his name had not been in the Gazette for two days when he characteristically changed his mind and withdrew it, with the result that Goschen was elected without a contest.

In 1905 the Campbell-Bannerman Government came into office, and at once rumours began to circulate that another Commission

[1] Cf. Mosley, L.: Curzon, The End of an Epoch, p. 134.

for the two older universities was in the offing: reform was everywhere in the air, and there was no reason why Oxford and Cambridge should be excepted. Goschen quickly realized from what quarter the wind was blowing, and he called for an enquiry to show what was being done by the colleges voluntarily to assist the University in learning and science, in teaching and research. The relevant statistics were duly produced, and they showed that the colleges, according to their means, had been most generous in these respects. Such was the position when, in February, 1907, Goschen died.

By this time Curzon was back from India, and at once there was a demand that his name should go forward. Christ Church was by no means wholly in his favour, and Case[1] at Corpus was a little doubtful of the soundness of his Toryism. On the other hand All Souls, with Sir William Anson at its head, rallied to his support, as did Trinity, while there was naturally considerable backing for him in his own college of Balliol. The Liberals, possibly with the potential Commission at the back of their minds, were determined not to let a Tory go unopposed again, so they once more put Rosebery forward. In an attempt to secure another compromise Warren, then Vice-Chancellor, called a non-party meeting at Magdalen, when other names were suggested, among them those of Lord Milner and the Archbishop of Canterbury, Randall Davidson,[2] but they were not pressed, and in a straight fight Curzon beat Rosebery by 1,001 to 440 votes, though the latter obtained the support of the majority of the resident electors.

Possibly the defeated candidate's appeal was a little too academic for the graduate who was no longer in residence, and his style of oratory was admirably parodied by Sir John Squire in his imaginary speech to the House of Lords on the subject of dogs:

> Rather, my Lords, has this nameless longing for the society of dumb and faithful beasts been regarded as something worthy in a man, something to be reverently cherished, something reminiscent of that infinitude from which trailing clouds of glory do

[1] Who, incidentally, always declared himself to be a Palmerstonian Liberal.
[2] The Archbishop's name was put forward again after Curzon's death in 1925, but he declined on the ground that the last clerical Chancellor had been Laud, and he did not find the precedent encouraging.

we come. Many a man has been better for the companionship of a dog. (Cheers.) Many a sombre and tenebrous deed has been killed before it was born by the naive and half-divine appeal in the eyes of some devoted mastiff or bloodhound. (Cheers.) I have not a word to say against the dog. I have not a word to say against the dog keeper. In my own small way I have kept dogs myself. (Laughter and prolonged cheers.)

From that moment the new Chancellor began to make an impression on the University. No Chancellor had been admitted in Oxford itself since the Earl of Arran in September, 1715, when the event was made the occasion for great Jacobite demonstrations, and several supporters of the exiled dynasty were given honorary degrees. Possibly because of this the custom had developed of admitting the Chancellor by deputation in his own house, but by 1907 a body of opinion had grown up which held that this procedure was hardly worthy of a great historic university, and that recourse might well be had to the practice of an earlier day: it was therefore suggested to Curzon that he should be admitted, in full conclave, by a real Convocation and in the Sheldonian Theatre; to this he readily agreed, and the ceremony took place in May.

All this time, however, the opponents of Curzon and the advocates of a Commission had only been holding their hands, and on the eve of the holidays, July 24th, 1907, to be precise, they struck. On that day, without a word of previous warning to the Chancellor or the Vice-Chancellor of either of the two older universities, Dr Gore, the Bishop of Birmingham, rose in his place in the House of Lords and asked for a Commission to deal with the Universities of Oxford and Cambridge. His main *gravamen* was not that they did not contribute much to learning, science, and education, but that they were the preserve and playground of the 'idle rich', and had little sympathy with the poor: his speech was, in effect, a blatant appeal to class-predudice, for about the industrious rich he said very little. The Bishop also took the line that the colleges were rich while the University was poor, a statement which may have been true of Cambridge, but which was certainly not so of Oxford, as Goschen's investigations had shown.

It was then seen that however unpleasing Curzon's personality might be the University had done well to have him for its Chancellor. He took action at once, and was able to point out that he had begun to consider reform 'from within'. Asquith, still Chancellor of the Exchequer, but shortly to be Prime Minister, was, like Gladstone, a whole-hearted and conservative believer in Oxford, and so was Crewe, the Lord President of the Council, though himself a Cambridge man: to him Curzon addressed a lengthy and persuasive memorandum in which he pleaded with much weight the steps which he had already taken. As a result of his efforts Crewe announced that the Government considered that it would be unfair to deprive a young and vigorous Chancellor of the opportunity to try his hand at reform 'from within', and that in consequence the question of appointing a Commission would be deferred for the present.

Nothing is so dead as the academic politics of half a century ago, but it is difficult to resist the conclusion that had Curzon displayed as much finesse on the national stage as he did on the academic he would have left a much more savoury political reputation behind him. His policy was to cut the ground from under the reformers' feet, and he secured a very considerable success at the outset, for it was a happy but ironical coincidence that the first act of the Vice-Chancellor and Council when the University reassembled in October, 1907, was to welcome what was constitutionally a revolution, namely the recognition of the Workers' Educational Association. The Vice-Chancellor immediately expressed his willingness to nominate the first representatives of this body, seven in number, to sit with the same number of members of the Extension Delegacy on a composite committee and on equal terms; and the University, with like readiness, legalized the arrangement which worked excellently, thus making it plain for all to see that sympathy with the poor student and the working man was not the monopoly of the reformers. 'It had, too, a very great effect on the attitude of the Labour Party.'[1]

For the next eighteen months proposals for reform 'from within' were carefully elaborated, and in April, 1909, they were pub-

[1] Ronaldshay, Earl of: *The Life of Lord Curzon*, vol. III, p. 100.

lished in the form of a Red Book, or 'Scarlet Letter' as it was termed by the more irreverent. The document received a very good press, and it also had an excellent reception in somewhat unexpected quarters, for even such reformers as Gilbert Murray, Arthur Sidgwick, and Estlin Carpenter were laudatory, as were Strachan-Davidson and A. L. Smith. Walter Raleigh was loud in its praise, and W. H. Gamben, the cautious Secretary to the Chest, pronounced it 'a monument of industry, knowledge, and statesmanship, and also full of literary charm', while Morley thought it a 'very effective piece of work'. The ladies were equally enthusiastic, for Miss Wordsworth wrote that it was 'lucid, interesting, and opportune', and Miss Penrose spoke with the same cordiality. During the relatively short period which elapsed before the outbreak of the First World War a beginning was made with the projected reforms, and no Commission was set up until after its termination.

Among the more eccentric Dons of those days was Turner of B.N.C. whose sense of the fitness of things can be gauged from a letter which he wrote to the parents of an undergraduate who had died in the middle of his first term: the last sentence of this epistle ran, 'It may be of some consolation to you to know that the young man would in any case have had to go down at the end of the present term owing to his failure to pass Responsions.' Another odd character was Cuthbert Shields of Corpus, whose reputation for eccentricity kept his memory alive at least until the Second World War. His real name was Robert Laing, but during one Long Vacation he changed it for the other, which was meant to signify that he had placed himself under the protection of St Cuthbert of Durham; another version was that the change was due to a sudden realization of the fact that he had been born on the feast of St Cuthbert at Shields. He was a firm believer in the reincarnation of the dead, and he founded a body which he called the Society of the Grain of Mustard Seed, of which his friends and acquaintances were liable to find themselve members. Shields once made a bonfire in his rooms in the Fellows' Buildings, but it was fortunately discovered by Plummer who lived opposite to him, and was able to extinguish it before any serious damage had been done. By the younger generation he was adored, for he used to give strawberry feasts in Corpus hall to the children of his colleagues, when they were allowed to eat as much of the fruit as they could get inside them regardless of the consequences. Eventually his mind gave way altogether, and after being decoyed into a cab in the House Meadows he, like the Scholar Gipsy, 'came to Oxford and his friends no more'.

Then there was E. P. Warren, an American from Rhode Island, who, after being an undergraduate at New College, came to live in England, where he made his home in Lewes; during term time he always lived in Oxford, where he was made a Fellow of Corpus. His hospitality was lavish but on an old-fashioned scale, with beer and cutlets for breakfast. Warren was a man of real classical culture,[1] which was probably his reason for settling down in England, for he was very critical of the way of life in his own country. In particular he was scornful of the social and intellectual pretensions of the Bostonians, and one of his favourite verses was the following:

> There was an old lady of Boston,
> And a great sea of doubt she was tossed on,
>> As to if it were best
>> To be rich in the West
> Or poor and peculiar at Boston.

Warren was also fond of reproducing a saying of a Bostonian on Shakespeare: 'Yes, Sir, William Shakespeare was a very great man. I don't think there are twenty men in Boston who could have written what William Shakespeare has written.' The alleged Bostonian snobbery which he derided recalls the story of the young man from that city who in his application for a job in New York mentioned by way of recommendation that he was closely connected with the Cabot, Lowell, and Lodge families, only, however, to receive an unsympathetic reply to the effect that 'we propose to employ, not to breed from you.'

As may be supposed Warren disliked the free and easy ways of American democracy, and another set of verses of which he was very fond ran as follows:

[1] He was well known as a collector of the sculpture of Rodin.

This is the country of the free,
    The cocktail and the ten cent chew,
Where you're as good a man as me,
    And I'm a better man than you.
O Liberty! How free we make!
Freedom! What liberties we take!

When Prohibition was introduced Warren was extremely scornful, and there was one story in particular about it which he often told. A traveller arrived by rail at a town in the Middle West, and on leaving the station he asked a native if he could tell him where he could find a house in which he could get a drink. The native said he could. He told him to follow the street in which they were, and take the third turning on the left; follow that street for three blocks and turn to the left; then, after turning, he would see a house painted white. 'Got it?' said the native. 'Yes,' said the traveller. 'Well,' said the native, 'that's the only house in this town where you can't get a drink.'

Undergraduate Oxford in the Edwardian era was the Oxford of *Sinister Street*. 'Every college,' Douglas Jerrold has written, 'except Magdalen and the House, which were dominated by Eton and Westminster, who wear their ties with a difference, was in its corporate aspect an appendage of the Public School system, with their organized games and their phalanx of industrious athletes whose fees and fines kept the University and college exchequers filled, and whose athletic achievements ensured the University a good press.' He found, however, New College a little strange after Westminster.

At New College I was plunged into the heart of the Public School system at its worst, which is also its very best, for Winchester, judged from almost any standpoint, is the quintessential Public School. In the days when the Public School was for the public, the making of manners was necessary to the making of men, but the one thing necessary, it seems to me, in a private school for the sons of the well-to-do is to break the mould in which the English caste system encases its victims. It is not enough that beneath every old school tie there should beat a heart of gold: somewhere there must be some individual trait, some strain of eccentricity, some divine madness, for which the world is waiting, but for which if the owner be an old Wykehamist, it must wait in vain. I found at New College that art and science, literature and history, were all "work" to be undertaken with a sincerity and a whole-heartedness quite foreign to the Westminster habit. I found also a ready acceptance of the strange hierarchies into which Winchester divides each year's progeny: the world, one felt, and was indeed told, would pass a different judgment at its peril. Other schools, worse manners, but we barbarians could, it was hinted, learn. Even Wykehamist bridge was orthodox.[1]

From the Public Schools came the tradition of ragging, for this was rife, and some of it was reminiscent of *Tom Brown's Schooldays*. It was no uncommon thing for Freshmen to be flogged round college with wet knotted towels, and this was, indeed, the fate of the late Leslie Hore-Belisha every Saturday night during his first year at St John's; others were turned out into the street without their nether garments. One institution which did unquestionably give rise to ragging and general indiscipline was the smoking concert, which sounds harmless enough but in actual fact was the cause of widespread disorder, because a large number of guests were invited and their names were unknown to the college authorities. On the other hand the undergraduates were often at a loss to know how far they could go, as an incident at B.N.C. abundantly testifies. The senior members of the college were invited to be present at the first part of one concert at which the star performer was a Christ Church man who did nigger business, and was notorious for the introduction of risky jokes into his patter. On this occasion he said, 'You know my sister Annie. She's a bad girl. At dinner the other day Mother said to her, "Annie, if you do that again I shall smack you." And Annie answered, "You can't Ma, I'm sitting on it".' Heberden, the Principal, was furious, and vetoed the appearance of that particular performer at any future concert at B.N.C. Next year, however, a Univ. man, Paul Rubens by name, sang a song which contained the lines:

> She was fat; she was fat;
> She was awful, awful fat:
> She weighed at least some twenty stone in nothing but her hat.

[1] *Georgian Adventure*, p. 63.

Whereupon the Principal was heard to remark to his neighbour, 'What I like about Paul Rubens is that he is so amusing without being at all vulgar.'

Life was still pretty free-and-easy, and there was a story about a Freshman at Corpus which well illustrates the fact, though it may relate to a slightly earlier period. He had obtained rooms in the right-hand corner, ground floor, of the front quad, but he did not think it necessary to thrust himself upon the attention of any of the authorities. He took matters very easily for some weeks until the Dean began to notice him, and finally asked the porter the name of the gentleman whom he constantly saw walking about the quad. 'That, Sir, is Mr Gordon, a member of the college,' he replied, and thus it came about that Gordon's attendance at lectures was secured before the end of term. Later on, Gordon brought about an important change in the life of Corpus: not that he was anything of a reformer himself – he was only the cause of reforms. He was far from regular in his attendance at lectures even after he had been reminded of their existence, and one day he rashly made the excuse for not putting in an appearance at one at eleven o'clock that he had not had time to finish his breakfast. Enquiries were made by those in authority, when it transpired that not only Gordon, but several other members of the college, were in the habit of lying in bed until midday. Compulsory roll-call was thereupon instituted, but there was no compulsory chapel until the middle years of Case's Presidency.

On the other hand there was a sharp distinction between the 'years', and a third-year, let alone a fourth-year, man was a very important person indeed. If he condescended to call on a Freshman, and the latter was not in his rooms, all he had to do was to leave his card upon the other's table; but in returning the call the Freshman was allowed no such latitude, for convention demanded that he went on calling until he was fortunate enough to find the magnifico at home, and this applied even if the two men were relatives or their parents were the closest of friends. Even in the street it was possible to distinguish men of different years, at any rate if they were gowned, for the Freshman would have his gown up to his neck, the second-year man would wear his on his shoulders, and the third-year man would sport it draped non-chalantly round his upper arms.

It was the exception for a man to have his university career, whether it were at Oxford or Cambridge, paid for by anyone save his parents, and the average undergraduate hardly gave a thought to what he was going to do when he went down. Motor-cars were very expensive, and so beyond the reach of all save a very small minority, with the result that the undergraduate rarely went more than a mile or two from the University during term; in consequence the outside world meant little to him during the three or four years that he was in residence – Abingdon and Woodstock were likely to be his furthest limits unless he was a hunting-man. Whether life was more austere than it later became is a matter of opinion. The habit of going out to breakfast, especially on Sunday morning, was still very widely observed, but, on the contrary, lunch was a very meagre affair, and in many colleges permission to have a hot lunch was not by any means easy to obtain, such applications being regarded as evidence of an effeminacy reprehensible in a young man; indeed, a distinguished member of the House of Lords at the present time earned the nickname of 'Hot Lunch' when he was at New College owing to his aversion to a cold meal in the middle of the day, though this was after the First World War. The hotels, too, played a much smaller part in the Edwardian undergraduate's life than they would appear to do in that of his Elizabethan successor, possibly because in the outside world the day of the hotel as a social centre was not yet. There was little to choose between the *Randolph* and the *Mitre*, and each had its partisans, though the junior members of the University rarely entered them except when their parents were up. The *Clarendon* still existed, and as it was under some managements understood to be prepared to allow the use of its bedrooms for an hour or two in the daytime for a small fee it had an appeal to certain quarters.

The late Kenneth Hare, himself at Wadham, complained of 'the unnaturally sexless life' of the Edwardian undergraduate, and declared that 'one over-exercised habitually' as 'an indirect effect of repression'. However, on his own showing, before long 'a tall

1. King Edward and Queen Alexandra in the grounds of
Buckingham Palace

2a. King Edward visits the Dublin slums—as arranged for his visit?

2b. King Edward and the Duke of Devonshire at the Royal Agricultural Show, Derby, 1906

3. King Edward and the Kaiser at Homburg, 1908

4. 'Can you see the difference between the Free Trade loaf and
the Protectionist loaf?' Joseph Chamberlain at Bingley Hall,
Birmingham, 1904

5a. The Asquiths departing for a holiday

5b. Balfour and his motor-car

6a. Viscount Haldane

6b. The Liverpool Overhead Railway

7a. Keir Hardie speaking on behalf of the suffragettes
in Trafalgar Square

7b. Suffragettes arrested in Whitehall, 1906

8a. 'Jackie' Fisher

8b. Sir Henry Campbell
Bannerman

9. Waterloo Station, 1906

10. Oxford Circus, 1901

11a. Women at work making bicycles

11b. Ice-cream vendor

12a. A Salvation Army procession in the East End of London

12b. A typical doss-house, 1906

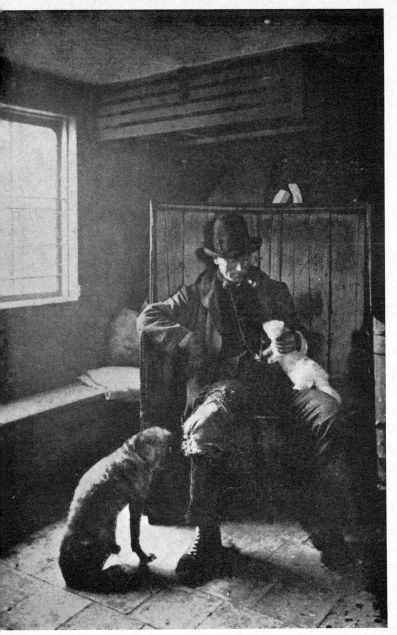

13. A country rat-catcher

14a. Henley

14b. Southend

Newsboys at Charing Cross

Lemonade seller

Muffin man

15. STREET SCENES

16. The highbrow
and the lowbrow
of the Edwardian
stage (*above*)
Beerbohm Tree;
(*below*)
George Robey

blonde provided the very necessary escape for a monk *malgré lui*', and a recess in an old bridge supplied them with the necessary scope for their amatory activities.[1] These restrictions probably irked the full-blooded Hare more than most of his contemporaries, but there can be no question that they were overdone, and they were, of course, the legacy of the Public School system. It was almost impossible for an undergraduate to meet even a respectable girl, for the members of the women's colleges were so chaperoned as to be practically unapproachable; this drove the more uninhibited to affairs with shop-girls and domestic servants, while one young reprobate went so far as to share a mistress with a friend at Cambridge, the lady spending alternate weeks at either university. Yet strangely enough little was heard of homosexuality outside a very narrow circle. It was a strange and artificial atmosphere considering that the Empire Promenade was in its heyday only sixty miles away.

One of the outstanding features of Oxford life was the 'Britter', short for 'British Working Man', a nickname given him owing to the singularity of his attire. He claimed that he never walked, except to the Union, and that he had his trousers cut accordingly, namely not for walking but for sitting, so that there was no need for him to pull them up before subsiding into an armchair. His legs were thus encased in voluminous triangles of cloth, the bases of which were at the waist, and the apices, shorn of their points, at the ankles. Instead of a starched collar the 'Britter' wore a muffler made out of material so rough that there was a school of thought which averred that it had been cut from a bath-towel. Yet, withal, he was a man of the most elaborate courtesy and no inconsiderable scholar, being in fact a Hebrew coach. The 'Britter', it may be added, was never seen to read anything except newspapers, but for these his appetite was insatiable, and their political views were quite immaterial.

One particular claim to fame enjoyed by the 'Britter' is that he once prompted a question in verse at the Union: it ran as follows:

---

[1] *Cf. No Quarrel with Fate*, pp. 83–84.

Mr President, are you aware,
That the cosiest smoking-room chair
    Is used by the 'Britter'
    For bedder and sitter,
And if you disturb him, he'll swear?

There were many wits in Edwardian Oxford, though how the number compared with that in earlier and later times is another matter; prominent among them was Hugh Kingsmill, of New College, who there acquired a reputation which he continued to enhance until his untimely death after the Second World War. One of the earlier instances of his gift of phrase was in the report of a Union debate, when he observed that 'the speaker entertained grave doubts, but not his audience'. He was, however, run close by the contemporary dramatic critic of the *Isis* when the musical comedy, *The Arcadians*, was put on at the theatre. A live horse was produced on the stage, and the music and bright lights rendered him restless: when the members of the beauty chorus endeavoured to calm him down the result was the reverse of what had been intended, and it became disconcertingly evident that the animal was by no means indifferent to feminine charm even when displayed by human beings. With considerable delicacy the *Isis* critic referred to the incident in these felicitous words – 'Although the cast, as a whole, is excellent, the palm for the best performance of the evening must go to the horse, who sustained to admiration the tradition of the great Toole.'

Oxford was defined by Douglas Jerrold as an oasis of university in a desert of clubs, and the remark is peculiarly applicable to the state of affairs existing in the Edwardian era. Pre-eminent among them was the Union, and it will hardly be denied that this was one of its great periods when it had men like Walter Monckton and Ronnie Knox for its office-bearers, as well as many another whose names would assuredly be household-words today but for the fact that they lie in their graves in Gallipoli or on the Somme. The party machines had not yet fastened their tentacles on undergraduates, and the political clubs were much more modest affairs than they were subsequently to become, being chiefly discussion groups which met in the rooms of one of their members, and held an annual dinner at the *Randolph* or the *Claren-don*. On the Tory side were the Canning, which tended to draw its membership from Christ Church, Magdalen, and New College, and the Chatham, which looked rather to Balliol, Trinity, and the Turl colleges. Opposed to them in the Liberal camp were the Russell and Palmerston, the former tending to be 'Little England' and the latter Liberal Imperialist in its outlook. There was also the Fabian Society, though this was a study group rather than a club, and membership was by no means confined to the Labour Party. Vincent's catered for the athlete, and the Grid for the *gourmet* – both of these had premises of their own, while the Bullingdon was the preserve of those who ' 'acked and 'unted'.

The Union, as we have seen, was passing through one of its better phases during these years, and it is not uninteresting to hear a contemporary view, albeit a Tory[1] one, on its outlook at that time:

> Wisdom is always reasonable, and Oxford is very wise. Accord-ingly it does not presume to suppose that all political truth can be expressed in a few *formulae*, however vague. It is profoundly conscious that there are two sides to every question. The Oxford man may champion one side or the other with con-siderable vigour, but he is not a bigot. No better illustration of the Oxford attitude can be found than the behaviour of the Union. The Union is at heart profoundly Conservative and Imperialist; but when a distinguished visitor comes down to advocate Home Rule, to attack the House of Lords, or to defend Free Trade, he will carry his motion if he makes a good speech. The Society feels that, judged by the evening's per-formance, his side has the best of the argument, and votes accordingly. Afterwards it thoroughly enjoys the comments of the Radical press which does not understand these things.
>
> Most of the popular misunderstandings of undergraduate politics are due to the neglect of the cardinal fact here indicated, that the Union is only a stage whereon are given exhibitions of epigram and dialectic; the real work is done elsewhere. The

[1] That of Harold Stannard, of Christ Church, in *The History of the Oxford Canning Club*, pp. 483–484.

true political thought of Oxford is secluded. It is not propagandist as is, for instance, the student opinion of modern Russia. It is elaborated in the political clubs with which Oxford is honeycombed.

The records of most of these institutions have perished, but those of the Canning have proved an exception, and a glance at them throws a good deal of light on the outlook of at any rate one school of undergraduate thought during the reign of Edward the Peacemaker. Of the club's early history, as of the early history of Rome, there is an unfortunate dearth of contemporary records, but there can be little doubt that its founder was that eccentric character, the Hon. Auberon Herbert, of whom *The Times* was to say in its obituary notice that his place in modern history might have been higher if he had been more in touch with the spirit of the age in which he lived. The historian of the Canning, the late Harold Stannard, always took the view that the foundation meeting was held in Herbert's rooms in St John's on December 9th, 1861, and that date may therefore stand. The peculiar brand of Toryism which it subsequently advocated tended to vary according either to its composition or the character of the Hon. Secretary for the time being: probably the best known of the Canning's Hon. Secretaries in Victorian times was Lord Curzon, and he left his mark upon it as upon every other institution with which he came in contact.

In the Edwardian era, as was not unnatural, the members of the Canning were much preoccupied with fiscal questions and with the conditions of their party – indeed they see to have been more appreciative of the parlous condition of Toryism under the Balfour régime than was the Cabinet in Downing Street. One of the protagonists of Tory Democracy was Maurice Woods of Trinity, whose father was Master of the Temple, and whom Joseph Chamberlain's advocacy of Tariff Reform had converted from Liberalism. Indeed, he began the Michaelmas Term of 1903 as a member of the Russell and finished it as a member of the Canning. Such being the case it was in no way remarkable that he should for some time have been an object of suspicion, not to say of hostility, to the more old-fashioned members of the club. Woods was, in effect, the protagonist of a rejuvenated and progressive Conservatism, and of that party he made the Canning Club the citadel.

On May 18th, 1904, Woods read a paper to its members on *Disraeli and the Tory Democracy* in which he went to the root of the matter. 'The problem of the moment for the Conservative Party was how to handle democracy and yet survive. Disraeli had suggested a solution, and with that Mr Woods was concerned.' The reader then 'led up to the main problem by a historical restrospect', showing how feudalism had been replaced by a strong central Government which had become utterly out-of-date at the close of the eighteenth century. 'Mr Woods then depicted a veritable Armageddon from which emerged nineteenth-century England crying for reform. No remedy was suggested by the Conservative Party; the Radicals, however, were ready with one which in time proved to be worse than the disease. The first Reform Bill was the outcome of their creed that man can live by votes alone. Its fallacies were revealed in the troubles – the Chartism and anarchy – which followed it. It was at this moment that Disraeli appeared upon the stage. He had a profound sympathy, as we see in the pages of *Sybil*, with the sufferings of the masses; but he had an equally profound distrust of the remedies advocated. His own solution was the Tory democracy. This remedy did not rely on a visionary future, but on a return to all that was best in the past. The people were not to lead but to follow their natural leaders. These, again, were to remember that *noblesse oblige*, and to be mindful of the lessons of the eighteenth century. Such was Disraeli's ideal, and to it Mr Woods traced all the best principles of modern Conservatism. Its policy in the future must not be one of mere concessions; it must consist of a vigorous counter-attack on what he described as "the obstinate shibboleths of middle-class Liberalism".'

On October 26th, Maurice Woods returned to the charge with a paper entitled *Chamberlain and Chamberlainism*. 'The French Revolution – there is the chronological and real beginning of the movement of which the permanent product is the French Republic and the democratic parties in Europe. The reaction of that movement is traceable throughout the last century in the Liberal Party. In the writer's words, "the mental attitude of the official Liberal is stamped with the hall-mark of its origin." In England, following upon the great national effort of the early nineteenth century, came the rise of Liberalism. The creed of this philosophic Liberalism was mighty in phrases and formulae, and productive undeniably of reforms which the situation demanded; but in its attempt to destroy all existing conventions, in its half-hearted parody of Rousseau, in its apotheosis of the Natural Man and Pure Reason, it became Individualist to the core. It landed its adherents in a political *cul-de-sac*, through which the forces of progress and the evolution of a nation could find no thoroughfare. . . .'

'After 1870 the Liberals remained in bed with their favourite toy, Individualism, for a longer night than they imagined, but meanwhile the new Conservatism was surely gaining ground, though not the ground that would have been gained had his party listened to Disraeli. . . . However successful abroad and inspired in his Imperial foresight, Disraeli was before his time, and the ideas of which he is the author had to wait for a new exponent in Chamberlain and a new name in Chamberlainism. The pause was marked by the Liberal victory of 1880. This victory was but a sunset red with the shame of national humiliation; it was followed by the dawn of the Imperial movement. . . . Efficient Imperialism drew all reformers to it. The country rejected Home Rule, and, enabled by the extension of the franchise in 1884, subscribed definitely to the cause of Imperialism, in which Lord Randolph Churchill might have shone, and of which Mr Chamberlain became the representative. New ideas under him took shape in a vigorous naval policy, in a consideration of working-class interests, in an efficient Colonial Office, in British supremacy in South Africa. Nor was the change in the Conservative Party only from without, but mainly from within. Fixity in politics and defence of vested interests had been left far behind.'

'Thus Mr Woods brought his story down to the beginning of the fiscal movement. Preference, he said, had long been foreshadowed, and when it was enunciated all true Chamberlainites rallied to it. . . . But the main purpose of his instructive paper was to show that Chamberlainism is no new product of fiscal reform, that it is not fairly represented by a Mr Chaplin and an interested manufacturer – no mere one-man movement, but the product of last century's history in England, the Imperialism which has distinguished all Conservative policy, the ideal to which other nations, too, have turned, to which they and England will turn long after its present opponents are dead.'

On the subject of the monarchy the young men of the Canning Club sixty years ago seem to have felt no qualms, and a few months before the death of the Queen a Mr W. M. Bouch, of B.N.C., pointed out that democracy necessitated delegation, so that the delegation of Royal power to a single family was quite in accordance with its tenets, and served to protect the people from the ambitions of a would-be tyrant. Other speakers assured their colleagues that loyalty to the throne had never been so intense, and that the danger of the future was not republicanism but the tyranny of the House of Commons. The reader of one paper went so far as to declare that 'Democracy always seeks to put away its burdens; we must see that those to whom they are delegated do not become our masters instead of our servants, and in this task the monarchy stands out as the Palladium of our menaced liberties.' There was, indeed, general agreement that all was not well with Parliament, but concerning what was actually wrong there was no sort of unanimity. Mr Jay, of New College, in a paper on *The Effeteness of Parliament,* suggested a system of committees as a remedy, but another speaker gave it as his opinion that 'the character of the House of Commons had completely changed within the last hundred years. Members had become delegates, whose duty was not so much to inform public opinion as to give expression to the views of their constituents. Again, practically all power of legislation had passed into the hands of the Cabinet. Whereas the duties of Government had once been mainly administrative, they had now become primarily legislative.'

As always when a Conservative administration is in office there was considerable difference of opinion among Conservatives during the opening years of the present century, and the members of the Canning Club were no exception: when, however, Sir Henry Campbell-Bannerman came into power at the end of 1905 there was a definite closing of the ranks and a discernible move to the Right, as may be gathered from the following short list of special toasts in chronological order: 'The Lords – more power to them', 'Damnation to the Land Tenure Bill', 'King Charles I', 'Mr Chaplin and the Whole Hog', 'The Archbishop of Canterbury', 'Damnation to the Education Bill', and 'The Future Prospects of the Barmaid' – this last being presumably in some way connected with the Licensing Bill. Among those who often spoke at the annual dinners, often held in conjunction with the Chatham, were Sir Samuel Hoare, Sir Edward Carson, Leo Maxse, F. E. Smith, and Austen Chamberlain, while those of its members during these years who later acquired national fame were Ronnie Knox, Duff Cooper, Edward Wood, and Walter Monckton.[1]

The Chatham came into existence not long after the Canning, but what if any doctrinal differences originally existed between them is wrapped in mystery: anyhow, like the differences between the Cherubim and the Seraphim according to Father Healey, they must have resolved them, since, as we have seen, early in their careers they acquired the habit of holding a joint annual dinner. However this may be it would almost certainly be true to say that the division between them was nothing like so great as that which for some years separated the Russell and Palmerston. There was also, with premises of its own, an organization called the New Tory Club, which was a very fashionable institution, so fashionable in fact that when war came, and it closed down, it owed a hundred pounds to its fishmonger alone.

When one turns to Cambridge it is to find a very different state of affairs. For some inexplicable reason the club habit has never made any great appeal there, even when, in the Edwardian and neo-Georgian eras, it was at its most flourishing at Oxford. The usual explanation is the size of Trinity, but as this is generally given as the reason for any difference between the universities it probably need not be taken very seriously. The Pitt Club was an

[1] *History of the Oxford Canning Club*, pp. 425–489.

exception, and it had very attractive premises of its own. It was –
and is – incidentally, together with the Pitt Clubs of London and
Chester, the only survivor of the numerous institutions of that
name which were founded in the statesman's memory during the
early years of last century. There was, too, the Hawks', which was
comparable with Vincent's at Oxford, but, generally speaking, it
would appear that at that time when a group of men on the Cam
found that they had the same ideas, habits, or interests, there was
not the same urge as on the Isis to found a club and design a tie.
Certainly no Oxford club was complete without one, and the
tradition survived the First World War: the original tie of the
Oxford Carlton Club, for intance, was selected in the summer of
1919 in the Corpus quad by the light of a waning moon by a
group of ardent Tories one of whom was a future Lord Chancellor
of England, when the colours chosen were purple for Church and
King, blue for Toryism, and white to symbolize the purity of the
wearer's political principles. Its life was short.

One of the Cambridge clubs which deserves more than a passing
mention is the Fish and Chimney Club, of which Jack, later Sir
John, Squire was a prominent member. The name was supposed to
indicate that the members drank like fish and smoked like chim-
neys, and among the rules were the following:

That this Society shall not necessarily be called the Chish and
Fimney;

That none shall be debarred from initiation into the mysteries
of the Society on account of sex, belief in the immortality of the
soul, membership of the Tariff Reform League, or membership
of the Society for the Prevention of Christian Knowledge;

That there shall be no officers;

That members shall be allowed to grow beards during a
meeting.

Within these terms of reference the members engaged in reading
plays and poetry, and the variety of their inclinations is attested by
the fact that in one year they read Sudermann, Beaumont and
Fletcher, Maeterlinck, Swinburne, and Yeats.

Squire was at St John's, and he has left on record his final conversation with his tutor, J. R. Tanner:

'Well, Squire, now you're going down, what are you going to do?'

'I'm going to write, sir,' I replied.

His reply was encouraging.

'You are,' he said, 'eminently fitted for that, and eminently unfitted for anything else whatever.'[1]

Those were all university clubs, but there were also an infinite number of college clubs and societies both at Oxford and Cambridge. How old they were in difficult to say, but at a guess it is doubtful if many of them dated back further than the eighties and nineties of the previous century. Undergraduate generations are short, and in consequence a reputation for immemorial antiquity is easily acquired. The Claret Club at Trinity, Oxford, claimed to date back to the Civil War, and there was a dining-club at Exeter with similar pretensions. St John's had the King Charles Club, and it claimed to have had its origin when that monarch made Oxford his headquarters, for tradition had it that he used to have twenty-four St John's men to dine with him once a week, presumably because it was Laud's college. Sometimes these clubs were forced into abeyance, or even killed, by authority if their activities were extended too far: the Wasps at Corpus Christi, Oxford, was a notable example, for its stings more than once led to its enforced suspension, though it always revived to sting another day. The Bullingdon was another club which experienced the same vicissitudes for the same reasons.

There was very little contact between the two older universities, at any rate at the undergraduate level, save in the matter of sport. The only means of physical communication was, of course, by rail, and that involved a weary journey with a change, and generally a long wait, at Bletchley. It was rare for families to be divided in their allegiance, so Oxford and Cambridge men tended only to meet at parties during the vacations, and the less social

---

[1] Cf. Howarth, P.: *Squire, Most Generous of Men*, p. 28.

never met at all. As to the latest developments in 'the other place', most undergraduates were better informed about the Balkans.

Sir Shane Leslie has written disparagingly of the Heads of Houses at Cambridge during the Edwardian era:

> Colleges still retained Patriarchal heads, fossil survivals of a bygone race. There was the ancient Master of Corpus, driving round the lanes like a ghost that could not slough itself of this delectable world. There was the old Master of Magdalene, whose office had only been filled once in ninety years, a Mastership that was something between a family living and a Rotten Borough. His College, after producing Charles Kingsley and Charles Parnell, had consequently gone to seed. Then there was the venerable bathchair-riding Master of Clare, who had been Master since the Crimean War, and the Master of Trinity, a bland Olympian in a black skull-cap with a white Jarine beard, and an untiring flow of lengthy anecdotes that are told in Heaven after the nectar has gone round twice. They were the grand old men, so grand in their own Colleges that the world knew them not, and so old that their Colleges had forgotten they were ever young! To hurrying youth they made dumb cry that youth was not lasting, a salutary lesson in a city of everlasting youth![1]

On the other hand Cambridge could boast 'The O.B.' – Oscar Browning – who was of the same *genus* as Herbert Warren at Oxford and John Mahaffy of Trinity College, Dublin, but as a snob was infinitely superior to either of them. Shane Leslie has written of him as 'Oliver Brownlow' in *The Cantab*, and he tells how 'the O.B.'s luggage made an ostentatious appearance in the Front Court for several days labelled "Oliver Brownlow – guest of the Hereditary Duke of Speintopz-Heilmarou".' What may be described as his full-length portrait could not be happier:

> It was extraordinary in how many portraits and phases the O.B. was able to appear to his guests. At the mention of any politics or philosophy he immediately spoke as one having oecumenical authority. The coming Elections were broached, and the O.B. rapidly described two personal experiences at the

[1] *The Cantab*, ch. XII.

Polls.[1] Religion was mentioned, and the O.B. acclaimed himself a distinguished convert to Christian Science. 'I had to adopt an American form of religion. It would have caused too much jealousy if I had adopted a European one.' A historical turn brought the conversation to the Papacy. The O.B. immediately described his presence, and hinted a personal part at the Vatican Council. Edward was left with the impression that the O.B. believed in his own Infallibility, and less tolerantly accepted that of the Pope.

He seemed one of the earth's supremely happy people, for whatever reverses or contradictions he received he always knew that he was right. If doubts crossed his mind, he gave them slight quarter. He was rather like a Leviathan. He bulked mightily and he was one of the most buoyant swimmers in the University. He was unique and at once universal. King's College was known to Europe as the O.B.'s resting-place, and Europe was largely interpreted to King's in terms of the O.B.'s stamping-ground. Courts and countries where the O.B. could not stamp were not worth stamping upon. Such was the insatiable and unsatisfying O.B., lovable and quarrelsome, exuding hates and loves, swollen with uncooked knowledge, portentous with vociferous ignorance, capable of playing any part and assuming any rôle, including the colossal misrepresentation of himself, which could be described as Falstaff playing Hamlet. From week to week the College was amused, tickled, or enraged by the O.B. If it happened that he had failed to utter something outrageous during the week, it was invented for him. The wits of the College would rise to a crescendo of creative caricature, which might perhaps reach the O.B. in time for him to rush out and explode in the Combination-room as original![2]

On May 30th, 1908, King's gave a dinner in honour of the O.B., and one of the speakers was Austen Chamberlain, his East Worcestershire opponent of sixteen years earlier, who has left a record of the occasion:

[1] Standing as a Liberal he had been defeated in East Worcestershire by Austen Chamberlain in 1892, and in the West Derby division of Liverpool by Walter Long in 1895.
[2] *The Cantab*, ch. VII.

I attended the dinner in King's Coll. Hall in honour of O.B., and made them a short speech which satisfied me, though I found it very difficult. For whilst I have a very friendly feeling towards O.B., and a great deal of sympathy with his ideas about what the History Tripos ought to be, one cannot conceal from oneself that O.B. with all his gifts has been a failure, and one sees only too clearly the reason why. However I managed to say enough without saying anything more than I felt to be true. It was a pleasant and successful dinner, but oh! it was long. We met at eight, sat down at eight-fifteen, finished dinner at ten, and rose at a quarter past midnight.

Austen certainly had need of all his powers of endurance during this visit to his old university, for next morning he was back at King's breakfasting with the Slade Professor, Sir Charles Waldstein, to meet Count Metternich, the German ambassador. The German clearly envisaged a return of the Conservatives to power in the near future, and he wished to avail himself of this opportunity to discover their attitude towards his own country.[1]

It would, however, be a serious mistake to imagine that the O.B. was merely a snob and a figure of fun, for he did a great deal to modernize the History School at Cambridge. In the previous century its outstanding figure had been Sir John Seeley, who regarded the study of history primarily as a training for statesmanship, while the O.B. and his contemporaries concentrated rather on training for historical research. The Edwardian period witnessed a general broadening of scope in all fields of academic life, not least in those of physics and chemistry whose needs, until 1907, had been catered for by a mere forty-six teachers and five lecture-rooms. It was not, however, that the older studies were being ignored, and until 1905 Sir Richard Jebb was Regius Professor of Greek.

At the same time it would be impossible to deny that during the twenty years between 1894 and 1914 the worship of athletics was at its height, as was also the case in the Public Schools – a tendency, one may add, which was deeply deplored by the O.B. and H. M. Butler. Many men came up with the avowed intention of playing

[1] *Cf.* Petrie, Sir Charles: *The Life and Letters of the Right Hon. Sir Austen Chamberlain*, vol. I, p. 215.

rather than working, and in April, 1914, Stuart Donaldson, Master of Magdalene, stated that of those who came up in 1909 a quarter had not taken a degree. 'He ventured to think that of that 25 per cent to whom he had alluded a very large number consisted of men who came up to have a good time, and did not care to read or work hard.'[1] The cost of living at Oxford and Cambridge was much the same, and it was estimated that a careful man need not spend more than £160 minimum a year, though this figure would exclude his expenses in the vacations, on clothes, and for travelling. Again at both universities a good many undergraduates undoubtedly got into debt, but shopkeepers held their hands, and there was more than a little truth in Douglas Jerrold's toast, 'The tradesmen of Oxford – to whom we all owe so much.' It was generally considered satisfactory if a man had paid his bills by the time that his eldest son came into residence.

Finally, it is difficult to resist the conclusion that at neither Oxford nor Cambridge did religion exercise much hold over the undergraduates during these years. Nor is this surprising, for they were mostly the product of the Public Schools, where the religion taught was that which is Established by Law, and where enthusiasm of any sort was sternly discouraged. It is not that there was much militant atheism in either university, but rather that the general attitude was one of indifference, though nineteenth-century rationalism had its followers. The senior members in the main made little or no effort to counteract this tendency, and since as often as not they professed agnostic views themselves their presence in chapel by virtue of their office was hardly calculated to stimulate piety in the young. In effect, most undergraduates would probably have declared that they belonged to the Church of England, without giving much thought to the matter, and certainly without doing anything about it.

[1] *Camb. Univ. Repr., 1913–14*, p. 886.

CHAPTER VI

Ireland

————◦◉◦————

IN all the tragic history of Ireland there have been few occasions
when the fairest of horizons has become so rapidly overcast
as in the early years of the present century. When Queen Victoria died it seemed as if the old bitterness was disappearing from
Irish politics: gone were the days of 'buckshot' Forster and
'bloody' Balfour, and in their place was a sweet reasonableness on
the part of the British Government which seemed to have become
wedded to a policy of killing Home Rule by kindness, forgetful
of the fact that down the ages the desire for autonomy has rarely
been exorcised by material prosperity. Nearer home Arthur
Griffith had begun to publish *The United Irishman*; the Irish Dramatic Movement had been launched; John Redmond had been
elected Chairman of the reunited Irish Parliamentary Party; and
the census of 1901 gave the figure of 4,447,085 as the population.

The man who was apparently indicated as the harbinger of the
new dawn was no less a person than the new Chief Secretary,
George Wyndham, and at first he possessed every qualification for
the part. He was on the right side of forty; he was a scholar and a
gentleman; and he was an enthusiast for Ireland and all things
Irish. He was undoubtedly one of the most brilliant men who have
ever appeared on the British political stage, but his very brilliance
kept him apart from the mass of his colleagues in the House of
Commons. In private he was the best of company, but few knew
him in such intimate surroundings, and it cannot be denied that he
suffered for his genius in that it cut him off from the rank-and-
file of his own party. He thus by nature and circumstances tended
to be out of touch with current opinion, and he was inclined to

take it for granted that the mental processes of others were as rapid as his own. Balfour – of all people – complained that Wyndham was obscure. 'I wonder why,' he once remarked to Austen Chamberlain. 'For one thing he talks in metaphors. I believe it's his natural way of talking, but it's a great bore for a person with a non-literary mind like mine.'[1]

As ever, the outstanding Irish problem was the land, and to this Wyndham at once addressed himself. Accordingly in the spring of 1902 he introduced a bill to facilitate land purchase, but it proved to be no great advance upon previous measures with the same objective, for it did not provide for the completion of purchase on anything like an adequate scale, and it did not afford any remedy for the sufferings of evicted tenants. In effect, its provisions would have operated so slowly, even under the most favourable conditions, that a century would have passed before land purchase was completed. Even John Redmond, who was always in favour of accepting practical concessions where possible, would have none of it, but, to quote William O'Brien, the situation 'was saved in 1902, as in 1898, by calling the robust sense of the country into council. The National Directory[2] of the League was still in the vigour of its original constitution, free as the air of the mountains, and strong with the strength of the people's arm. . . . Their instinct was not for a moment at fault in proclaiming that to allow the Wyndham Bill to pass would be to abjure the abolition of landlordism, the redistribution of the grazing lands, and the rescue of the evicted tenants until the Greek Kalends.'[3]

If the object of the bill was to pacify the country then it was a dismal failure from the beginning, for during the summer of 1902 there was a great deal of agitation and violent disturbance of one sort and another. Large areas, including the cities of Dublin, Cork, and Limerick, were proclaimed under the Crimes Act; public meetings were suppressed; and a number of Members of Parliament were imprisoned. In these circumstances Wyndham quietly dropped his bill.

[1] Chamberlain, Sir Austen: *Politics from Inside*, p. 255.
[2] *I.e.* the United Irish League.
[3] *An Olive Branch in Ireland*, p. 136.

There the matter would probably have rested had not the following letter made its appearance in the Irish newspapers almost immediately afterwards:

Sir,

For the last two hundred years the land war in this country has raged fiercely and continuously, bearing in its train stagnation of trade, paralysis of commerical business and enterprise, and producing hatred and bitterness between the various sections and classes of the community. Today the United Irish League is confronted by the Irish Land Trust, and we see both combinations eager and ready to renew the unending conflict. I do not believe there is an Irishman, whatever his political feeling, creed, or position, who does not yearn to see a true settlement of the present chaotic, disastrous, and ruinous struggle.

In the best interests, therefore, of Ireland and my countrymen I beg most earnestly to invite the Duke of Abercorn, Mr John Redmond, M.P., Lord Barrymore, Colonel Saunderson, M.P., the Lord Mayor of Dublin, The O'Conor Don, Mr William O'Brien, M.P., and Mr T. W. Russell, M.P., to a conference to be held in Dublin within one month from this date. An honest, simple, and practical suggestion will be submitted, and I am confident that a settlement on terms alike satisfactory to landlords and tenants will be arrived at.

I have the honour to be your most obedient servant,

JOHN SHAWE-TAYLOR,
Captain.

September 3rd, 1902

The author of this remarkable letter had not consulted any one of the people whom he thus publicly invited to meet him within a month's time, and his name conveyed nothing whatever to most of them. He was, in fact, the younger son of a Galway squire, who, to quote William O'Brien once again, 'from the hunting field of the "Galway Blazers" and the camps of the South African War, had evolved into a gentle fanatic, with all the simple chivalry of a Don Quixote, and some gleams of the divine mission of a Savonarola, and, having begun to win over his own troopers into the ways of teetotalism and sanctification, soared eventually to refulgent and wholly disinterested dreams for the regeneration of his country'.[1] Even so, it is doubtful if the letter would have pro-

---

[1] *An Olive Branch in Ireland*, p. 140.

duced much effect but for a statement by the Chief Secretary two days later to the effect that in his opinion 'no Government can settle the Irish land question' and that 'any conference is a step in the right direction'.

Thereafter matters began to move apace. The four Nationalists named in the letter promptly accepted the invitation, but Dillon and Davitt, who had not been included in it, suspected a trap: the four landowners refused. Moderating influences were, however, at work, and the Catholic hierarchy came out in support of Shawe-Taylor's proposal, as did Lords Dunraven, Castletown, Mayo, Powerscourt, and Meath, Colonel Hutcheson-Poë, and Mr Talbot, who formed a Conciliation Committee, and were determined that the conference should take place.

Rather more preliminary negotiation proved necessary than Captain Shawe-Taylor had envisaged, and it was not until December 20th, 1902, that the Land Conference held its first meeting at the Mansion House in Dublin: those present were Lords Dunraven, and Mayo, Colonel Hutcheson-Poë, and Colonel Nugent Everard for the landowners, and John Redmond, William O'Brien, the Lord Mayor of Dublin, and T. W. Russell for he tenants. Lord Dunraven was voted into the chair and Captain Shawe-Taylor was appointed honorary secretary.

Subsequent sittings took place on December 22nd, 23rd, and 31st, and on January 3rd, 1903; all these meetings were in private, and practically no information was given to the Press. A basis of agreement was very quickly found, for the truth was that since the abolition of the grand juries by the Local Government Act of 1898 the status of Irish landownership had lost the last vestiges of its old prestige. The Land Courts had brought down rents to levels far below the extortionate rack-rents of twenty years earlier, while the principle of State-aided land purchase had been introduced and developed in several of the many Land Acts, so that there was a general disposition on the part of the landlords all over the country to sell their estates, except the demesnes, if they could obtain attractive terms. In effect, it was soon clear that everything depended upon the extent to which the Treasury could be expected to assist a measure of land purchase on a really extensive scale.

'To the joy and amazement of the country,' as William O'Brien put it, the Land Conference presented a unanimous report on January 4th. In substance, the solution produced was quite simple. The landlords were to sell their estates to the existing tenants on terms which involved an average of either $18\frac{1}{2}$ or $21\frac{1}{2}$ years' purchase on the prevalent revised scale of judicial rents, according to whether they were first-term or second-term. The Treasury was to advance the capital to pay the landowners, and was to recover by a series of annuities payable, in lieu of the previous rents, to the Land Commission over a period of $68\frac{1}{2}$ years. The Treasury was also to provide as a gift a bonus of 12 per cent on the amount of every such sale, as an inducement to the landlords to sell quickly, thus providing an ample margin to cover any possible loss of income on the transaction in each case.

The report was received by the Irish people as a whole with immense approval, and the landlords, too, were well satisfied with what had been done. At a meeting of the Executive Committee of the Landowners' Convention on January 7th, a resolution, moved by the Duke of Abercorn and seconded by The O'Conor Don, was unanimously adopted, recognizing the report as 'a valuable addition to the various suggestions that have been made for removing the grave difficulties of the Irish Land Question by bringing the Land Purchase Acts into more general operation on the voluntary principle', and it expressed a hope that, in spite of certain points which invited criticism, 'the whole report will receive the serious consideration of the Government'. The O'Conor Don also wrote to the *Irish Times* that, as one who had questioned the utility of holding a Conference, he rejoiced that his doubts had not been substantiated, and he defended the financial proposals of the report.

There remained the obstacle of the Treasury, for although England was heavily in Ireland's debt it did not necessarily follow that she was prepared to finance the proposals in the report. Nevertheless Wyndham, with Balfour's encouragement, was determined to carry the matter through, and he wrote to Dunraven, 'I am confident that 1903 will mark an epoch in Irish history'.[1]

[1] Mackail, J. W., and Wyndham, Guy: *Life and Letters of George Wyndham*, vol. I, p. 82.

On March 25th he introduced a bill which embodied the Conference's proposals, and not a single Irish Member spoke against it on its second reading, though in committee Redmond proposed certain amendments which were accepted. In the House of Lords it was passed without any division being taken, and on August 14th it received the Royal assent. Redmond rightly hailed it as 'the most substantial victory gained for centuries by the Irish race for the reconquest of the soil of Ireland by the people.'

Unhappily in this clear sky there was a small cloud which was to grow until it covered the whole horizon. In the autumn of 1902 it was announced that the post of Under-Secretary for Ireland had been offered to Sir Antony MacDonnell, until recently Governor of Bengal, and brother of Dr MacDonnell, the Nationalist Member for Queen's County. Sir Antony had had a brilliant career in India, where he had been specially concerned with the land and its problems; it was therefore felt in Whitehall that he would be extremely useful in Dublin at that particular moment. There was something in this reasoning, but not a great deal, for Indian experience had often proved to be a handicap in Ireland, since it was liable to suggest analogies which subsequently proved to be false. In view of the complications which were so soon to ensue it is well to realize that from the beginning this was no ordinary appointment.

MacDonnell had originally been brought to Wyndham's notice by Lansdowne, and he and the Chief Secretary had several discussions as to the terms on which he should take the post: these conversations were embodied in two letters which Wyndham read in the House of Commons on February 22nd, 1905. In the first of these communications, in which Sir Antony accepted 'under the colours and conditions he had mentioned', he went on to say, 'I have been anxiously thinking over the difficulty; I am an Irishman, a Roman Catholic, and a Liberal in politics. I have strong Irish sympathies.' He further informed the Chief Secretary that in taking the office he would not only be 'abused by the Orangemen as a Roman Catholic and a Home Ruler', but also 'denounced by the Home Rulers as a renegade'. It was certainly a curious appointment to be made by a Unionist Chief Secretary.

'It was, therefore, with full notice of Sir Antony's anti-Unionist convictions that Mr Wyndham singled him out from the whole number of possible candidates for the most important post in his gift – a post which, even when held by the usual tenure, confers upon its occupant control of the whole administration of Ireland, limited only by the intervention of the Chief Secretary, and gives him constant opportunities, direct and indirect, of influencing the general Irish policy of the Government.'[1]

If Sir Antony was hardly the man whom one would have expected a Conservative and Unionist administration to appoint as Under-Secretary to the Lord-Lieutenant, the conditions of his nomination were also exceptional. 'It is understood between us,' wrote Wyndham, 'that I make and you accept this appointment on the lines and under the conditions laid down in your letter.' That these conditions were abnormal was admitted by the Chief Secretary himself: 'These letters,' he said, 'make it perfectly plain and clear that Sir Antony MacDonnell was invited by me rather as a colleague than as a mere Under-Secretary to register my will.' Lansdowne went even further, and thought it almost a matter of course that a man of such antecedents 'could hardly be expected to be bound by the narrow rules of routine which are applicable to an ordinary member of the Civil Service', and he told the House of Lords that 'when Sir Antony MacDonnell took up his appointment it was understood, both by himself and the Chief Secretary, that he was to have greater freedom of action, greater opportunities of initiative, than he would have expected if he had been a candidate in the ordinary course'. Sir Antony, he added, 'was justified in assuming that he had a certain scope of action, and he certainly acted upon that assumption, and acted upon it with the knowledge and approval of the Chief-Secretary'. In these circumstances it is not surprising that in the eyes of the more extreme Unionists Wyndham and MacDonnell were working hand-in-glove.

MacDonnell's appointment, it is to be noted, met with the warm approval of the King. He appreciated Sir Antony's sincerity and ability, and sympathized with him in the difficulties of his position.

[1] A correspondent in *The Times*, September 18th, 1906.

In him the Sovereign discovered an influence which sought to raise the long-standing Irish Question above the bitterness of party strife, and throughout the differences which soon arose between him and the North Sir Antony found a firm supporter in the wearer of the Crown.

In that year of hope and promise, 1903, King Edward himself paid a visit to Ireland, and in the light of what had gone before and of what was to come afterwards he met with a surprisingly enthusiastic reception, even though by a majority of forty votes to thirty-seven the Corporation of Dublin refused to present an address. The fact was that the Irish of all creeds and classes had a soft spot in their hearts for him, not only because he was a sportsman, but also because it was reported that he was very friendly to the Irish people, which had certainly not been the case with his mother. The story went the rounds that he had asked MacDonnell, 'Are the Irish disloyal?'

'No, Sir,' came the answer, 'but they are discontented.'

'What do they want?'

'They want education and they want security in their land.'

'I shall come to Ireland with an Education Bill in one hand and a Land Bill in the other.'

King Edward and Queen Alexandra landed at Dun Laoghaire, then called Kingstown, and drove the eleven miles from there to the Viceregal Lodge through decorated streets and cheering crowds: in spite of the attitude of the Dublin Corporation no political ill-feeling dimmed the brilliance of the popular reception. It was at this time that Pope Leo XIII died, and with considerable tact the King entrusted Cardinal Logue, the Catholic Primate of Ireland, with a message of condolence for the Sacred College. No less than eighty-two deputations presented addresses of welcome, and among them was one brought by two carmen signed by twelve hundred jarveys. Throughout the ceremony of receiving these the King, who was in excellent spirits and no hurry, talked with many of those who presented the addresses, and, as Wyndham put it, he was 'happy and dead on the bull's eye'. There was also a military review in Phoenix Park, and a visit to Trinity, both occasions being marked by wild enthusiasm.

Outside the capital the King and Queen visited Maynooth, Belfast, Derry, and Cork, and during the course of this tour they sailed down the West Coast, landing on several occasions and driving to remote villages. Throughout the visit there was a noticeable absence of unpleasant incidents, and all sects and creeds united in welcoming the King: in Cork he was received at the City Hall by the Lord Mayor. On leaving Ireland he issued an address, 'To My Irish People', thanking them for their tokens of loyalty and affection, adding on behalf of the Queen, as well as for himself, 'For a country so attractive and a people so gifted we cherish the warmest regard, and it is with supreme satisfaction that I have during our stay so often heard the hope expressed that a brighter day is dawning upon Ireland.'

In the present age Heads of State are so numerous, so many of them are nonentities, and they are so continuously on the move, that it is permissible to doubt whether their peregrinations have any effect at all, but such may well not have been the case sixty years ago, and even his most severe critics would hardly deny that King Edward VII was a dominating personality. Certainly so acute an observer of the Irish scene as Sir Horace Plunkett had no doubt that the Royal visit had served a useful purpose, for in the following November, when he had had time to assess the results, he wrote to Knollys:

> That the immediate effect was altogether good was so obvious and so generally admitted as to leave no room for doubt. . . . In this case I have been able to detect no reaction whatsoever from what I would venture to characterize as the irrepressible loyalty of the Irish people, which found so gratifying an expression during His Majesty's visit. . . .

> What I now find among the people is the feeling that the King recognizes that he is, and prides himself on being, the ruler of Ireland: that he is not the people's leader, but that he is in real sympathy with them: that he felt for them in their sorrow when they lost the head of their church, and that he went to extraordinary exertions in order to see for himself the darker side of their poverty.

> I find a very general belief in the country that His Majesty

exercised his personal influence in getting the Land Bill through Parliament. It is also thought that he is quite open-minded on the subject of any constitutional change which may be required. On the whole I have gained the impression that no King has ever been so popular among the majority of the Irish as His Majesty since the days of James II, and there is this great difference between the two cases, that the affection for James II soon came to lack the element of respect.

Looking to the future, it appears to me that the several speeches of His Majesty while in Ireland, and still more the valedictory address 'To My Irish People', have laid the foundations for a lasting understanding between the Sovereign and all that is worthy in the Irish people. These utterances have been of great value in stimulating the people to new and progressive effort, and they are cited by, and carry weight among, people who would not previously have believed that the Sovereign had any personal knowledge of, or interest in, the practical affairs of the people's life. . . .[1]

King Edward and Queen Alexandra paid two more visits to Ireland during their brief reign. The first was in 1904, when they attended Punchestown and Leopardstown races, and also visited Waterford and Kilkenny. The second was three years later, but this was somewhat marred by the fact that four days before the King's arrival it was discovered that the state jewels of the Order of St Patrick, including the Diamond Star of the Grand Master, had been missing for a month from a safe in the Office of Arms at Dublin Castle. King Edward was in the capital when he learnt the particulars of the theft, and we are told that 'his language on that occasion was vigorous and forceful, partly for the reason that in the particular circumstances he could do nothing, and partly because of the feeble efforts that were being made to elucidate the mystery'.[2] This, however, is to anticipate.

The Land Act had been intended by Wyndham, MacDonnell, and those who thought with them as a beginning, but the more extreme Unionists, particularly in the North, intended that it

---

[1] Quoted by Lee, Sir S.: *King Edward VII: A Biography*, vol. II, pp. 169–170.
[2] *Ibid.*, p. 473.

should be an end, and when the Chief Secretary showed a disposition to deal in the same spirit with the demand for a Catholic university he was soon made to realize that he had gone too far. The Marquess of Londonderry, then President of the Board of Education, announced at the beginning of 1904 that the Government had no intention of introducing any such measure, and soon afterwards Wyndham had to state openly that he had not been able to commit the Cabinet to his own views on the subject. The strain of office was in any case beginning to tell upon him, and in August he departed on a prolonged holiday. In spite of the time of year matters now proceeded to move very fast.

For some time a number of the more progressive landlords had been continuing on a wider basis the discussions which had been so successful at the Land Conference of 1902–3, and in that same August of 1904 they formed the Irish Reform Association with Colonel Hutcheson-Poë as its honorary secretary. On the 25th its members issued a report of their first meetings, which declared that 'while firmly maintaining that the Parliamentary union between Great Britain and Ireland is essential to the political stability of the Empire and to the prosperity of the two islands, we believe that such union is compatible with the devolution to Ireland of a larger measure of self-government than she now possesses'. Dunraven was the chief promoter of the new movement, and he worked closely with MacDonnell: both men firmly believed that Wyndham shared their views.

The discussions continued during the Chief Secretary's holiday, and on September 24th a long manifesto from the Reform Association made its appearance in the newspapers. A suggested solution of the Irish Question was presented under two heads: (a) administrative control over purely Irish finance; and (b) certain Parliamentary functions connected with local business. Briefly, it proposed the creation of an Irish Financial Council, partly nominated and partly elective, and the establishment by Parliament of a statutory body to deal with such Irish affairs as were considered unsuitable for the attention of the Imperial Parliament. From the beginning it was clear that the Association's proposals did not go far enough to please one section of Irish opinion, while they went far too far for the other. Redmond himself was not unsympathetic, but Dillon saw in it the discreditable climax of a long campaign 'to kill Home Rule with kindness', and Davitt denounced it at once as a 'wooden-horse stratagem'. On the other side Sir Edward Carson, Attorney-General for Ireland, publicly referred to the scheme as 'a gross betrayal', and declared that 'he preferred the repeal of the Union to any such tampering'.

Wyndham was in London when the storm broke, and as Parliament was in recess he took the somewhat unusual course for a minister of writing a letter to *The Times* in which he repudiated any knowledge of the Irish Reform Association, and announced the opposition of the Unionist Party to 'any plan for the multiplication of Legislative Assemblies within the limits of the United Kingdom'. *The Times* itself published a leading article on the same day in which 'this insidious project' was denounced, and its authorship openly ascribed to 'an influential clique in Dublin Castle, of which Sir Antony MacDonnell is regarded by numbers of Irish Unionists as the head'. The Chief Secretary deluded himself into the belief that the incident would soon be forgotten. On October 1st he had an interview with MacDonnell during the course of which he deplored the discussion of impracticable schemes which could only raise false hopes, and he refused to concern himself with the suggestions of the Irish Reform Association: on this MacDonnell wrote to Dunraven to say that he could have no further consultations with him.

Far, however, from blowing itself out the storm increased in intensity, and it soon became clear that either Wyndham or MacDonnell would be forced to resign, but the latter refused to budge. He took the line that he had informed the Chief Secretary of all that he was doing, and the fact Wyndham did not reply to his letters was, he held, tantamount to approval of a course of which he had long been aware. In adopting this attitude it was generally believed that he had the support of the King.

When Parliament met the crisis was accentuated. Captain Craig, later Lord Craigavon, put a series of questions on behalf of the Ulster Unionists, and Wyndham replied with a laboured but unconvincing, explanation, while on the following day Dunraven made a full statement in the House of Lords by way of protest against the 'sinister' interpretation which had been placed upon his activities. So it went on. On February 19th, 1905, a Nationalist amendment to the Address was debated, and the storm broke with a vengeance. Wyndham had to face fierce hostility from his own party, for he was accused of having made a scapegoat of his Under-Secretary. His position had clearly become impossible, and at the beginning of March he resigned.

From that day to this it has been stated that Balfour threw Wyndham to the wolves as his uncle had thrown Carnarvon twenty years before, but Balfour's latest biographer, Kenneth Young, will have none of it,[1] and he quotes a letter dated September 1st, 1906, which would seem to prove his case: in it Wyndham wrote to Balfour, 'It is more to the point that both you and Lansdowne warned me that the appointment[2] might get me into trouble. That I offered, to both of you, "to stand the racket".' As for the ordinary English supporter of the Government in Parliament and in the Carlton Club, he felt that Wyndham had been going too fast and was becoming involved in large unknown commitments, and he was therefore not sorry to see him replaced by Walter Long, who had been President of the Local Government Board, and who had a wide and deserved reputation as a very able administrator, firm and level-headed. At the same time it would be idle to deny that there was a good deal of personal sympathy for Wyndham.

Long's views on Ireland are contained in a letter which he wrote to Sandars (incidentally one of his bitterest enemies though he never guessed it) soon after his arrival in the country:

> *Chief Secretary's Lodge*
> *Phoenix Park*
> *Dublin*

My dear Jack

All has so far gone well. Things are not so bad as some thought tho' there is a great deal of deep-seated dissatisfaction, but I am *quite certain* if we were to part with Sir A.M. it wd. cause profound dissatisfaction in many quarters and would most assuredly cause great

---

[1] *Cf. Arthur James Balfour*, p. 246.   [2] Of MacDonnell.

deal of trouble in the country, everybody would believe he was being sacked because he is a R.C. – I feel sure I can get on with him. I am certain he will be *thoroughly loyal* – I believe we can put things right by a firm application of the existing law – and this can, I am satisfied, be secured by almost imperceptible change in administration. What the country wants now is rest and peace, steady quiet but firm administration, wholesome food and drink, she has had too much quack medicine lately! The Act 1903 is working well & having immense indirect effect – it wants a little pushing – this can be done easily now! Don't think I am optimistic, I am only *relieved* by my personal investigation.

I have had a long day, have seen people of all sorts, including two L.U.s from Belfast, and what I write to you is the result of all I have heard, knowing my weakness you won't believe me, but it is true, I have *listened* & said very little myself. Every moment makes me feel more strongly my own incompetence, & makes me regret more and more and more deeply that by one act of mistaken enthusiasm George Wyndham has deprived the country of his splendid talents, & has no longer the chance of reaping in person the rich harvest wh. is now being gathered from the seed he so well sowed. I have much more to say but I must keep it. Tell the Chief as much or none of this, as you think best. I won't bother him with a letter, but I thought it might be a relief to his mind if you could tell him that so far as I know I have made no great blunder to-day, probably because I have *said* so little & that I am convinced patience and firmness will put things right. *On all sides* the *respect* for Sir A.M. is deep and real.

I arrive Friday morning & will come & see you. We had an awful crossing – 1 h. 25 m. late, did not affect me except to make me swear at being woke up and bruised, but poor Monteith suffered heavily.

Yours,

W.

15.III.05

In view of the sharp change in the policy of the British Government it is only natural that there should have been 'a great deal of deep-seated dissatisfaction' in the country, and what is surprising is that it should have taken no more violent a form than a little cattle-driving in Galway. This letter, too, proves that Long was no extremist, but the Nationalists welcomed neither the policy nor the methods of the new Chief Secretary, and they become extremely vocal on the subject in the House of Commons. Toby,

M.P., pictured Long reflecting 'why did he leave the pleasant pastures of the Board of Agriculture, passing through the portals of the Local Government Board, to tread the hot pavement of Dublin Castle? He who once walked through the ripening cornland hand-in-hand with Ceres, was now condemned to listen to John Dillon by the hour.'[1]

There can be few people alive today who have witnessed the old Irish Party in action in the House of Commons, so it may not be out of place to quote once again the inimitable, if somewhat prejudiced, Toby, M.P.:

House of Commons

Monday, May 15

Apparently there are few Sabbath afternoon exercises that give the Irish Constabulary purer joy, greater comfort, than rolling in the roadway one of the representatives of the People. To set upon an ordinary shop-keeper or farmer may serve to fill up time; 'tis poor sport compared with the handling of one of the hon. gentlemen who go to Westminster and, in the sanctuary of the House of Commons, speak disrespectfully of their fellow-countrymen who answer for law and order in Ireland.

There are few Irish members, even of the Party as at present constituted, who have not from time to time told a sympathetic House how on such occasion they fared. Under George Wyndham's rule there was surcease of this kind of diversion. Disposed to kill Home Rule by kindness, he discouraged Sunday afternoon athletics by the constabulary. A new era, or rather revival of an old one, appears coincidentally with the succession of Walter Long to the Chief Secretaryship.

Anyhow Mr Roche[2] this afternoon up and told how, paying a Sunday afternoon visit to his constituents in the musically named hamlet of Cappatagle, co. Galway, he was swooped down upon by the constabulary, who lifted him bodily out of the cart, dragging him along the road for fifty yards. 'Me askin' thim to lave go,' Mr Roche added by way of making it clear that he was not a consenting party to the performance.

Owing to natural excitement, rapid utterance, and something

---

[1] *Punch*, August 2nd, 1905.
[2] M.P. for East Galway.

quite novel in the way of brogue, it was difficult to follow Mr Roche through the full details of the Sabbath afternoon scene. The conversation opened in dry, formal manner by a question on the paper. It invited the Chief Secretary to state whether he was aware that at the place on the date named 'the Member for the Division, while addressing his constituents, was dragged and pulled about by the police?'

The fashion of framing the question endowed it with a certain peaceful, prim formality. It appeared that Mr Roche had no personal interest in the matter, was merely making inquiry on behalf of another Member. That was, however, a matter of style. Just as when Royal Proclamation is made the Sovereign is alluded to in the third person as 'His Majesty', or as under the ancient French monarchy announcements were made *de par le roi*, so Mr Roche, still smarting from his pummelling in the highway of Cappatagle, alluded to the victim of the outrage as 'the Member for the Division'. Later, when he supplemented the question by a speech, he disdained this courtly circumlocution, and, fiercely facing the blushing Chief Secretary, challenged him to deny that 'I was dragged about, me askin' thim to lave go.'

That was ever Mr Roche's strong point. An ordinary man, say a Unionist Member, thus dealt with by the police, might have quietly reconciled himself to participation in their Sunday afternoon service, might even have affected to have enjoyed his share in it. Not so Mr Roche. He was not going to leave the criminal constabulary any loophole of escape on the ground that 'the Member for the Division' was a consenting party. Several times during his fifty yards' excursion down the main street of Cappatagle he 'asked thim to lave go'. Was the right hon. gentleman aware of this?

Walter Long, his blushes more than ever completing his resemblance to a maiden of seventeen, showed a disposition to rise and state the extent of his knowledge on this particular point. But the Deputy Speaker was on his feet by way of indication that the incident had closed. By indulgence of the House, Mr Roche had been permitted to make a personal statement. No debate could follow.

Thereupon the unrelenting advocates of law and order in Cappatagle burst all bounds, turning the House of Commons into a den of wild beasts. The Deputy Speaker stood with a copy of the Orders of the Day in hand waiting to name the first. Below the gangway on his left the Irish Members, tossing like the salt estranging Channel in a westerly gale, incessantly bellowed 'Long! Long!' For fully two minutes the tumult lasted, the Deputy Speaker standing mutely waiting for an opening. At times the turbulent throng surged towards the Treasury Bench as if with intent to seize the Chief Secretary and afford practical illustration of the way things are managed at Cappatagle on Sabbath afternoons. Short of that, it seemed that the scene must have violent end.

It was Winston Churchill who came to the rescue, adroitly suggesting that if the Chief Secretary desired to make a personal statement surely the House would hear him. The Deputy Speaker promptly followed this friendly lead. He had ruled, in accordance with unbroken precedent, that there could be no debate on a personal question. If the Chief Secretary had a statement to make on his own account he should be heard.

It was delightfully in keeping with the scene that Walter Long prefaced his remarks by emphatic declaration that he had no personal statement to make. Of course he accepted the hon. Member's narrative of what took place. His own was based upon the reports of the police.

'Then someone's a liar,' cried Mr Kilbride.[1] With which incontestable summing up of the situation the storm cleared away, and the mere business of the Budget Bill was taken in hand.

Business done – Not much.[2]

In Ireland itself Long soon became far more popular with all classes than might be gathered from the storms in the House of Commons of which he was so often the centre. His loyalty to the Union once more rallied to the side of the Government those who had been estranged by Wyndham's policies, and the Duke of Abercorn was of great help to him in allaying suspicion in Ulster. His own Irish connections rendered him popular with the man-in-the-street, and in this connection a further asset was the charm of

[1] M.P. for South Kildare.
[2] *Punch*, May 24th, 1905.

his wife, Lady Doreen, a daughter of the ninth Earl of Cork. Long hunted with the Meath whenever opportunity occurred, and for several weeks he stayed at Humewood in County Wicklow which had been his grandfather's home.

His troubles were by no means confined to the necessity of facing his Nationalist opponents or of allaying Orange suspicions, for there soon arose no inconsiderable amount of friction between the Lord-Lieutenant, the second Earl of Dudley – not the easiest of men with whom to deal[1] – and himself, chiefly owing to the ambiguity which existed as to their respective positions under the Constitution. There was no settled rule as to whether the Lord-Lieutenant or the Chief Secretary should, or should not, be a member of the Cabinet. In the present instance Long was a Cabinet Minister, while Dudley was not, but in the last Salisbury administration the Lord-Lieutenant had been included in the Cabinet, while the Chief Secretary had been left outside. In these circumstances it was not unnatural that there should be considerable doubt as to who, in the last resort, was responsible for the administration of Ireland.

The letters exchanged between Long and Dudley were marked by an increasing asperity.

> *Woodside*
> *Chenies*
> *Rickmansworth*
>
> May 8th, 1905
>
> My dear Long
>
> If you have time, I wish you would send me a line and tell me what impressions you formed during your trip in Ireland. I read of it with much interest. How do you think of the situation in the West? And what do you think of the justice of the demand for the grass lands?
>
> Yours sincerely
> DUDLEY

Long had no doubt as to the relative positions of the Lord-Lieutenant and himself, and he determined to make his views clear from the beginning:

---

[1] Walter Long himself could be peppery on occasion.

Irish Office

11th May, 1905

My dear Lord Lieutenant

I had a very interesting time in the West, but I can't say I saw anything very new. The condition of the cottier tenants is very bad, in some cases awful, and the saddest part of it is that while I believe it to be impossible to obtain enough land to make the holdings "economic", it is also impossible to get the people to migrate – the local people told me themselves that their people would not migrate, and would not know what to do if they found themselves put into a good farm in a strange country. I believe the only possible policy is to do all we can to extend and improve railway, steamer, and other means of communication and to deal with the land question prudently and carefully. I regard the demands for the grass lands as a question which must be very cautiously dealt with – it is cruel and even wicked to raise hopes in the hearts of these poor peasants which we know cannot be realized; and if it is sought to force the graziers out by intimidation and boycotting I am determined that the full strength of the law shall be employed to stop anything of the kind, and that the law shall be supported by the *administrative* policy of all branches of the Executive.

As I am on this subject will you forgive me if I say plainly why I deplored and objected to the speech you made on the land question during the interregnum – It was not because I do not sympathize with the object you have in view and which you have laboured so hard to effect, but because I hold firmly that Ministers ought not when they are speaking in their Ministerial capacity, and therefore for their colleagues as well as themselves, to hold out hopes which they do not believe can be realized. See how we have been flogged in the House of Commons over your speech about "Government in accordance with Irish ideas" – this is applauded by the Nationalists and derided and flouted by Unionists – and it produces a very difficult situation; as you and I exist as Ministers by Unionist votes, it is of course an impossible policy to use language of the kind.

As we have got to work together in the discharge of a very difficult task I have taken the opportunity which your letter has afforded me to express myself frankly as I always believe in plain dealing. I beg you will forgive me.

There is another aspect of the grazing farm question which calls for serious consideration. Ireland depends largely upon the cattle trade, she exports annually to Great Britain some 800,000 cattle, with probably as many millions – if the grass farms are divided and large parts brought under cultivation, what must be the fate of this large and prosperous branch of the agricultural industry?

Yours sincerely

W. H. LONG.

There is another point which deserves attention. Section 27 of Act of 1881 and Section 7 of Act of 1885 have been repealed by the Act of 1903, thereby clearly showing that untenanted lands were only to be acquired for the benefit of the persons named in Section 2 of Act of 1903, that is mainly for the enlargement of uneconomic holdings and the re-instatement of evicted tenants. So far as I can see it is scarcely possible to obtain untenanted land to effect these objects, yet by some means or other the idea has got abroad that Tradesmen and others living in towns, *i.e. landless* men, are entitled to be converted into farmers and be installed in farms carved out of grazing lands at the expense of the State. The result is that persons of this class joined the forces of disorder, have promoted, or aided in the system of intimidation which has been resorted to in order to obtain possession of grazing lands. If any countenance were given to such a project the problem of congestion would be aggravated, not remedied, and drastic measures must be taken to prevent any administrative action calculated to encourage men to entertain illegitimate hopes of this kind.

W.H.L.

The situation was clearly growing more tense, and it was unfortunate that ill-health on the part of the Lord-Lieutenant prevented him from having that personal discussion with the Chief Secretary which might have done much to obviate the subsequent crisis in their official relations.

House of Commons

6.VI.05

CONFIDENTIAL

My dear Lord-Lieutenant

I am very sorry to hear from Eddy Stanley that you are so unwell. I hope you will soon throw it all off. I had hoped to hear from you before this in answer to my two letters, and I am writing now to suggest that we should have some talk as soon as possible about matters of general policy, and some other questions of minor importance. The Lord Chancellor has just shown me your letter about the Recordership. I wrote to you some time ago to say I had undertaken to recommend the Recorder's name to H.M. for a Privy Councillorship on his *retirement*: his letter of resignation was brought to me and by my direction was of course sent on to you. I have decided views as to the selection of his successor, and I shall be delighted to discuss the matter with you with whom the actual appointment rests.

I also promised that the resignation should not take effect till July for reasons connected with the business of the Court.

When are you going over to Ireland? There are one or two matters which are important and may be controversial, and I think should come before you and not before the Lords Justices.

I am very anxious to see you and discuss these and other matters.

Sincerely yours

WALTER H. LONG.

His Excellency The Earl of Dudley

A month elapsed, and during that period the relations between the two men became even further strained.

Inver Lodge
Maam X., Galway

July 8, 1905

Dear Long

Although I signed the "Instructions" to the Estates Commissioners at your request, I feel bound to tell you that I do not like No. 2 or agree with the policy underlying it.

I need hardly say that I quite appreciate your desire to check intimidation designed to compel a landlord to sell at an unfair price, and I would support any attempt made through the ordinary police channels to prevent it. But I do not think that it is wise to make such an attempt through the medium of an instruction to the Estate Commissioners. If the Act is to work smoothly and quickly, those administering it must keep clear, in my opinion, of anything that can be considered as a threatening attitude, for the odium that will be aroused by any such attitude will hamper them and frustrate them throughout their negotiations.

The whole basis of the Act, as you truly said to me the other day, is its voluntary character and it would be fatal to invest it with a coercionist tinge.

But there is another point of view of even greater importance, as it seems to me – You will never cure intimidation by the policy of postponing sales.

You will only incur the danger of making it ten times worse, of fanning and fomenting local irritation, until the old methods of "no rent campaign" and physical violence are resorted to, and the character of the agitation changed from one of comparative harmlessness to that of violent and active organization.

To my mind an absolutely opposite course should be followed, and no chance should be lost of accelerating sales on those estates where the trouble has become almost chronic and traditional, and by that means, as in the case of the Dunsandle and De Freyne Estates, of cutting out from the very roots the disease from which the trouble springs.

Some people may call that "conceding to the forces of lawlessness and disorder", but if one thing *is* proved in Ireland, it is the failure of the policy of the "big stick", and it is because of that failure that I dislike and disagree with a policy which looks like a return to it.

Yours sincerely

DUDLEY.

From this letter it is obvious that the Lord-Lieutenant approached the problems of Ireland from the standpoint of Wyndham rather than that of Long, and in the circumstances one might have thought that he would have resigned as a fundamental principle of policy was at stake, but he did no such thing. What he did get was a blistering reply from the Chief Secretary.

House of Commons

12.VII.05

Dear Lord Lieutenant

I beg to acknowledge the receipt of your letter of the 8th inst. I am, of course, always glad to have your views on any question of policy; but in this instance I don't quite understand the object of your letter, as the Regulations having been issued and signed by you, your views on their contents can now only have an academic interest. Your position as a member of the Irish Executive makes you jointly responsible both for their terms and for their loyal administration.

Yours sincerely

H.E. The L.L.   W.H.L.

A few days after this letter was written the differences between the two men were temporarily overshadowed by a misfortune which concerned them both, namely the defeat, on July 20th, of the Government in the House of Commons by 200 votes to 196 on an Opposition amendment to reduce the Irish estimates, though the real blame rested with the Chief Whip. Long at once wrote two letters to the Prime Minister, the first being an offer of resignation as was customary in those days from the Head of a Department in his circumstances.

Irish Office
Old Queen St., S.W.

My dear Prime Minister

I do not want to add to your worries so I merely write to say that my resignation is in your hands & and that if you decide to carry on you may rely upon my unfailing & constant support. I am very sorry this has happened.

Sincerely Yours

21.VII.05 WALTER H. LONG.

The second letter throws some light upon the meeting of the Cabinet which had been called to discuss the crisis.

Irish Office
Old Queen St., S.W.

My dear Prime Minister

I am very reluctant to trouble you, the more so as I feel I said more than I was entitled to do at the Cabinet. I still hold that there are only two courses.

    1st. Immediate resignation facing all the consequences, including an August election.

    2nd. Absolute defiance & carrying on to next Session.

The latter would, I am sure, be full of difficulty but yet could, I think, be carried out.

I am afraid of the October plan, or Sept., because of our men who will be taken by surprise. On these grounds I would ask you (& C.[1] agrees with me), whether we might not meet, say at 12.30 on Monday, & have some further talks: *unless you are quite clear that you yourself entirely approve* the course you are going to adopt, in which case I am satisfied. You, & you alone are to be considered: this decision will, of course, hereafter be regarded as yours: & if you have any strong view which differs from ours I will support it heart & soul.

I can't say how wretched it makes me that this trouble should have arisen over my estimates & I still feel that I ought to go – but in this as in all else your wish will be my law.

Yours sincerely

21.VII.05 WALTER H. LONG.

Two days later Balfour decided that he would neither resign nor

[1] Either Lord Cawdor or Austen Chamberlain.

ask for a Dissolution. Of course he was immediately accused by the Liberals of having acted unconstitutionally, but as all Oppositions accuse all Governments, irrespective of party, of acting unconstitutionally no serious attention was paid to the charge. Once the crisis was over the Lord-Lieutenant and the Chief Secretary returned to their more personal differences, and at the end of July and the beginning of August their relations reached a stage when the intervention of the Prime Minister became necessary as an important constitutional question had by this time arisen.

House of Commons

My dear Lord Lieutenant

I am very sorry to have to trouble you about the appointments to the N.E.B.[1] but the position of this Board and its work call forth so much criticism here that it is impossible for me to consent to any appointments being made other than those I recommend: for these reasons I wired you today.

I see they propose to memorialize you on behalf of the Galway Prisoners – as this case involves the general policy of the Government I am sure you will not deal with it without communicating with me.

Yours sincerely

26.VII.05   WALTER H. LONG.

His Excellency The Lord Lieutenant

An exchange of somewhat embittered telegrams followed. Dudley was still at Maam Cross, and on July 27th Long wired to him there:

Must ask Your Excellency to be so good as to approve of appointments I have suggested. It would, I think, be unfortunate if a difficulty were to arise between us in this matter, in respect of which I could not possibly alter my recommendations. If, however, Your Excellency desires matter to be submitted to Prime Minister I am quite willing to do so. – CHIEF SECRETARY.

To this Dudley replied:

I am coming to London on Monday night and will see you Tuesday with reference to subject of your telegram. I presume if we are unable to agree I am willing to refer matter as you suggest. Please telegraph on this.

Long was clearly none too pleased judging by his reply:

[1] National Education Board.

Last part of telegram not clear. Assume your question is if you are unwilling to accept my suggestions case shall be referred to Prime Minister. To this I agree. – CHIEF SECRETARY.

The Lord-Lieutenant in his next telegram put his finger upon the real problem:

Question is whether fact of your being in Cabinet and I not, compels me to accept your recommendations with regard to patronage in Ireland without seeing papers or knowing on what grounds your recommendations are based. If we hold divergent views on this Prime Minister must decide but we had better discuss matters in order to arrive at an understanding. – DUDLEY.

The Lord-Lieutenant came to London[1] a couple of days later, and had a talk with Long which showed that there was no personal bitterness between the two men.

Friday night
7 Carlton Gardens, S.W.

My dear Long

Before going back to Ireland to-morrow, I want to write you one line to tell you how grateful I feel to you for the kind and considerate way in which you met me yesterday and listened to what I tried to say.

We have not seen much of each other in the past and therefore probably do not know each other very well, and I very much feared that you might misunderstand my point of view, and think either that I was trying to pick a quarrel or that I was trying to claim a voice in matters that properly belong to you.

But thanks to your patience and consideration, my task was far easier than I had anticipated, and I came away from our interview with the feeling that I knew you better and with the hope that I had succeeded a little in showing you some of the difficulties and doubts that had been in my mind.

It was only a little cloud that had arisen above us – but I hope and believe that it will be the only one that will ever appear, and I at any rate certainly think that as we know each other better and under-

[1] Whenever the Lord-Lieutenant left Ireland two or three Lords Justices, usually judges, were appointed to carry on the Government in his absence. On his return a curious ceremony always took place. Arriving at the Castle from Holyhead about 9.0 a.m., he would walk straight to the Throne Room, which was empty except for the Lords Justices sitting tightly wedged together in the Chair of State and wearing their top hats. As he entered the room they rose, bowed, and vacated their seats, which the Lord-Lieutenant then took, putting on his hat as he sat down. He thus resumed the functions of his office.

stand each other's points of view that there will be less and less likelihood of any differences of opinion between us.

We shall have an opportunity this autumn for many talks together, and to that I look forward very much.

Yours sincerely

DUDLEY.

The 'little cloud', however, was not long in making its reappearance, this time in connection with the filling of a vacancy upon the Senate of the Royal University.

Irish Office

7.VIII.05

My dear Lord Lieutenant

I thank you for your letter and I am very glad our meeting tended to relieve your mind. I can assure you I am most anxious to do anything I can to make your position agreeable to you – but, while I am at all times ready to discuss questions of all kinds with you, I cannot undertake, for obvious reasons, to write to you before I come to a decision when you are absent from London. It is also impossible for me to subordinate my views, when deliberately arrived at, to anybody save the Prime Minister or the Cabinet. As regards the question of patronage, I have examined the precedents since I saw you, and I have every reason to believe that it has been customary for Chief Secretaries to write privately as I did to you, thus avoiding the recording on the files of discordant opinions; however, I am quite ready to adopt the form which you prefer and which is no doubt the strictly regular one: but when it comes to the adoption of a principle I cannot assent to your proposal that your opinion should be paramount.

Policy is often indicated by the appointments made, this is especially the case in Ireland, and if I, as the Minister responsible for the Government of Ireland, come, after careful and full consideration, to the conclusion that the selection of a particular individual is necessary, I must ask you to be so good as to act upon my advice unless you can show me that some other individual would be a better selection and would represent the same principle. In the case before us it is not so, you desire to increase the Catholic Clerical representation, I, agreeing with my predecessor, desire to maintain the present proportions of Lay and Clerical representation.

I cannot recede from my position, and I sincerely hope you will not think it necessary to force a crisis between us, as I should deeply regret such a result both on personal and public grounds. I am only asking you to follow the course adopted by all your predecessors, when the present Prime Minister was Chief Secretary both Londonderry and Zetland invariably accepted his decisions and carried out his wishes. I pass by the time when our opponents were in office, when as you know Morley claimed full and absolute independence of action in all matters, and I come to the time when the Lord Lieutenant was in the Cabinet and the Chief Secretary was not, when, to my knowledge, almost invariably, if differences arose, the Lord Lieutenant gave way to the Chief Secretary on the ground that he was really the Minister who, having to defend, ought to control all acts of the Government. I must therefore ask you to be so good as to signify your approval of the name I have submitted to you.

Believe me I have no personal object to serve. I am most anxious to work on terms of confidence and friendship with you, but, above and beyond all, I am determined so long as I hold my office to be really responsible for the administration.

I am,

My dear Lord Lieutenant

Yours sincerely

WALTER H. LONG.

His Excellency The Lord Lieutenant

The Lord-Lieutenant would not agree, so there was nothing for it but to refer the problem to Balfour, who, in a letter to Dudley, gave a reply which was virtually a State Paper, for it prescribed the régime in Ireland which continued until the end of British rule in that country.

10 Downing Street
Whitehall, S.W.1

15.8.05

My dear Eddy Dudley

You ask me whether "it is my wish that . . . the views of the Chief Secretary should always prevail". The question is a very natural one and goes to the root of that practical paradox – the present system of Irish Government.

It is of course obvious that, could we start afresh, no such system would be proposed by the wildest visionary. The Lord Lieutenancy was originally contrived when Parliamentary Government was in its infancy – when Ireland was as far off (measuring distance in time) as Constantinople – when the British immigrants were regarded as colonists and the natives as barbarians. The Lord Lieutenant was then and for long after what the Viceroy of India is now – a great officer dependent indeed upon the Home Government for his tenure, but with a large measure of practical freedom both from Parliamentary criticism and Cabinet control as regards administrative details.

All this has suffered inevitable change. The perpetual interference of the H. of C. in the pettiest subjects, the "tightening up" of the doctrine of Cabinet responsibility, the Union, and, finally, the telegraph, have now transferred the real headship of the Irish Government to the Minister who happens both to be in the Cabinet *and* in the House of Commons. When, as in the case of Lord Spencer and Lord Cadogan, the man in the Cabinet is not the man in the House of Commons, the change from the old system to the new is not so violent, but the system itself is even more difficult to work: for nothing can deprive the man in the H. of C. both of power and responsibility so long as Irish subjects are the occasion of daily Parliamentary skirmishing – and divided power is fruitful in friction.

The result of all this is that while the legal status and the social duties of the Lord Lieutenant remain what they were, his political responsibilities are quite altered – altered, not deliberately or of set purpose, but by the unconquerable force of circumstances. If therefore you ask me whether, in case of difference, the views of the Chief Secretary should prevail, I can only answer *yes*. There can be but one head of the Irish administration. Do not however suppose that the true deduction from this is that the Lord Lieutenant is nothing more than an Under Secretary. He much more resembles (though of course with many differences) a constitutional monarch – and it would be a shallow view indeed which would regard even the most constitutionally limited monarch as no more than an historic figure head. I am not arguing for or against the retention of the Viceroyalty as an integral part of our system; this is much too large a subject. All I am contending for is that, *while it exists*, a Viceroy who works harmoniously with his Chief Secretary can and does perform in virtue both of his social and of his legal position, a most valuable work, such as no Under Secretary could even attempt.

This is an inordinately long letter. But I am anxious that you should have my full thoughts on a complex problem. I admit the difficulties of a Viceroy's position; but though difficult it is both important and useful, and I earnestly trust that you will not abandon it.

Yours,

ARTHUR JAMES BALFOUR.

This, of course, decided the controversy in favour of Long Dudley did not resign, but he wrote, 'I am bound to say that I regret his (*i.e.* the Prime Minister's) decision for the sake of my office, but personally I am, of course, prepared to fully carry out his desires.' Balfour tried to pour some oil on the troubled waters by writing to the Chief Secretary that 'Dudley is really a good fellow, and I am sure means to do his best', but he was not wholly successful, for Long replied, 'I am sure Dudley is a good fellow. As to his intentions, they may be well meant, but if so they are very badly carried out from the Unionist point of view; but I am quite certain that however good a fellow he may be in private life he is a very bad colleague in Government.'[1]

While this crisis was taking place in Dublin the Prime Minister also had on his hands the contemporary dispute between Curzon and Kitchener, so it is hardly surprising to find him writing at this time to Sandars, 'Life would be tolerable but for its Viceroys.' Incidentally, the relations between Sandars and Long throw further light upon the former's position, for the Chief Secretary was certainly not the man to fawn on another, but shortly after his appointment to the Irish Office he wrote to Sandars, 'I will be at the Office at 11, and shall be glad if I can have half an hour to discuss the following points.' Equally illuminating on this score is a sentence Sandars wrote to Balfour, 'I have told Walter to go steadily just now – two Viceroys at once would be too much.'

Little of interest occurred where Ireland was concerned during the next few months, and on December 4th, 1905, Balfour tendered his resignation to the King. There was one incident in connection with this event which is best told in Long's own words. 'Before dismissing me he (*i.e.* the King) said that he had a request to make which he hoped I would be able to grant. I need hardly say that I replied I felt certain that His Majesty had only to make a request for me to be prepared to carry out his wishes. However he pointed out that he felt he was asking me to do something quite out of the common. He said, "I know, when Governments change, the out-going Ministers do not treat their successors in the same way as they would if it was a mere change of office under the same Government, and they were to be followed by Members of their own Party. This is, of course, natural, and,

[1] *Cf.* Petrie, Sir Charles: *Walter Long and His Times*, pp. 81–97.

163

as a rule, no doubt right, but the case of Ireland is an exceptional one, and I want you to go and see Mr Bryce, your successor, tell him quite frankly and freely what are your views of the difficulties connected with the Government of Ireland quite apart from the question of Home Rule, what you believe to be the most essential details of administration, and, in other words, give him the benefit of your knowledge and experience just as you would if you were being followed by some political friend of your own." Of course, I at once told His Majesty that if Mr Bryce cared to receive me, I would be only too glad to carry out His Majesty's wishes. The path was accordingly prepared for the interview, and I had two long mornings with Mr Bryce, during which I endeavoured to put everything before him, without, of course, trespassing in any way upon party political ground.'[1]

If English statesmen were continually ruining the hopes of Ireland by deliberately entangling her problems in their politics King Edward VII was not among their number.

As we have seen the King paid one visit to Ireland during the Liberal régime, but it was somewhat marred by the theft of the state jewels of the Order of St Patrick, to which allusion has already been made. Dudley had been succeeded as Lord-Lieutenant by the Marquess of Aberdeen, who had held the office for a brief space twenty years earlier: he was a good deal of an eccentric, and the King considered him to be lacking in dignity. Accordingly he was neither displeased nor surprised when, in urging the advisability of a Royal visit to Ireland, the Lord-Lieutenant said that there might be some difficulty about staying at the Viceregal Lodge. The Sovereign readily agreed in a curt autograph note, 'All right. I look on it as a settled matter that we live on board the yacht'. The visit took place in the second week of July, 1907, and as usual the King and Queen received a popular and cordial welcome.

The change of Government soon proved to have made little difference where Ireland was concerned. Long experience had shown that there was little enough to choose between the two English parties, and Redmond well put the Irish point of view when he

[1] *Memories*, pp. 169–170.

said, 'The sooner that this Government understands that to us Whig, Tory, Liberal, Conservative, are but as names, and that British Governments are judged by us by what they do and not by their professions of sympathy, the better it will be for them and for every one concerned.'[1] Mindful of their defeats in 1886 and 1895 on the subject of Home Rule the Liberal leaders were fearful of introducing any measure with that end in view, and as they possessed an independent majority in the House of Commons they were under no necessity of placating Redmond and his followers: they went, however, so far as to introduce a Bill to establish an Irish Council having wide administrative powers but with no power to make laws or to control finance. This emasculated form of Home Rule was referred by the Irish Party to a convention in Dublin which contemptuously flung it back in the Liberal Government's face. As a contemporary parody of an old Irish patriotic song ran:

> Is it this you call Home Rule?
>> Says the Shan Van Vocht.
> Do you take me for a fool?
>> Says the Shan Van Vocht.
>
> To be sending round the hat
> Five-and-twenty years for that
> Isn't good enough for Pat,
>> Says the Shan Van Vocht.
>
> And the Lord-Lieutenant too,
>> Says the Shan Van Vocht,
> Is he still to be on view?
>> Says the Shan Van Vocht.
>
> And all them big police,
> Monumentally obese,
> Must I go on feeding these?
>> Says the Shan Van Vocht.[2]

There was, however another Ireland – the Ireland of the future – coming into existence, and it was in more ways than one a reaction against Lords-Lieutenant, Chief Secretaries, political action

[1] Gwynn, Denis: *The Life of John Redmond*, pp. 133.
[2] *Cf.* Robinson, Lennox: *Bryan Cooper*, pp. 63–64.

at Westminster, and all that these things implied. While the old Queen was still on the throne Arthur Griffith had started Sinn Fein and Douglas Hyde had founded the Gaelic League, and to them turned the young people who felt themselves frustrated by the fact that Irish ambitions had so obviously became the plaything of English politicians. As for the Parliamentary Party,

> Faith it's growing clear to me,
>   Says the Shan Van Vocht,
> That ye like being absentee,
>   Says the Shan Van Vocht,
>
> At Westminster to appear
>   On two hundred pounds a year;
> Ye'd have empty stomachs here,
>   Says the Shan Van Vocht.
>
> All your promises were vain,
>   Says the Shan Van Vocht.
> I'm turning to Sinn Fein,
>   Says the Shan Van Vocht.

As so often in the better days of nationalism it was contemporary with a literary renaissance, for the turn of the century was marked by the appearance of the Irish Literary Theatre, a name soon to be changed to the Irish National Theatre. On May 8th, 1899, W. B. Yeats's *The Countess Cathleen* was given its first performance at the Ancient Concert Rooms in Dublin, and in the same year Edward Martyn's *The Heather Field* was produced. In 1900 three plays were staged at the Gaiety Theatre, namely George Moore's *Bending of the Bough*, Alice Milligan's *Last Feast*, and Edward Martyn's *Maeve*: in 1901 the number was again two, that is to say *Diarmuid and Grania* in which Yeats and Moore collaborated, and, most significant of all, *Casadh An tSúgáin* by Douglas Hyde which was the first Irish Gaelic play ever produced in any theatre. These were presented at the Gaiety, for the Abbey did not come into existence until three years later. So the modern Irish dramatic movement – the movement that had the widest appeal and attracted the most attention – was born, but it was only part of a more general cultural renaissance of which the birth can be dated at least a decade earlier. That renaissance was the result of a confluence of many streams, some of which had nothing to do with the theatre and not very much with literary or artistic circles. The late M. J. MacManus was of the opinion that 'it was given its first outward expression within the covers of a little book of verse, bound in white linen, published by Gill of Dublin in 1888. Its title was *Poems and Ballads of Young Ireland*.'[1]

At the same time tribute must be paid to an earlier pioneer, George Petrie, who died in 1866. Together with John O'Donovan and Eugene O'Curry he revealed that heroic and glorious past of Ireland which gave birth to the best poetry of the movement. Petrie was a many-sided scholar, for he was an artist of no little merit, a collector of folk-music, and no inconsiderable archaeologist. 'His part in the revival of Irish studies was to organize, guide, and stimulate, and it was indispensable.'[2]

With the foundation of the Abbey Theatre in 1904 an extremely clever school of acting grew up under the Brothers Fay, by whom the utmost was made of heroic and poetic plays, of social satires, peasant dramas, tragedies, and burlesques. Indeed, the actors were second to none in their natural art, fine voices, and good team work, though it must be admitted that the richness of Irish dialogue gave them opportunities denied to those who are called upon to deliver the uninspiring speech of English and American cities. For twenty years the Abbey was the centre of Irish artistic endeavour, and of political controversy, and it provided a powerful stimulus which was not without its influence upon the history of Ireland. Later it incurred a good deal of criticism, and de Blacam wrote of 'the general Abbey defect' which was that it was 'interested in the vagaries of life rather than in the grand central principles'.[3]

Patriotic, even nationalist, though the new movement may have been in intention it had to encounter a great deal of hostility in its earlier days, and particularly was this the case with J. M. Synge's play, *The Playboy of the Western World*, which was produced for the first time at the Abbey in January, 1907. Even before it appeared

[1] *Adventures of an Irish Bookman*, p. 176.
[2] Blacam, Aodh de: *A First Book of Irish Literature*, p. 176.
[3] *Ibid*, pp. 218–219.

on the stage it was attacked in the Press as an insult to Ireland, and the first night was pandemonium. To quote Professor Starkie:

> Although I tried very hard to concentrate upon the play it was impossible to hear the actors after the first few minutes because of the interruptions and disturbances which took place all over the auditorium. When these reached a climax, one of the company advanced to the footlights and tried to appeal for silence. He said, as far as I could make out, that anyone in the audience who did not like the play was at liberty to get up and leave, but nobody left. Instead, pandemonium broke loose, and my wizened neighbour, whom I had considered an inoffensive old man, jumped to his feet shouting, "Clear the decks! Down with Willie Fay!" And his shouts were taken up in chorus by the gallery. Then came shouts from the pit below, and many started to sing the revolutionary song, *The West's Awake*.
>
> While all this rumpus was going on the actors and actresses on the stage continued valiantly to act their parts, but they were puppets; I could see their lips move but hardly a word reached me.

Professor Starkie goes on to say that in spite of all this disorder 'Lady Gregory stood at the door of the Green Room as calm and collected as Queen Victoria about to open a charity bazaar': as for the author:

> While we were munching our cake we observed the author, J. M. Synge, mooning about among the actors like a lost soul. I had seen him on various occasions in Kingstown, and when I passed him striding along the Dalkey Road swinging his stick I used to wonder whether he was French or Austrian, for he had moustaches and a little goatee or 'imperial'. When I saw him on the night of the Abbey riot his face was pale and sunken, and he looked like a ghost of the sun-tanned wanderer I had seen walking by the sea. I watched him closely as he sat motionless through the dumb-show of his play, amidst the rioting and insults of the mob, but not a trace of emotion could I discern in his pale, mask-like face that gazed unseeing at the raging auditorium.[1]

[1] *Scholars and Gypsies*, pp. 37–59.

If the movement had a patron and a centre they were Lady Gregory and Coole, the house of which Yeats wrote the prophetic lines:

> Here, traveller, scholar, poet, take your stand,
> When all these rooms and passages are gone,
> When nettles wave upon a shapeless mound
> And saplings root among the broken stone,
> And dedicate – eyes bent upon the ground,
> Back turned upon the brightness of the sun
> And all the sensuality of the shade –
> A moment's memory to that laurelled head.

These verses were written in 1929 when the house which had played so large a part in the resurgent literary movement was still standing, but within less than fifteen years it was a ruin, for, as Yeats had foretold, the nettles and saplings had been allowed to work their will.

The Gregorys had come to Galway in the eighteenth century after making a fortune in the service of the East India Company, and towards the end of Queen Victoria's reign they were still at Coole in the person of Sir William Gregory, who had at one time been Governor of Ceylon as well as a Member of Parliament. He married, as his second wife, Augusta Persse, who came from the neighbouring big house at Roxborough, and who had been born in 1852. That was in 1880, and twelve years later Sir William died. There was nothing in all this which gave any promise of what lay ahead, nor had either the Persses or the Gregorys up to then displayed any Nationalist sympathies. Both familes had been good landlords, and a Gregory had died of the plague in 1847 while ministering to his stricken tenants; the storms of the Land League left them virtually untouched, but all the same they remained pure Ascendancy, loyal to the Imperial tradition, and stout defenders of the British connection. In these circumstances when Lady Gregory became a widow and sold her London house it would only have been natural if she had, in her retirement at Coole, settled down to a country-house existence entertaining from time to time the neighbouring gentry or high officials from Dublin Castle and the Viceregal Lodge.

Then the unexpected happened, and in 1896 she met Yeats.

At that time, the poet wrote afterwards, she was 'a plainly dressed woman of forty-five, without obvious good looks, except the charm that comes from strength, intelligence, and kindness'. The attraction was mutual and complete, and Coole became a cultural centre where poets, dramatists, and artists foregathered. Yeats spent the whole summer of 1897 there: at that time he was, he has told us, involved in 'a miserable love affair', and distressed by finding that his devotion 'might as well have been offered to an image in a milliner's window or to a statue in a museum'. He could not concentrate, and to distract his mind from himself Lady Gregory took him out into the open air, going from cottage to cottage gathering folklore, while each evening they noted down what they had heard during the day. Yeats 'was tremendously excited; his health improved, and he was able to work. Coole became a place of great literary activity. The Celtic Renaissance was being born.'[1]

As the years went by and Lady Gregory grew older, she herself became almost a national institution, for not only had she founded the Abbey Theatre, but she had written some of the most successful products of the Abbey stage, such as *Hyacinth Halvey*, *The Workhouse Ward*, *The Rising of the Moon*, and *Cathleen-ni-Houlihan*, which last was hers in all save the suggestion. From Coole, too, Lady Gregory conducted a tireless, but in her lifetime unsuccessful, campaign, to have that wonderful collection of pictures bequeathed to Ireland by her nephew, Sir Hugh Lane, taken out of English hands and brought home. She tended Coole with a mother's care for her son Robert, but he was killed in the First World War, and she died in 1932. Soon afterwards her home disappeared, but the Seven Woods have changed little since Yeats wrote of them.

> Shanwalla, where a willow-bordered pond
> Gathers the wild duck from the winter dawn;
> Dim Pairc-na-Carraig where the wild bees fling
> Their sudden fragrances on the green air,
> Seven odours, seven murmurs, seven woods.

Finally, those who did not know Edwardian Ireland are likely to

---

[1] MacManus, M. J.: *Adventures of an Irish Bookman*, p. 129.

see it it in a wrong perspective. Was not this the time, they will ask, when the Home Rule agitation was sweeping the country, and did not this issue set everybody by the ears? The answer is in the affirmative, but contrary to what is generally supposed in England the Irish are interested in other things than politics, and it was these latter, of which sport in all its forms was the most important, that brought men and women together. Political feeling too, varied in intensity in different parts of the country; Mayo and Sligo, for example, took their politics more easily than, say, Clare on the one hand and Derry on the other. Memories in the former were still fresh at only one remove of the landing of the French at Killala, and Humbert's soldiers had not been so popular as legend would have us believe, for it was by no means forgotten how they had left their Irish allies in the lurch at Ballinamuck: while as for the Connaught Unionists, not only were they few in number, but they were far from holding to their faith with the grim fanaticism of the Black North, and Lord Dunraven had a number of followers among them.

Not for the first – or the last – time in her chequered history in Edwardian days in Ireland appearances were liable to be deceptive.

CHAPTER VII

Scotland

————◦◉◦————

THE turn of the century, and the transition from Queen Victoria to her son, found public opinion in Scotland more concerned with religious, than with political or social, problems, and the centripetal forces seemed to be gaining ground, especially where the non-established Presbyterian Churches were concerned. The Free Church had been joined in 1876 by the bulk of the Reformed Presbyterians or Cameronians, and now, after a quarter of a century, negotiations with the United Presbyterian Church were resumed, with the result that in 1900 the Free Church and the United Presbyterian Church became one under the name of the United Free Church. The Free Church, it is to be noted, had had experience since the Disruption in 1843 that, though it 'went out' to secure it spiritual independence from the interference of the civil courts, these courts never hesitated to adjudicate upon any case brought by a minister or member alleging breach of contract against the Church; it therefore took a great risk as a Church which had hitherto maintained the 'establishment principle' when it united with a confessedly voluntary body.

In these circumstances it is not surprising that some thirty of its ministers and a certain proportion of its members refused to enter the Union, and became colloquially known as 'Wee Frees'. Cross-actions were brought between the uniting majority and the dissentient minority, and both parties asked to be declared the rightful holder in trust of the Free Church property. The Scottish courts decided in favour of the majority, but in 1904 the House of Lords reversed this decision. Their lordships held that by passing a certain Declaratory Act in which the doctrine of the Confession had been modified, and by ceasing to maintain the principle of an Established Church, the majority had ceased to represent the Free Church: in consequence the ministers and congregations who held to the ancient standards unmodified were declared to be the Free Church of Scotland, and thus entitled to hold its eleven hundred churches and other property both at home and abroad. In effect, the case had really turned on the point whether a Trust for a Church was a Trust to promulgate a rigid doctrine, or whether it might be a Trust for an organization free to mould its own doctrine and its own constitution: the Law Lords had taken the former view.

This decision created an impossible situation, for the minority was manifestly unable to discharge its trust, so recourse was perforce had to Parliament. Accordingly the Scottish Churches Bill was introduced to give the Free Church the relief necessary to allow her to retain the bulk of her property, and there was no opposition to its provisions in principle. It was another thing, however, when to the same Bill a fifth clause was added, which dealt, not with the Free, but with the Established Church of Scotland, empowering her without recourse to Parliament to alter the form of subscription to the Confession of Faith laid down in the Act of 1690. Campbell-Bannerman took strong exception to this; he described Clause V as an 'undesirable alien', a phrase which was highly topical at the moment owing to the controversy over the Aliens Act; and demanded that it should be introduced, if at all, in a separate Bill.

This was just the sort of controversy in which Balfour delighted, and he took Clause V through Committee himself. He particularly resisted the suggestion that it should be introduced as a separate Bill, for he knew full well that a dying Government could never force a second controversial measure on this subject through a dying Parliament. 'Clause V', he declared, 'was no intruder.' It was relevant to the general interest of Presbyterianism in Scotland. All the Scottish Presbyterian Churches had the same origin, and their reunion was something to which all looked forward. The decision of the House of Lords, by which relief had just been given to the Free Church, had made many people feel that its

Established brother was left handicapped, and that a barrier had been raised against unity. 'I shall always be found,' declared the Prime Minister, 'on the side of freedom and the side of unity.' His most formidable opponent was James Bryce, who fought hard to exclude Professors of Theology in the universities from the authority of the Ecclesiastical Assemblies. Balfour continued this argument by admitting his sympathy for the unfettered freedom of theological teaching, but he deprecated the raising of the big question of University Tests on this particular occasion.[1] The Bill passed into law on July 20th, 1905. Thus accorded a new-found liberty the General Assembly of the Established Church in 1910 framed the following formula, 'I hereby subscribe the Confession of Faith, declaring that I accept it as the Confession of this Church, and that I believe the fundamental doctrines of the Christian Faith contained therein.'

The essential justice of this action on the part of Parliament was generally admitted, and by none more heartily than the members of the Church of Scotland. At the same time, the case showed how futile it was to expect that a Church which holds property, collects funds, and has a settled constitution can keep its affairs out of the civil courts, if in any of its activities it may be held to infringe the rights of a minority or of an individual.

Incidentally, when Balfour spoke of freedom and unity in respect of ecclesiastical institutions he was using no mere catchphrase, but was giving expression to a deeply-rooted opinion.

One race, many nations, a universal Church, many ecclesiastical organizations – those are the facts we have got to take and make the best of. . . . I have no hope that these divisions among us will be healed by being abolished. Nay, I say that if Christianity is going to be what we all think it ought to be, and will be – the world religion – if it is really going to attack successfully those great populations in the Far East . . . it must be by the help of teachers of their own race, who are going to lead them, and in leading them, will probably add something to the apparent divisions of the Christian world, although they will add, I trust, greatly to that universal Church to which every one

[1] *Cf.* Dugdale, Blanche E. C.: *Arthur James Balfour*, vol. I, pp. 285-287.

of us, whatever his ecclesiastical allegiance, belongs. . . . Therefore I have to face the fact, and I do face it, that Christendom is and must remain ecclesiastically divided . . . and that what we have to do is to see beyond the separate organization to which we all belong, that greater whole of which we are all members.[1]

However detrimental to the best religious interests of the country were the dissensions of the Victorian era, there can be no doubt but that at the beginning of the twentieth century the Churches still maintained their hold upon the people. In 1843, before the Disruption, the communicants of the Church of Scotland did not number more than 14 per cent of the population, but in 1908 they numbered nearly 15 per cent, while those of the United Free Church were over 10 per cent: in other words, taken together they amounted to 25 per cent, while their activities and their contributions were estimated to have increased in a still greater proportion.[2]

Lord Balfour of Burleigh admirably summed up the situation when he wrote at the beginning of the reign of King George V:

However widely the Scotland of the twentieth century may differ from the Scotland of Knox and Melville, it cannot be denied that their principles, shorn of some rigour and brought into proportion by experience, rule the ecclesiastical life of Scotland today. The government is Presbyterian – orderly, simple, and capable of meeting every crisis by its inherent strength, its close touch with the people, and by its store of precedents accumulated during centuries of development. The happy combination of the clergy and the representatives of the laity in the same courts has kept the Church in constant sympathy with the mind and needs of the country. Presbyterianism has justified itself in Scotland by its adaptation to the religious needs of three centuries and a half.[3]

[1] Speech at the City Temple, June 19th, 1906.
[2] To arrive at a figure for the practising Christian inhabitants of the kingdom there must, of course, be added the communicating members of the Roman Catholic and Episcopalian Churches.
[3] *The Rise and Development of Presbyterianism in Scotland*, p. 162.

At the same time it is satisfactory to add that if sixty years ago Scotland was as Protestant as ever the intolerant zeal of earlier days had been replaced by a more charitable temper, and there was a relaxation in the suspicion of the Church of Rome which made it possible to sanction as lawful to Christian liberty what might once have been construed as a concession to Popery.

It was certainly owing to her Church that Scotland avoided those controversies over educational policy which were dividing contemporary England, for the zeal of Knox and Melville for education had never been wanting. Left at the Reformation with the merest pittance from its ancient patrimony to maintain its ministry, the Church and individual churchmen, out of their poverty and with little countenance from the State, did much to establish schools for the people. It was not until 1696 that Parliament came effectually to their aid, but from then until 1872, when the parish schools were handed over to form the basis of a national compulsory system of education, the alliance between Church and school in Scotland was perhaps the nation's greatest blessing. Even after that date the Church exercised a constant and friendly influence upon the whole detail of instruction and administration, but no ecclesiastical differences embittered educational affairs in Scotland.

Yet in spite of the hold which the Church had upon the country many a superstition lingered in the more remote districts as Dr McNair Wilson discovered when he had a practice in Argyllshire. There was still a belief in witches, and one man 'who possessed, and deserved, a reputation for shrewdness and common sense told me that his father had seen one of these women turn herself into a hare that she might draw milk from the udders of cows'.

> My father shot at the hare, but of course he couldn't kill her with a lead bullet; he put a three-penny piece in the gun and took a second shot. The hare was wounded. He followed it to the witch's cottage. It jumped through the window, and there was the old woman lying in bed with a broken leg.[1]

[1] This recalls the legend that Dundee, in Covenanting eyes very much in league with the Devil, was killed with a silver bullet at Killiecrankie.

Dr Wilson was far too courteous to cast any doubt on this story, and he was rewarded with another concerning witchcraft in one of the islands, where an English family had rented the shooting. There was a witch living near the lodge, and one evening the butler and a footman decided to play a trick on her; so they carried a gramophone to her cottage, and set it going in a thick bush close to her door. The old woman came out and looked round in evident alarm, whereupon the two men began to laugh. 'You can laugh tonight,' she told the butler, 'but you will not see the light of tomorrow morning.' He died in his sleep.

This was by no means an isolated instance of a belief in the supernatural, for Dr Wilson had a medical friend who practised in Inverness-shire, and who owed many a good night's rest to the fact that there was a small lake by the roadside near his house: little white horses were reputed to gallop round the lake at night, and no one would pass the place between dusk and dawn.

As late as 1900 an Inspector of Poor in the North Highland District sought advice from the Local Government Board. In his parish there was an old woman who was chargeable to another parish, and her house had been pronounced by the Medical Officer to be unfit for habitation, and dangerous to the lives of its inhabitants. Her parish of settlement had offered her alternative accommodation, and she was quite willing to go to it; but the neighbours asserted that she was a witch, and refused to allow her to come there, while she, for her part, refused to go to the poorhouse, and persisted in remaining in her dangerous dwelling. Even more recently officials in another area were hesitant about evicting another old woman from her derelict Highland home for fear that she might put the 'evil eye' on them.[1]

To one who had come from a busy centre of population like Glasgow, and who had Highland blood in his veins, Edwardian Argyllshire was a sorry spectacle. 'The Highlands died in the '45,' an old minister told him. 'You see nothing today but the ruins.' Dr Wilson had much sympathy with the old lairds who were left,

---

[1] *Cf.* Ferguson, T.: *Scottish Social Welfare, 1864–1914*, p. 13. This admirable book is a veritable encyclopaedia on the subject with which it deals, and the present author has drawn largely upon it in the succeeding pages.

and who were compelled by financial pressure to find tenants each year for their grouse moor or forest. He found them doing all that lay in their power to help the people, but 'poverty was everywhere. It showed itself in declining fisheries and agriculture, and in the industries which are dependent upon them. The young people, here as in England, migrated as quickly as possible to the towns; when the old people died the roofs of the cottages fell in. This steady depopulation of the Highlands is a spectacle so melancholy as to make one doubt the sanity of those who allow it to continue.'[1]

For many years emigration overseas from the Highland counties had, indeed, received official encouragement, for the aim was to bring about a measure of depopulation in parts of the country regarded as too overcrowded to be able to support the people living in them, but the results were by no means always as satisfactory as had been anticipated. The Royal Commission on conditions in the crofting counties had as long ago as 1884 recognized the difficulties, for they found that there were two main reasons why the crofters were averse from emigration: the first was that those who went abroad encountered serious risks, and the second was that while emigration had always been spoken of as a panacea for the ills of those who remained, in practice it left them exactly as they were.

> Emigration offers few difficulties to the young and able-bodied, but it is obvious that it can be of no benefit to a country to lose its workers alone, and that it is only by the removal of entire families that any serviceable relief from congestion will be experienced. Comparatively few, however, of the crofters in the districts under consideration are likely to have the means of moving their families to a new home across the seas, and starting themselves there with something approaching a certainty of success, nor can much direct assistance be expected from the proprietors of these impoverished parts.

The Commission accordingly recommended further Government encouragement of emigration along 'family' lines, but, as Professor Ferguson has written, 'receiving countries have never

[1] Wilson, R. McNair: *Doctor's Progress*, pp. 107–110.

shown any great enthusiasm for grandmothers'. The traffic, however, was not all one way, and the census of 1901 showed an increase of 14,117 in the number of aliens resident in Scotland over the figure for 1891: most of them seem to have been Russians and Poles who had come to find employment in the coal mines and iron works of Lanarkshire.

All the same emigration was an important factor in the national life. During the last decade of the nineteenth century it continued at the rate of 16,000 a year, but thereafter there was a sharp rise, and in 1907 no fewer than 66,355 Scots left home for destinations outside Europe. There was also a change in the new domicile of their choice, for although the United States was still the most popular Canada was now not far behind.

It is in no way surprising that there should have been this emigration, for behind a façade of well-being there was a good deal that was unsatisfactory in contemporary Scotland, both in the Highlands and Lowlands. In the former even the coming of the motor-car did not at once mitigate the difficulties of communication, and not long before the First World War a general practitioner could write of his hardships:

The patient's house was set in a glen that embouched on to the main road at the head of a loch. The message was received on a stormy evening in February. Horse and trap were employed to the entrance to the glen; but unluckily, before reaching the point, the horse stumbled into a hole on the road, the shafts were smashed, and both doctor and driver were thrown into the ditch. After 'splicing' and tying up, it was necessary to retrace steps to the nearest dwelling – a gamekeeper's. The good man offered to accompany the doctor on foot with a lantern. He advised climbing a hill on the other side of the glen in order the quicker to reach the patient's house. By then wind and rain had risen to a tempest and deluge. The light frequently gave out. But for the foot-sureness of the guide and his accurate knowledge of the ground, not that night could the objective have been attained. Possibly neither of the party would have returned alive. In the end the shepherd's house was reached. No nurse – only a neighbour woman. The baby had been born for a couple of hours. . . . The return journey was accomplished by the longer route along the glen. Driver and trap were found in a more or less serviceable condition on arrival at the game-keeper's house.[1]

In 1883 a Royal Commission had been appointed to enquire into the conditions of the crofters and cottars of the Highlands and Islands. The Commissioners commenced their work by defining a 'crofter' as a small tenant of land, with or without a lease, who found in the cultivation and produce of his poor holding a material proportion of his occupation, earnings, and sustenance, and who paid rent directly to the proprietor; and a 'cottar' as the occupier of a dwelling with or without some portion of land, whose main subsistence was by wages of labour, and whose rent, if any, was paid to a tenant, and not to the landlord. As may be supposed the Commissioners received many complaints against the deer forests, which it was alleged in some quarters were the cause of most of the ills from which the Highlands were suffering. They were told that the deer forests had been to a great extent created by the evictions or removal of the inhabitants, and this had caused de-population; that the land now cleared for deer might be made available for profitable occupation by crofters; that it might at all events be occupied by sheep farmers, and that a great loss of mutton and wool might thus be avoided; that in some places where deer forests were contiguous to arable land in the occupa-tion of crofters, damage was done to crops by deer; and that deer deteriorated the pasture, and that the temporary employment of ghillies and others in connection with deer forests had a demoral-izing effect. Finally, the critics maintained that 395,000 sheep might be grazed on land then occupied by deer forests.

The Commissioners examined these charges carefully, and on balance they were inclined to favour the continuance of the exis-tence of the existing deer forests so long as there was no 'unjusti-fiable extension'. What they did feel was that one serious objec-tion to the deer forests lay in the fact that they contributed to the absence of a graduated local representation of the various orders of society, and never was this more marked than in the Edwardian era. For a brief space each year the sporting tenant appeared at the

[1] *Cf.* Ferguson, T. L.: *Scottish Social Welfare, 1864–1914*, p. 450.

lodge with guests, servants, and money in his wake: this was all very well, but local affairs meant nothing to him; he was divided by a great gulf from the local people who were only interested in his purchasing power as he was only interested in their services; and at the end of the season he departed, not to return for another twelve months, if at all. In 1892 another Commission was set up specifically to enquire what land in the crofting counties, then devoted to sporting purposes, was capable of being cultivated for profit or otherwise advantageously occupied by crofters or other small tenants. Nowhere was the problem more acute than in Lewis but all the same the Commissioners reported:

> We are of opinion that were the whole forests and farm lands of the Island of Lewis made available for crofters in some form or other, this step, while it might allay or mitigate the more serious evils arising from the existing condition of matters, would not effect a permanent remedy, and would only relieve the urgency for a limited number of years.

All the same, and in spite of the conclusions of the Commissioners of 1883, the deer forests continued to grow, and in the twenty-five years between 1883 and 1908 the acreage under deer in the counties of Caithness, Sutherland, Ross and Cromarty, Inverness and Argyll increased by $1\frac{1}{4}$ million acres, or some 60 per cent.

The truth is that for long the Highlands and Islands lagged far behind the rest of Scotland in all that related to social welfare. An instance of this occurred in 1897, when the Local Government Board commissioned Sheriff Campbell of Stornoway to inquire into some unhappy events associated with an outbreak of typhoid fever in South Uist. One distressing feature of the outbreak had been that the victims were left unattended by their neighbours and relatives, doubtless because of the widespread fear of infection that was so prevalent in the Islands. The Sheriff reported:

> Now the people of the West Islands are not of a callous disposition. They are naturally unsophisticated, simple-minded, and kindly to friends and neighbours. Their habits of life, as a rule, are unfortunately not guided by sanitary and hygienic rules and considerations. The benefits of the newer systems of

education have not yet had time to remove old prejudices and habits, of which they are unfortunately so conservative.

The low general level of housing was itself a serious bar to progress, and housing was fundamental, and the District Medical Officer of Harris is found writing as late as 1905:

> The mischief done by these black houses and the filth inseparable from them is so great that all causes become insignificant in comparison, and any attempt at improving the sanitary condition of Harris, and, for that matter, of the Outer Islands generally, must begin with the houses.

In those days St Kilda was still inhabited, and lying 140 miles from the mainland it was, in spite of the fact of being a mere three miles by two, a source of continual anxiety to those in authority. The very mention of the island, says Professor Ferguson, 'must often have spelt qualms for a Civil Servant faced with an emergency dash in time of storm to deal with some emergency, perhaps in response to a message brought in by some passing trawler, that the islanders were starving, or stricken by some strange disease. St Kilda typified many Highland problems, and St Kilda was always "news".'[1]

The inhabitants were very much a law unto themselves. In 1877 an official of the Highland and Island Agricultural Society arrived at St Kilda at 9.30 p.m. on a Saturday, but as it was drawing near Sunday, and the people were preparing themselves for the devotions of the Sabbath, they would not think of unloading the boat in spite of the insecurity of the anchorage. At that time conditions were somewhat primitive, for there were only two watches and one clock on the island; to avail themselves of these amenities there was a population of seventy-five, including about a dozen marriageable women, but only two unmarried men. All the islanders read the Gaelic Bible, and there were several copies of this in each house. It was further reported that the islanders seemed to be contented with their lot, and very much attached to their home: there was no inclination to emigrate.

In the mid-eighties a Civil Servant from Edinburgh of the name

[1] *Op. cit.*, p. 47.

of McNeill visited St Kilda, and he reported several changes for the better in the inhabitants' condition: there was now a resident nurse, and during the short summer season some two hundred or more tourists visited the island each year. The local atmosphere, however, was changing, for McNeill reported that during the year 1884 a former emigrant from St Kilda to Australia had returned and spent several months on the island: he seemed 'to have occupied himself in spreading discontent among the people, and in striving to place them in antagonism to their indulgent landlord'.[1] The arguments of this man had created, within the past eighteen months, a strong desire to emigrate and, 'with the exception of one or two old men I found none who were not anxious to be transferred either to the mainland or to Australia'. McNeill added that the idea might well be worth the consideration of the Government.

Accompanying McNeill's report was one by Dr Acheson, the Surgeon on H.M.S. *Jackal*, which in no small measure explains the growing interest in emigration as the news of the higher standard of civilization in the outside world reached the island. Dr Acheson found the children to be anaemic and languid, suffering in his opinion from symptoms of incipient scurvy: in consequence he suggested that an attempt should be made to grow cabbages, turnips, carrots, and other vegetables on the island; that fowls might well be introduced; and that preserved vegetables and lime juice might be made available when no fresh vegetables could be procured. The water supply he found to be derived from springs which issued from the base of the hill close to the houses, and it was of excellent quality and unlimited quantity. As for the houses themselves, Dr Acheson said they were eighteen in number, one storey high, with zinc roofs, glass windows, hearth and chimney, and clay floors. They were in the main dirty, but were dry and comfortable, though the furniture was sparse and primitive. There were no domestic animals in the dwelling-houses except cats and dogs, and the cattle wintered in the old thatched houses which had been the original dwellings. To improve the amenities of life for the younger people Dr

---

[1] Macleod of Macleod, who lived in Paris.

Acheson suggested that the schoolmaster might be supplied with some simple games for the children; that he might also teach singing; and even introduce some instrumental music, 'for at present there are no games or music on the island, and whistling is strictly forbidden'.

The Board of Supervision found themselves in substantial agreement with the views of McNeill and Acheson, and they urged the Secretary for Scotland[1] to implement them, especially in what related to the removal of the population from the island. 'The Board are of opinion,' they stated, 'that emigration is the only practicable mode of securing the people against periodically recurring seasons of scarcity and destitution, and that advantage should be taken of opportunity, when the people appear to be willing to go.'

A very different attitude was adopted by Macleod when these documents reached him in the French capital. His first comment was that he was surprised to see a recommendation that the people should be removed from St Kilda altogether, and he thought this was a very extraordinary proposal: there was not a single pauper on the island; the inhabitants were well-to-do people possessing cattle, sheep, and other property, and had only appealed on a recent occasion to some of their friends in consequence of a very exceptional misfortune, which had led them to fear that they might run short of meal before their spring supplies reached them. In any event if they wished to emigrate of their own free will and with their own means there was nothing to prevent them, and if some of them lacked the necessary financial resources they could always appeal for aid. The Laird felt that in any case only the younger portion of the community was suitable for emigration since they alone could speak English, while it had further to be remembered that if the young people were encouraged to emigrate their departure would be a most serious misfortune for those who remained. Lastly, if the islanders were largely reduced in numbers the minister, the teacher, and the midwife would have to be withdrawn. Taking all the circumstances into account, therefore, Macleod hoped that the Secretary for Scotland would leave

[1] At that time the seventh Duke of Richmond and Gordon.

these people, who were among the most religious and intelligent in the Highlands, free to follow their own inclinations. 'When they shall have sent to His Grace a petition asking for assistance to emigrate, I venture to think it will be time to consider whether effect can be given to their wishes.'

The Board of Supervision duly considered this reply, but it did not change their opinion. 'As Mr Macleod must know, similar appeals have been frequently made in previous years, and the inhabitants have, from time to time, received from outside sources much assistance of an eleemosynary character. Owing to the inaccessible nature of the island and the small amount of intercourse which the inhabitants have with the rest of the world, there is no security either that their wants in a time of pressure would be duly made known, or that their wants could be immediately supplied.' Nothing, however, was done.

Nevertheless conditions on the whole were improving, and when in 1900 the Medical Officer of Health for Harris visited St Kilda he reported that he was agreeably surprised at the advanced state of sanitation; the houses, he found, were kept very clean and tidy, and so were the inhabitants themselves. There was strong opposition to vaccination, and this feeling was displayed during a smallpox scare six years later. The Local Government Board sent a doctor to vaccinate such of the resident population as voluntarily consented, and forty-nine people out of a total of seventy-eight did consent, but none of them were over sixty. As excuses, women tended to plead family duties, and men the approach of the bird-catching season.

The history of St Kilda in the post-Edwardian period is soon told. In 1913 there was a serious outbreak of influenza, apparently of the type which was to sweep across the world in a few years' time, but there were no deaths: in the same year permanent communication with the mainland was established by the installation of wireless. In 1928 the remaining inhabitants were evacuated, and the island was left to the wild-fowl.

The vicissitudes of St Kilda have been recounted in some detail, not on account of their intrinsic importance, but because its problems were in many ways typical of those of the Highlands and Islands as a whole. Improvement in means of communication may have made many a remote area less isolated, but it has also brought news of conditions in the outside world to the local people, and thus rendered them increasingly discontented with their lot.

If the more remote parts of Scotland had difficulties peculiarly their own at the turn of the century this does not mean to say that elsewhere there were no problems at all. The later Victorian era had shown that godliness was by no means incompatible with fornication and drunkenness. In 1866, 10·27 per cent all the children born alive in the country were registered as illegitimate, and the distribution of these illegitimate births is somewhat curious. They were in general more prevalent in the rural areas on the mainland than in the urban districts, while in the islands there was very little illegitimacy at all. Thus, in 1884, when 8·1 per cent of all the births in Scotland were illegitimate, the proportion in the principal centres of population was 7·4, though in Aberdeen it was as high as 10·3. The blackest areas were Banff with 16·1 and Wigtown with 16. In some instances illegitimacy seems to have run in families, and a case is on record in a small Dumfries-shire parish where a domestic servant registered three illegitimate children; she had three sisters each of whom had given birth to three children born out of wedlock. Probably the reason for the higher rate in the country as contrasted with the towns was due to greater facilities as well as to the absence of prostitutes, but it undoubtedly occurred in an age of universal church-going.

The same was the case with drunkenness. In the sixties the consumption of alcohol was high, and it was estimated that in Edinburgh between 40 and 50 per cent of all those arrested by the police were drunk when they committed the crime for which they were taken into custody. As for Glasgow, it was reported that in the central districts of that city there were upwards of two hundred houses of ill-fame, in many of which both shebeening and thieving were common. 'Besides which there are about 150 shebeens conducting the illicit still of liquor on a more or less excessive scale, and against both these classes of houses numerous convictions have been recorded.'

The situation was, however, improving. In 1898, when he was President of the Royal Philosophical Society of Glasgow, and again in 1908, Dr Duncan, a physician in that city, reviewed the consumption of alcohol in Scotland, and he showed that between the years 1872 and 1896 it had steadily diminished. At the beginning of the period the Scot on an average drank more than the Englishman, and proportionately suffered more from alcoholic diseases, but at the end the position was reversed. By 1907 the consumption of alcoholic liquids per head of the population was equivalent to 1·4 gallons in Scotland, 1·6 gallons in Ireland, and 2·1 gallons in England, while the expenditure per head worked out at £3 3s 1d in Scotland, £3 3s 10d in Ireland, and £3 19s 0d in England. From this Dr Duncan came to the conclusion that in proportion to population more disease and more deaths were due to excessive consumption of beer among the people of England than by the excessive use of whisky in Scotland.

Having arrived at this conclusion the worthy doctor was faced with the enigma why there was so much open drunkenness in Scotland, and why there were, in proportion to the population, more convictions in Glasgow than in London. He found the solution of this problem in the contrast between the drinking habits of the two countries.

> In Scotland the whisky drinkers of the lower orders live in crowded tenements of houses, and so are concentrated in comparatively small areas. In the early stages of intoxication the whisky drinkers are violent and combative and require restraint and take their liquor in the public house where they are under the public eye. On the other hand, the beer drinkers take a large part of their liquor at home where they are not in the public eye. . . . They are not so much violent maniacs as stupid sots, so that they require assistance more than restraint, and do not become a danger so much to their neighbours as to themselves.

At the same time some Scots, like a good many other people, were apparently the better, rather than the worse, for drink. Anyhow, when in 1907 a Certifying Factory Surgeon was one day admiring some engineers earnestly at work fitting up an engine for a new vessel it seemed to him that no sculptor could have given more care and anxious application of mind and hand to his work. He observed to the foreman that he assumed all the men were total abstainers or they could never have executed such beautiful work. 'Deed no, sir,' came the reply, 'I don't think there is one of them who has not had his mornin' tae steady his hand.'

In that same year Bigham was sent by the Board of Trade to enquire into the prevalence of drink in Great Britain, and he found that drunkenness was definitely on the decrease in Scotland. 'Dundee,' he writes, 'was the worst place for drink; young women in the jute factories were wheeled home drunk in barrows on Saturday nights; they were only paid 10s a week. On the whole, however, it was clear that the abuse of alcohol and the money spent on it were rapidly decreasing all over the country, and that the population generally was much more sober than it had been ten years before.'[1]

What was reprehensible was the growing use of methylated spirit as an intoxicant, and to this the Medical Officer of Health for Aberdeen drew special attention in his Annual Report for 1902. The Labourers' Federation in that city were concerned at the evils arising from the growing addiction to the use of methylated spirit among their members, although the practice was said to be just as prevalent elsewhere. The fact was at that time it could be retailed at 4d a pint bottle, and if diluted to the same strength, in respect of alcohol, as cheap whisky, could be sold at 3d a pint, or less than a halfpenny a glass, which was no more than a quarter of the price of even the cheapest genuine whisky. Several grocers in Aberdeen, it was stated, held a licence to sell methylated spirits, though they were not licensed to sell ordinary spirit: there were practically no restrictions to its sale, except that it could not be sold on Sunday. Those who drank it mainly did so in halfpenny and pennyworths, but as much could be had for a penny as would be the equivalent of two glasses of whisky. At one grocer's shop in Aberdeen, where methylated spirit was freely retailed in small quantities, as many as seventy men had been seen to enter the premises within the space of two hours in

---

[1] *A Picture of Life, 1872–1940*, p. 222.

the morning; each of them carried the requisite bottle, and after leaving the shop proceeded to an adjacent water-tap to dilute the spirit and drink it.

The effects of drinking methylated spirits were reported as being worse than an excessive indulgence in whisky, for in addition to intoxication the result was often a severe stupor, with effects on the drinker that were apt to be at once profound and prolonged. The general social effect of this type of drinking was also bad, for it led to irregularity at work, neglect of family ties, loss of all moral sense, and rapid deterioration in health. The root of the trouble, in the opinion of social workers, was the cheapness of methylated spirits, for no man, however reduced his circumstances, was so poor that he did not possess the necessary halfpenny or penny, even if he had to borrow it from a fellow worker. Finally, investigation seemed to show that the drinker of methylated spirits was usually a man who had previously indulged in other forms of alcohol to excess, and who had turned to it, not so much out of preference, as because of its cheapness.

If there was much to criticize in Edwardian Scotland, there was equally much to admire, and her system of education was still one of the wonders of the world: indeed it is no exaggeration to say that Scotland had a national system of education when England was merely groping in the dark. Even as early as 1494 freeholders were required by a statute of James IV to send their heirs to school to acquire 'perfect Latin', and in 1646 an Act of Parliament laid down that a school should be founded, and a schoolmaster appointed, in every parish not already provided for; the matter was, as we have seen, carried further in 1696 when there was passed what has been called the Magna Carta of Scottish education, and the ideal was finally attained of a school in every parish. Some authorities have held that as the twentieth century progressed Scotland tended to lag behind her southern neighbour, but this was certainly not the case in the years immediately preceding the First World War.

After the postponement of the King's Coronation owing to his illness, and the strain to which he had been subjected both by the operation and the ceremony, it was deemed advisable that he

should go on a cruise, and the West of Scotland was selected for
the purpose. The other members of the party were the Queen,
Princess Victoria, and the Marquis de Soveral, the Portuguese
ambassador, with Austen Chamberlain, then Postmaster-General,
as Minister in attendance. They sailed from Cowes on August
22nd, 1902, and put in at Weymouth, Milford Haven, the Isle of
Man, Arran, Colonsay, Ballachuilish, Torloisk, Stornoway, and
Dunrobin, before arriving at Invergordon on September 8th.
As the *Victoria and Albert* approached the Scottish coast Austen
was fascinated to hear the King say to his valet, '*Un costume un
peu plus écossais demain*'; he evidently did not wish to make the
transition from English to Scottish attire too abrupt, Sir Philip
Magnus[1] notes. The weather left little to be desired, and the cruise
was thoroughly enjoyed by all the party.

A few extracts from the Postmaster-General's diary well illustrate the life aboard.

> The yacht is very comfortable. I have a nice roomy cabin,
> appertaining of right, as I learn from the key labels, to the
> "3rd lady". We breakfast at 9.30, lunch at 1.30 or 2, "high tea"
> at 5 with a little lobster (!), prawns, jams, etc., and dine at 9.45.
>
> I sit usually next Princess Victoria, occasionally next the
> Queen, who sits on the King's left – our places being only
> varied when guests are invited, and not always then. After
> dinner, if we are alone, the Queen usually retires to her drawing-
> room; the King smokes on deck or retires to his sitting-room,
> and then the rest of us sit about and smoke till midnight, and
> then turn in.

There was a complete absence of unnecessary formality. At Pem-
broke, for example, Austen describes their reception during a
drive while the *Victoria and Albert* was coaling.

> The people had gathered everywhere at the cross-roads, and
> the King and Queen in their hired landau (driven by the prin-
> cipal butcher of Pembroke Dock) were everywhere most
> warmly welcomed. No police about, and at one point as many
> as six little boys clinging on to the back of the carriage, en-
> couraged by the Queen.

[1] *King Edward the Seventh*, p. 364.

A few days later he wrote,

> After dinner we had a sing-song by the men. . . . The Com-
> mander looked very anxious, and the rest of us roared with
> laughter. You can imagine what it was like! It was a novel form
> of State Concert, and would have astonished Buckingham
> Palace.

And again:

> Nothing could be simpler or less formal than life on board or
> our parties ashore. The King and Queen are both in excellent
> health and spirits, thoroughly enjoying themselves, I think,
> and making the trip as pleasant as possible for other people.
> In short, it is a very pleasant, very jolly party on a particularly
> fine and comfortable yacht.

Politics seemed very far away, but occasionally they obtruded
themselves:

> The King says I must tell Father that as I was sitting in a
> carriage some way behind the King's at Ramsey, a man kept
> calling out, "God save the King and down with the Education
> Bill!" I got a small and embarrassing ovation of my own, how-
> ever, in Douglas, shouts of "good old Brum" and "good old
> Joe" and "Hullo, Austen", betraying the origin of some of
> the trippers. Yesterday as I drove on the box of the King's
> carriage a small boy, aged I should think about fourteen,
> saluted us with "Three cheers for Mr Chamberlain, and God
> save the King and Queen", to their great amusement.

To pass from the particular to the general, that is to say from
local affairs to national politics, one of the outstanding characteristics of Scottish life in the nineteenth century was the popular
devotion to the Liberal Party. At the General Election of 1880
of the sixty members returned by Scotland only seven were Conservatives: the position became modified when the split in the
Liberal ranks over Home Rule took place, and when Salisbury
appealed to the country in 1900 the proportion after the election
of that year was thirty-eight Conservatives and Liberal Unionists
to thirty-four Liberals: it was, however, a mere flash in the pan,

for in 1906 there were returned a mere twelve Conservatives and
Liberal Unionists to fifty-eight Liberals and two Labour. 'In
Scotland,' Austen Chamberlain wrote to Balfour, 'the class hatred
was very bitter and the animosity against landlords extreme.
Nothing else counted very much.'[1]

Mr Robert Blake, in his admirable biography of Bonar Law,
entitled, *The Unknown Prime Minister*, throws much light upon the
political and social life of Scotland at the turn of the century.
First of all he paints in the background against which the future
Prime Minister's career was set:

> The Kidstons'[2] world was very self-contained. The wealthy
> Scottish middle classes to which they belonged were divided
> by a clear line not only from the class below but from the class
> above also. Their attitude, their prejudices, their pleasures,
> their voices even, were quite different from those of the Scot-
> tish nobleman or laird. An even deeper gulf lay between them
> and the territorial aristocracy of England. They had their own
> values, and they had no desire to move up into a class of whose
> outlook upon many matters they strongly disapproved. The
> Kidstons were generous and rich. Had they wished, they
> could easily have sent Bonar Law to an expensive public
> school followed by Oxford or Cambridge. But they would
> have regarded such a choice as ridiculous. They considered it
> more sensible to send a boy who was destined to earn his living
> in business to Glasgow High School, and give him a clerkship
> in their office when he was sixteen.

For some unaccountable reason, the Kidstons, unlike most of
their contemporaries, were Conservatives, and consequently it
was in that atmosphere that Bonar Law was educated. When the
leaders of the Conservative party came to Glasgow they were
naturally delighted to accept the hospitality of members of a section of the community which was normally opposed to them, and
on these occasions young Bonar Law made their acquaintance.
There is even a tradition that Disraeli himself once visited the

---

[1] Petrie, Sir Charles: *Life and Letters of the Right Hon. Sir Austen Chamberlain*,
vol. I, p. 242.

[2] Bonar Law's cousins, with whom he spent his early life after leaving New
Brunswick.

Kidston establishment, but however this may be their youthful relative early acquired a great respect for that statesman, who remained one of his heroes to the end of his life.

For the aspiring young Glasgow politician, whatever his party, there was the Glasgow Parliamentary Debating Association which held its meetings at the Assembly Rooms in Bath Street. It was a mock Parliament, and had been founded by a number of enthusiastic young men as long ago as 1876; it copied as closely as possible the rules of procedure in the House of Commons, and its 'Speaker' spent some weeks at Westminster studying the proper way in which to manage debates. Members had imaginary constituencies; there was a Prime Minister and a Cabinet; and bills were introduced, carried, rejected, or amended. In effect, the Glasgow Parliamentary Debating Association was for the young businessman of that city what the Oxford and Cambridge Unions were for the undergraduates of the two senior English universities.

It even had its own organ, the *Mace*, which was at least as acid in its comments as the *Isis*, and among those who from time to time came under the lash was Bonar Law. On one occasion its reporter wrote:

> The hon. gentleman's style of delivery reminds one of the verses of the *Sexton's Daughter* as read aloud by its author and described by Carlyle. "A dreary pulpit or even conventicle manner; that flattest moaning hoo hoo of predetermined pathos, with a kind of rocking canter introduced by way of intonation, each stanza the exact fellow of the other, and the dull swing of the rocking horse duly in each." Why does not Staffordshire[1] give up this style which mars but does not altogether spoil the fine matter of his speeches?

Bonar Law was also accused of insufficient seriousness:

> It is a great mistake for members who possess ability, as North Staffordshire undoubtedly does, to devote themselves to uttering commonplaces or jocularities. Frivolities, even from an able speaker, are still frivolities, and are no assistance in furthering argument in debate.

[1] Bonar Law was 'member' for North Staffordshire in the Debating Association.

It was not a charge that was often to be brought against him in the years that lay ahead, and already the Prime Minister was to be detected in the young ironmaster:

> It is at once evident that he understands his business – down even to the by no means unimportant detail of where to take his position for speaking. He makes just enough of reference to preceding speeches to give a colour of spontaneity to the carefully prepared attack which he is going to deliver.[1]

He always expressed his debt to the Glasgow Parliament, and he said that what he learnt there had been of the greatest assistance to him when he got to Westminster, which happened in 1900. Two years earlier he had become prospective Conservative candidate for the Blackfriars and Hutchesontoun Division of Glasgow, a constituency which had been created in 1884, and which had ever since been a Liberal stronghold: the sitting member was one A. V. Provend, but Bonar Law succeeded in converting his majority of some five hundred into a minority of exactly a thousand. In spite of his training in the Glasgow Parliament his success in the House of Commons was not immediate, and his maiden speech, during the debate on the Address, passed unnoticed, possibly because Sir Winston Churchill also spoke for the first time on that day. Depression overtook him. 'He was sitting alone with me,' wrote the future Sir Austen Chamberlain, 'in the old smoking-room of the House of Commons, a prey to one of those moods of depression which beset him from time to time in his life. I tried to cheer him up. "No, Austen," he replied, "this is no place for me. It's all very well for men like you who came into it young; but, if I had known then what I know now, I would never have stood for Parliament".'[2]

Mr Blake is of the opinion that his disillusionment may well have been due to the circumstances of Parliamentary life, since 'much of the ritual and procedure of the House of Commons must have seemed at first maddeningly futile to someone accustomed to the brisk conduct of business in the Glasgow iron market'. As we have seen in the case of Liverpool, the provincial

[1] Quoted by Blake, R.: *The Unknown Prime Minister*, pp. 29–30.
[2] *Down the Years*, p. 224.

business-man worked hard in those days, and he did not leave
his office in the middle of the morning to get shaved, as was by
no means infrequently the case with the Londoner. Bonar Law
was no exception, for he would arrive at his office, 7 Royal Bank
Place, at 8.50 a.m. from the Helensburgh train; he opened all the
letters himself; and then he would summon the various heads of
departments, with whom he would discuss the impending business of the day. At this point the time sheet would be brought in,
and those clerks who had arrived after nine would receive a repri-
mand. Before eleven he was at the Royal Exchange where the
dealings in iron took place, and where, save for a quick lunch,
he remained until three, when he returned to the office to sign
letters: finally, he caught the 4.10 train back to Helensburgh,
where in the summer he liked a round of golf before dinner. It
was not, perhaps, a long day, but it was a strenuous one while it
lasted, and it was in marked contrast with the idle hours spent
hanging about the House of Commons. Such was the upbringing
of one who was to succeed a novelist, a landed proprietor, and a
philosopher as leader of the Conservative Party.

Bonar Law was not, however, destined to languish in obscurity
for long: the resignation of Salisbury resulted in a reshuffle of the
Government, and the Member for Blackfriars and Hutchesontoun was appointed Parliamentary Secretary to the Board of
Trade. For three years he held this not very arduous post, and
then at the General Election of 1906 he lost his seat, swept away
by the great Liberal flood; it proved impossible to find anything
else for him in Scotland, but before long he was safely ensconced
in Dulwich, and launched upon the career which was to take him
to Downing Street.

Meanwhile in another part of the country there was growing up,
though in very different circumstances, another young Scot who
was to tread the same path, namely Ramsay MacDonald. If
Asquith is possibly the most misjudged of recent Prime Ministers
there can be little question but that MacDonald is the most mis-
understood, and probably, today, the least known: not even Sir
Winston Churchill has been the victim of so many vicissitudes or
so often the sport of fate. Moreover, the events of 1931 left no

political party or section of public opinion with any particular interest in seeing that justice was done to his memory, while, like Gladstone and Baldwin, he remained in office a little too long for his reputation.

However this may be, Ramsay MacDonald was born on October 12th, 1866, in a two-roomed 'but and ben' at Lossiemouth in Morayshire, within a few hours' walk of the Highlands. His family background on the male side was irregular, for like so many of the world's great men he was illegitimate, being the son of a head ploughman, but he was devoted to his mother throughout his life, and he regarded her as a woman of exceptional character. However, Lord Elton was later to write in the *Dictionary of National Biography*, 'The peculiar circumstances of MacDonald's childhood may well have accounted for the unusual later combination of mental toughness, physical courage, and extreme sensitiveness in his character.'

The boy attended Drainie parish school, where the fees were eightpence a month, and there he studied Euclid and the Classics, and in his leisure hours a consumptive watchmaker introduced him to the works of Dickens. Before he was fifteen he was head of the school, and after he left it he worked for a short time on a farm: then when he was about sixteen the 'dominie' of Drainie invited him to become a pupil teacher at the salary of seven pounds ten shillings, a year. With the free run of the schoolmaster's shelves he had the world of Shakespeare, Carlyle, Ruskin, and Henry George open to him, but, to quote Lord Elton once again, 'although he was fundamentally of a religious turn of mind, with an unfailing reference for what he called "the grand, crowned authority of life", an obstinate streak of rationalism combined with that instinct of the insurgent, which sprang perhaps from his fatherless childhood, to prevent any of the rival Scottish orthodoxies from gaining his allegiance'. It was a very different upbringing from that of Bonar Law, but to the eternal credit of Scotland be it said that it was just as typically Scottish.

Ramsay MacDonald tried his luck in England twice before he finally settled there, and when, in 1906, he was returned to the House of Commons it was for Leicester. Bonar Law, as has been shown, only went South after he became a Member of Parliament, but from the date of his election for Dulwich he and his fellow-Scot sat there together. Of the third Scottish Prime Minister of the twentieth century, namely Campbell-Bannerman, mention has been made in another place. Meanwhile, by the time that King Edward was in his grave there were in existence two other young Scots who were to develop – and achieve – political ambitions, Harold Macmillan and Alec Douglas-Home.

With five potential Prime Ministers in her womb, one in Downing Street, and one in retirement, Scotland in the early years of the century had no reason to feel ashamed of her political position, and Radical though she was in her outlook it was to Scotland that Joseph Chamberlain came to launch his Tariff Reform campaign. On October 6th, 1903, he stated the case for a change at the St Andrew's Hall, Glasgow, in one of the most famous speeches of modern times, and he began with the words, 'I am in a great city, the second of the Empire; the city which by the enterprise and intelligence which it has always shown is entitled to claim something of a representative character in respect of British industry.' Liverpool and Chamberlain's native Birmingham might have disputed the contention that Glasgow was the second city of the Empire, but no contemporary would have questioned the great statesman's second claim on its behalf.

CHAPTER VIII

The Services

—————•◉•—————

THE first ten years of the twentieth century were marked by radical changes in both Services, and it was well that this should have been the case or they would have entered the First World War in a very sorry state. Where the Navy was concerned the motive force was Sir John Fisher, and personalities played no small part in the controversy; in the case of the Army the deficiencies exposed by the South African War had roused even a country notoriously indifferent alike to the efficiency and to the welfare of its soldiers.

Fisher had entered the Navy in 1854 at the age of thirteen, and at the date of the King's accession, which found him Commander-in-Chief in the Mediterranean, he had thus served continuously for nearly half a century. In 1902 he was recalled to the Admiralty as Second Sea Lord, and in that capacity he quickly made his reforming zeal felt. He devised a new system of naval education, and sketched out a scheme for rendering the fleet an effective weapon of war which should be ready to strike at a moment's notice. At his own request he was transferred in 1903 from the post of Second Sea Lord to that of Commander-in-Chief at Portsmouth, but while he held that office he was also busily engaged in drafting further plans for the reorganization of the country's fighting forces; nor was he by any means content with his own Service, for he readily accepted a seat on the Esher Committee whose task it was to reform the War Office.

His physical exuberance developed into literary and controversial profusion; he spoke, wrote, and thought in large type and italics; when writing he underlined his argument with two, three, or even four strokes with a broad-nibbed pen, and when talking with blows of his fist on the palm of the other hand. 'I wish you would stop shaking your fist in my face,' the King said to him on one occasion when being subjected to one of his more forceful arguments. Fisher never played field games or indulged in any form of athletics, and the only exercise he took was walking. This distaste for sport may have originated in the fact that in his younger days he had shot a butler in mistake for a rabbit, though his only recorded comment on the incident was that 'he was a pompous old fellow and it did him good'.

Admiral Bacon wrote of him at this time:

When Fisher went, full of energy, to the Admiralty as First Sea Lord, he was, for a masterful man, singularly free from great defects. His failings were in reality the exaggerations of his virtues. He was careless of the opinions of others. Always twenty years ahead of the age, in small things as well as in great, he would dance the whole of an evening, and perhaps several in succession, with the same partner. This in those days earned him the reputation of being a Don Juan, a reputation totally undeserved. In greater matters he was, as events showed, too confident; he had too great a belief in his powers to demolish obstruction and persuade dissentients. His conversation and writing tended too much towards exaggeration. But in 1904 he was singularly free from the defects which his subsequent service at the Admiralty developed in him. He had, up to that time, had little personal dealing with politicians; he had not learned from them the tricks and devious courses which are the arteries and veins of political life. He had not learned to bow the knee to expediency. As King Edward told him, "He had been round the world, but had never been in it."[1]

At the same time there was a kindly side to his character, at any rate in his earlier days, which has tended to be ignored. One instance of this will suffice. When he was Second Sea Lord he received a letter from a man of whom he had never heard saying that his son, a young midshipman, had written home that he was very

---

[1] *Lord Fisher*, vol. I, pp. 238–239.

unhappy in the ship in which he was serving, and that he would be driven to desert. Fisher at the time was away from London inspecting the various training-ships. He at once told the Secretary of the Admiralty, who was with him, to wire to the Admiralty and have the boy transferred to another ship, as he was convinced that he was being bullied; but the matter was not allowed to end there. That evening Fisher arrived at Dartmouth, and at once had the boy's record when a naval cadet in the *Britannia* looked up. It proved to be a good one. Fisher had been thinking a good deal about the case all day, and, on reading the record, he turned to the Secretary and said, 'Perhaps at the Admiralty they have not treated this case as urgent. Wire at once to the Commander of the station to have the boy transferred to his flagship. Who knows, the lad might desert tonight.'

In the course of 1904, largely under his inspiration, a reform in the distribution and methods of mobilization of the Fleet was put into practice, and in view of the growing rivalry with Germany concentration was its keynote. Fisher took the opportunity of this reorganization to effect a redistribution of British men-of-war all over the world in order to meet the altered conditions of the day. The policy was to make the squadrons on foreign stations more efficient and less vulnerable, while permitting the strengthening of the Home Fleet without any serious increase in the Naval Estimates. Fisher characteristically described his scheme in a letter to Lord Knollys as 'Napoleonic in its audacity, and Cromwellian in its thoroughness', and added that unless naval reform was 'ruthless and remorseless . . . we may as well pack up and hand over to Germany'.

All gunboats were withdrawn except those necessary for river service in China and on the west coast of Africa. The ships stationed permanently on the south-east coast of America were withdrawn, and this coast was in future to be visited annually by other ships. The Pacific Squadron was also withdrawn, with the exception of one vessel to police the Behring Sea seal fishery. The China, Australia, and East India Squadrons were formed entirely of cruisers, and, although retained as separate commands, their respective admirals or commodores met periodically to discuss the problems of their stations, and to arrange for joint action in the event of war. As it had become imperative to keep the strongest possible fleet in the Channel the old Home Fleet was increased to fourteen battleships together with six armoured cruisers, as well as a proportion of light cruisers and destroyers, and renamed the Channel Fleet.

The Mediterranean Fleet was fixed at nine battleships, with four armoured cruisers, smaller cruisers, and destroyers; while a third Fleet, based on Gibraltar, was formed, to act as a reinforcement either in the Channel or in the Mediterranean: this was given the name of the Atlantic Fleet, and was composed of nine battleships with six armoured cruisers and various smaller ships. Finally, a new Cruiser Squadron was formed of six ships, and was to be used for training purposes in time of peace: it was intended that this squadron should show the flag at the West Indian ports and on the coast of South America, while in wartime it was to join the Channel or Mediterranean Fleet as might be required. The new organization was designed to give a 10 per cent superiority over a combination either of France and Russia or of Germany and Russia, the United States not being regarded seriously as a naval Power at that time.

Great economies were effected by the abolition of unnecessary and obsolete ships on foreign stations, but, in addition, the withdrawal of these craft rendered several subsidiary dockyards useless, and here again money was saved. The naval bases at Halifax, Jamaica, St Lucia, Ascension, and Esquimault were abolished, although at Ascension a sufficient force of Marines was maintained to man the guns in order to prevent the anchorage being used by an enemy in wartime. The base at Trincomalee was closed. The bases on the China station, on the other hand, were expanded as circumstances required, and that at Gibraltar was enlarged so as to cope with the refits of the Atlantic Fleet, for it was assumed that in war Gibraltar would be a valuable repair base between England and Malta.

As may be supposed this reorganization caused a good deal of controversy, not only in Naval circles, but also in the Press, and one wag wrote:

On the 21st October, 1904, it was resolved that the venerable arrangements for the disposition of the Fleet then in force, which had lasted since 1812, should be brought up to date. The (old) arrangement pleased the Foreign Office and the Consuls' daughters, many of whom were extremely attractive girls who doted on the 1812 arrangement because, after all, there is no white male quite so agreeable as the British naval officer, whether he is a middy in his first commission or a retired Admiral, full of years and honours, who devotes a good deal of his life to attacks on the Admiralty. Though the old system of distribution was popular, there was one fatal mistake in it. For lawn tennis, waltzing, relief of distress, or ambulance work after an earthquake it was admirable; for war purposes it was useless, because the force was divided and subdivided, and was largely composed of ships that could neither fight an enemy nor escape him. The change was made on the principle that Germany, not earthquakes, was the objective; that Teutonic, not seismic, disturbances were the business of the Navy.

There had recently been some disturbances in Chile and Cuba, as well as a small mutiny of the police at Zanzibar, and there had been complaints that under the new dispensation the Navy had not played its part in their suppression. Fisher flatly refuted any such interpretation of its duties.

In the case of Cuba the protection of British interests was very properly entrusted to the United States Navy, as we are at any time ready to protect them in any part of the world where our ships have to be present and theirs have not. Cuba is almost a protectorate of the United States of America. Even if one of our ships had been present in Havana Harbour, it would have been very undesirable for her to land British bluejackets at a time when American intervention was in the balance.

Chile is a civilized country, and should be required to protect other nationalities resident within its territory. The Admiralty must distinctly refuse to be responsible for the policing of Chile.

Zanzibar is a British protectorate, and the military and police arrangements should be such as to make serious disturbances almost impossible. In any case the Admiralty cannot be expected to legislate for the totally unexpected.

Apart from the above, a good many of the individual applications for men-of-war deserved investigation, and it is worth while observing the *modus operandi* in these cases. Three typical ones had occurred recently:

(*a*) Lord Charles Beresford goes to Mexico on private business and sees the President. "In the course of conversation the Admiral mentioned that some British vessels were to visit American waters during the coming season, and the President signified with emphasis what satisfaction it would cause him were the vessels to pay a visit to Mexico." The British Minister therefore urges that a British squadron should visit Mexico, and the Foreign Office "hope that the Lords Commissioners may see their way to make arrangements for a visit". Luckily, Admiral Inglefield (with his squadron) happens to be in West Indian waters, and therefore, it is not necessary to send the First Cruiser Squadron to Vera Cruz; but no one except the Admiralty takes any account of the cost in coal and wear and tear of engines in the squadron steaming an extra 3,500 miles; nor apparently, till Lord Charles suggests the idea, was any necessity seen for the visit.

(*b*) Some American millionaires get up a race for motor-boats, to finish at Nassau, in the Bahamas. With transatlantic vivacity they call this a "flag-to-flag" race, and ask for a ship to look after the boats in case the weather is bad. The Governor of the Bahamas report this to the Colonial Office, giving the impression that an international sporting event of some importance is contemplated, and the Colonial Office ask the Admiralty to send the *Indefatigable* from Jamaica. The Admiralty comply, and the *Indefatigable* arrives to find that the race has been abandoned, and that, in any case, she had never really been wanted.

(*c*) In 1906 Commodore Paget is ordered to the Falkland Islands at the request of the Colonial Office, not because he is wanted there, but presumably to compensate the 2,050 inhabitants of the group for the withdrawal of the South Atlantic Squadron which used to visit there.

Result: This year, when the *Brilliant* is ordered to Buenos Aires, the Governor asks that she may be sent on to the Falklands (2,000 miles more) because Commodore Paget stayed there such a short time last year.

There was obviously too much of this sort of thing, and it had been encouraged in the very highest quarters, for Lord George Hamilton, who had been First Lord from 1886 to 1892, wrote to Fisher, 'During my term of office, Lord Salisbury, as Foreign Secretary, was frequently pressing for a wider and larger distribution of ships-of-war for diplomatic and other reasons; but this pressure was withstood by the Admiralty on the grounds that this peacetime distribution was extremely dangerous and undesirable, not only on grounds of resulting inefficiency following on the isolation of those vessels and their absence from fleet exercises and war training, but their concentration on the verge of war would be difficult, and often impracticable, because of precipitating the crisis when relations were strained, and when the slightest movement of ships-of-war would give rise to the idea of warlike purposes in so doing.'

At the same time we can see now in retrospect that Fisher's reforms marked the end of an era – an era when British men-of-war could enter any port in the world without the 'by your leave' of its owner.

> So they sought, explored, discovered, so they sailed
>   from day to day;
> When the Lizard dropped behind them there were
>   none might bid them stay:
> With Marconi yet undreamed of, none to call, or heed
>   their prayers,
> They had none of our good fortune; we, alas, have
>   none of theirs.[1]

For better or for worse 'showing the flag' was never quite the same thing again.

One of the greatest abuses in the Navy at this date was the length of time that some ships were kept in commission, and this was a cause of much dissatisfaction to officers and men alike. Three years was the usual term, but on some distant stations four years was frequent, and five years was by no means unknown. This meant that officers and men were separated from their families for periods considerably longer than was necessary, as one

---

[1] Hopwood, R.: *The Laws of the Navy*.

example will serve to prove. A lieutenant got married, and within three months he was sent abroad for a five-year commission: at its expiration he returned home, but he had only spent six months in England when he again went abroad, this time for a commission of over four years, which meant that during a period of nine years he spent a mere six months with his wife.

Such experiences put the maximum strain on the continence of any young married couple, and so far as the efficiency of the Navy was concerned they were quite unnecessary. The practice originated in the understandable desire of the Admiralty to safeguard every penny that it could screw out of a niggardly Treasury, for these long commissions avoided the expense of sending out a new crew in a mail steamer and bringing the old one home in the same way: it had become usual, therefore, to wait until some warship was proceeding to the station in question, and on board it the relief crew could be crowded. If commissions were shortened to two years, it was argued, there would be a serious wastage by having a larger number of relief crews on passage to and from foreign stations, and therefore more men would be required to keep ships on the distant stations supplied with crews. To his credit Fisher also regarded the problem from the human angle, and he therefore insisted that, whatever the cost, a period of two years should be adopted as the standard length of commission.

In all his reforms Fisher had the steady backing of the King, for whom he entertained feelings bordering on veneration, while the monarch also had a very high regard for the admiral. In Fisher's *Memories* and *Records* there are many good stories of the King, of which a couple will serve to show the footing upon which the two men stood with one another, they are best told in Fisher's own words:

On another occasion I went down to Sandringham with a great party; I think it was for one of Blessed Queen Alexandra's birthdays. (I hope Her Majesty will forgive me telling a lovely story presently about herself.) As I was zero in this grand party, I slunk off to my room to write an important letter, then took off my coat, got out my keys, unlocked my portmanteau, and began unpacking. I had a boot in each hand; I heard somebody fumbling with the door-handle; and, thinking it was the footman whom Hawkins had allocated to me, I said, "Come in; don't go humbugging with that door-handle!", and in walked King Edward, with a cigar about a yard long in his mouth. He said (I with a boot in each hand), "What on earth are you doing?" "Unpacking, Sir." "Where's your servant?" "Haven't got one." "Where is he?" "Never had one, Sir; couldn't afford it." "Put those boots down and sit in that armchair." And he went and sat in the other on the other side of the fire. I thought to myself, "This is a rum state of affairs. Here's the King of England sitting in my bedroom on one side of the fire, and I'm in my shirt-sleeves sitting in an armchair on the other side."

"Well," said His Majesty, "Why didn't you come and say 'How do you do?' when you arrived?" I said, "I had a letter to write, and with so many great people you were receiving I thought I had better come to my room." Then he went on with a long conversation, until it was only about a quarter of an hour from dinner time, and I hadn't unpacked. So I said to the King, "Sir, you'll be angry if I'm late for dinner, and no doubt Your Majesty has two or three gentlemen to dress you, but I have no one." And he gave me a sweet smile and went off.

Another time Fisher was very definitely put in his place:

On one occasion a certain Admiral approached – perhaps the biggest ass I ever met. The King shook hands with him and said something I thought quite unnecessarily loving to him; when he had gone, he turned on me like a tiger and said, "You ought to be ashamed of yourself!" I humbly said, "What for?" "Why," he replied, "when that man came up to me, your face was perfectly demoniacal! Everyone saw it! and the poor fellow couldn't kick you back! You're First Sea Lord and he is a ruined man! You've no business to show your hate."

And then Fisher remarks:

The lovely thing was that a man came up I knew the King did perfectly hate, and I'm blessed if he didn't smile on him and cuddle him as if he was his long-lost brother, and then he turned to me afterwards and said with joyful revenge, "Well, did you see that?" Isn't that a Great Heart? and is it to be wondered at that he was so popular?

It was not, however, always the King who got the better of it, for on one occasion he found fault with Fisher for having only one idea at a time, and he told him that it would be his ruin: to which observation the Admiral promptly retorted, 'Anyhow I am stopping with you at Balmoral, and I never expected that when I entered the Navy penniless, friendless, and forlorn.'[1]

If the King was a firm supporter of Fisher and his reforms the same was certainly not true of many of his personal friends, and particularly was this the case with Admiral Lord Charles Beresford, of whom Sir Winston Churchill said when he was a Member of Parliament, 'He is one of those orators of whom it is said that before they get up to speak they do not know what they are going to say, when they are speaking they do not know what they are saying, and when they have sat down they do not know what they have said.' Beresford was a man of great personal charm, to which his popularity with women testified, and he was also one of the leading wits and practical jokers of his day. Where the Royal Family was concerned he often ran considerable risks.[2] To Queen Alexandra he was 'Little Rascal', and when in 1870 she had been in a state of grave anxiety in case Denmark should yield to the blandishments of Napoleon III and come in on the side of France against Prussia, a course which might easily have resulted in the loss of her independence, it was he who brought her the news of her country's neutrality. 'Glad to tell you, ma'am,' he said, 'that Denmark has declared neutrality, and so has the Beadle of the Burlington Arcade. Great weight off our minds. Didn't know what either of them would do.' Again, when King Edward, as Prince of Wales, asked him to dine at Marlborough House, he telegraphed, 'Can't possibly. Lie follows by post.'[3]

One of Charlie Beresford's most famous bets was with Walter

---

[1] Cf. Bacon, Admiral R. H.: The Life of Lord Fisher of Kilverstone, vol. II, pp. 66–68.

[2] His relationship with the King was rather of the 'love-hate' variety, and there was more than one serious quarrel between them: on one occasion Lord Charles came within an ace of striking the Sovereign.

[3] Cf. Benson, E. F.: King Edward VII, p. 106.

Long, and related to an exploit in Hyde Park. The only persons who have the right to drive up Rotten Row are the Sovereign and the Duke of St Albans, the latter in his office as Hereditary Grand Falconer, but Beresford bet Long that he would do so between eleven and twelve on a certain morning. On the day in question Long kept a sharp look-out from eleven o'clock onwards, and just before noon he saw the watering-cart wending its way along the Row as usual; something prompted him to scan closely the man who was driving it, and there was Lord Charles who had bribed the driver to change clothes with him. Beresford was also no inconsiderable wit. One day at a race meeting King Edward greeted Sir Edward Sassoon with the remark, 'Hullo, Sassoon, your nose seems to get bigger each time I see you.' Whereupon Lord Charles observed, 'Can you be surprised, Sir, seeing how often he has to pay through it?'

Sir Winston Churchill has written with considerable truth of the controversy between Fisher and Beresford:

> There were . . . officers of social influence and independent means, who had access to Parliament and to the Press. In sympathy with them, though not with all their methods, was a much larger body of good and proved sea officers. At the head of the whole opposition stood Lord Charles Beresford, at that time Commander-in-Chief of the Channel or principal Fleet. . . . Whatever the First Sea Lord proposed the Commander-in-Chief opposed. . . . Neither side was strong enough to crush the other. . . . The lamentable situation thus created might easily have ruined the discipline of the Navy but for the fact that a third large body of officers resolutely refused, at whatever cost to themselves, to participate in the struggle.

In the eyes of the public the issue was further obscured by the demand of the Conservative Opposition for an extended building programme, especially where Dreadnoughts were concerned; a demand which was voiced in a popular jingle:

> Eight, eight, eight!
> We won't have less than eight!
> So we'll smash 'em flat
> If they won't give us that!
> We will have eight!

'In the end,' Churchill has recorded, 'a curious and characteristic solution was reached. The Admiralty had demanded six ships; the economists offered four; and we finally compromised on eight.'[1]

Only on one occasion during the Edwardian era did it look as if the Navy might be involved in serious hostilities, and that was in 1904. Russia and Japan were at war, and in October the Russian Baltic Fleet, under the command of Admiral Rozhdestvensky, was on its way to the Far East. On the night of the 21st in the North Sea it mistook some British trawlers who were fishing on the Dogger Bank for Japanese men-of-war, and promptly opened fire on them. A steam trawler was sunk and the captain and third hand killed, while other vessels were severely damaged and some of the crews injured: to render the situation worse the Russian fleet passed on without making the slightest attempt to render any assistance.

There was no wireless in those days, and it was not until the 24th that the news of the incident became generally known, causing widespread anger. In the conflict between Russia and Japan public opinion in Britain was overwhelmingly on the side of the latter, and the attack on the Hull fishing fleet added fuel to the fire of popular hatred of Russia. The Tsar endeavoured to pour oil on the troubled waters with the following telegram to the King:

> Through foreign source have heard of sad incident in North Sea. Deplore loss of lives of innocent fishermen. Our fleet being at sea I have not yet received any direct information from Admiral. Having had many warnings that Japanese were lurking in fishing smacks and other vessels for purpose of destroying our Squadron on its way out, great precautions were ordered to be taken, especially by night. Trust no complications will arise between our countries owing to this occurrence.
>
> Best love. NICKY.

This was not good enough for King Edward, who replied:

> I have received your telegram and am surprised that only

[1] *Cf.* McKenna, Stephen: *Reginald McKenna, 1863–1943,* p. 66.

through a foreign source you heard of the untoward incident which occurred in the North Sea. Knowing your kind heart I felt sure you would deplore the loss of innocent lives. But what has caused me and my Country so painful an impression is that your Squadron did not stop to offer assistance to the wounded, as searchlights must have revealed to your Admiral that the ships were British fishing vessels.

For a brief space it looked like war, and the British Press adopted a very truculent tone; but in the highest circles it was quickly realized that if hostilities did ensue the *tertius gaudens* would be Germany. The Russian Government showed no disposition to escape the consequences of its admiral's mistake, and Balfour, in spite of the excited state of public feeling, had no intention of proceeding to extremities. Recourse was accordingly had to the Hague Court, which set up an International Commission of Inquiry consisting of British and Russian admirals, together with representatives of the navies of Austria, France, and the United States. It met in Paris, and on February 25th, 1905, the Commissioners found in favour of Great Britain, condemning Russia to pay £65,000 by way of compensation.

For the Army the last years of Queen Victoria, and the Edwardian era, were a period of change at the hands of reformers and of some chastening experiences at those of the Boers. In 1895 the Duke of Cambridge, a cousin of the Queen, ceased to be Commander-in-Chief, a post which he had held since 1856, though he was to live for another nine years. In his youth he had some progressive ideas in military matters, but he had long forgotten them. He was definitely an eccentric, but there was something not unattractive about his eccentricity, unlike that of so many other members of the House of Hanover. For instance, his comments on his inspections were not seldom a joy to those who heard them. He once reviewed in Hyde Park the three battalions of Grenadiers who happened to be in London together, and he thus summed up the impression which they made upon him. 'In all my experience of reviews in England, Ireland, or on the Continent of Europe,' he declared, 'I have never witnessed such a damnable exhibition of incompetence as has been shown by the Grenadier

Guards today. When the Cease Fire sounded, the First Battalion was firing at the Serpentine; the Second Battalion was firing at the Marble Arch; and God Almighty knows where the Third Battalion was firing, I don't.' Once on parade he was inveighing against the habit of swearing in the Army, and he wound up his tirade with the words, 'I was talking it over with the Queen last night, and Her Majesty says she is damned if she will have it.'

The commanding officer of a battalion which had incurred the Duke's displeasure was asked where the pioneers were. 'In front of the leading company, Your Royal Highness,' was the reply. 'Have they got their picks and shovels with them?' 'Certainly, Your Royal Highness. Do you want them to do anything?' 'Yes,' said the Duke, 'I want them to dig a very deep and very wide hole, and then bury this bloody battalion in it.' To a member of the Gunter family of wedding-cake fame who was in command of a Dragoon Guards Regiment, and who appeared on parade with his horse in a lather, H.R.H. bellowed, 'Ice him, damn you; ice him.'

Yet he would never have been so popular with all ranks, as was unquestionably the case, had there not been a considerable amount of humanity behind the façade of bluffness. In the Franco-Prussian War a young Sapper officer had fought with the French Army of the Loire, and on returning to England he was summoned to the Horse Guards, where he was severely rated by the Duke in his capacity as Commander-in-Chief. The offender was told that he had behaved abominably, had broken countless Queen's Regulations, had disgraced the Service, and was extremely fortunate not to be court-martialled. When he had finished the Duke muttered under his breath, 'I am bound to say in your place I should have done the same.' The young officer's name was Kitchener.

In the Crimean War the Duke commanded the 1st Division, but although no one ever questioned his personal courage he lacked several of the qualities necessary in a successful general. In the words of his latest biographer:

"The first quality of the soldier," said Napoleon, "is constancy in enduring fatigues and privations. Courage is only the second." In the heat of action, the Duke had displayed a gallant disregard of danger and sought the thick of the fight. But he did not possess the sustained fortitude which enables men to endure discomfort, fatigue, nights without sleep, cold, hunger, and the sight of suffering. Overwhelmed by responsibility and worn out by anxiety he succumbed to fear and depression. . . . The Duke was always overwhelmed by grief after a battle. On the evening of the Alma he described in his Diary the awful sights he saw, "When all was over I could not help crying like a child." After Inkerman, he was even more deeply affected.[1]

Down the years, however, criticism was fastened on the Duke of Cambridge not for his conduct in the field but for his alleged obscurantism as Commander-in-Chief of the Army, for his tenure of that office was marked by an extremely conservative spirit when any innovation was in question, combined with a warm interest in the welfare of the ordinary soldier. The result was that he was extremely popular with the vast majority of the officers and men, but he incurred the hostility of a small group of reformers led by Sir Garnet, later Lord, Wolseley, who were known as the 'Garnet Ring'. It may, indeed, be that Wolseley and his circle wished to go too far, but there was certainly much room for improvement in the training of the Army, where manoeuvres were so rarely held that special Acts of Parliament had to be passed each time they took place. Those of 1871 were, it is to be feared, typical in that they reflected the unpreparedness of the country for war, at any rate until the outbreak of hostilities in South Africa in 1899. It was with the greatest difficulty that the men pitched their tents, so ignorant were they of the very rudiments of fieldcraft; the horses of the 1st Life Guards were frightened by a flock of geese, and stampeded before operations began; and so sober an organ of opinion as the *Quarterly Review* described the manoeuvres as 'a shameful performance' and 'a spectacle of open humiliation'.

At the same time the blame for this state of affairs must be laid fairly and squarely at the door, not of the Army, but of the British people and of the politicians of all parties to whom the British people had entrusted its destinies. There was on all sides far too

[1] St Aubyn, The Hon. Giles: *The Royal George, 1819–1904,* p. 90.

much reliance on the argument that if Britain lost the opening engagement of a war she always won the last battle. A further piece of 'wishful thinking' was to the effect that the sea was Britain's best defence against a foreign foe, and that the Navy could always be relied upon to ward off invasion. Fortified with these fallacies statesmen, Conservative and Liberal alike, who should have known better, proceeded to cheese-pare where the Army was concerned, and when inevitable disaster followed in time of war, they complacently heaped abuse on the commanders in the field. As for the attitude of the British public, it was well summed up by Kipling in the lines:

> For it's Tommy this, an' Tommy that, an'
> "Chuck him out, the brute!"
> But it's "Saviour of 'is country" when the
> Guns begin to shoot.

The interest of the Royal Family in the Army during the nineteenth century was very considerable, and it was invaluable in counterbalancing the neglect of the politicians, but all the evidence goes to show that the Queen and the Prince Consort tended to regard it as designed at least as much to repress revolution at home as to fight the country's enemies abroad, and for this reason the link between Buckingham Palace and the Horse Guards could not be too strong or too close: possibly this attitude of mind originated in the course of events in the German States in 1848 and in the memory of the difficulty experienced in getting George IV safely back to Carlton House after his Coronation Banquet in Westminster Hall.

The Duke of Cambridge was succeeded as Commander-in-Chief, though with diminished powers, by his critic Wolseley, but the latter had little time to put his ideas into practice before the South African War broke out in the autumn of 1899. It was destined to be a far longer and more arduous conflict than either side had anticipated, for each party to it undervalued both the resources and the resolution of its antagonist. The Boers, who had the most vivid recollection of their earlier struggle with Great Britain, who knew the extent of their own armaments, and who were well aware of the insignificant number of British troops in

South Africa before the outbreak of hostilities, believed that the Imperial Government would prove to have neither the means nor the will to wear down their determined resistance, and that in any event it would not be long before some European Power came to their aid. On the other hand the British Cabinet had convinced itself that the Boers would yield to pressure without fighting, and so had paid little attention to the advice of its military advisers: what preparations it did make were at once tardy and inadequate.

There was also complete ignorance in high places as to the nature of the warfare which was about to take place. Regular troops are always at a disadvantage in dealing with a mobile force of irregulars on its own ground, and the farmers of the Dutch republics were irregulars of quite exceptional quality. Born and bred on the African veldt they were familiar from boyhood with the rifle, the saddle, and the transport-waggon; they possessed, too, the obstinate patience of their race, and on their hardy ponies they could move at a speed which baffled the British generals, at any rate until the latter had learnt many lessons from them.[1] Nor was this all, for they had the good fortune to produce some re- markable generals such as Christian de Wet, a Free State farmer, who merits comparison with Garibaldi as a daring and resourceful *guerrillero*; J. H. Delarey, a Transvaaler, who distinguished him- self as a skilful leader of mounted infantry; and, above all, Louis Botha, who displayed both strategical and tactical ability of the highest order. Indeed, had it not been for the lax discipline of the Boers, their incapacity to act on a large combined plan, and their excessive caution, the war might have lasted a great deal longer than was actually the case.

In the small battles fought during the opening months of the campaign it became apparent that, due to the use of smokeless powder, the old terror of a visible foe had been replaced by the paralysing sensation of advancing on an invisible one. A foretaste of this had been noted a year earlier in the Spanish-American War, and Theodore Roosevelt had written, 'As the Spaniards used

---

[1] The lessons learned were not forgotten in 1914 when 'British tactics, schooled by Boer marksmanship, proved distinctly superior to those of the Continental Armies' (Terraine, John: *Mons*, p. 91).

smokeless powder, their artillery had an enormous advantage over ours.'[1] A universal terror, rather than a localized danger, now enveloped the attacker, while the defender, who was always ready to protect himself by some rough earth- or stone-work, was enabled, because of the rapidity of rifle fire, to use extensions unheard of in former battles, and in consequence overlap every frontal infantry attack. Thus at the battle of the Modder River the Boers extended 3,000 men on a frontage of 7,700 yards; at Magersfontein 5,000 on 11,000; and at Colenso 4,500 on 13,000; yet in spite of this human thinness these fronts could not be penetrated.

After the battle of Paardeberg on February 18th, 1900, the Boers took to guerrilla warfare, when the war proper may be said to have begun, and by the time it finished on May 31st 1902, it had absorbed in all 450,000 British soldiers, many of whom were mounted infantry. It was brought to a successful conclusion by an audacious scheme which struck at the Boer mobility, for a vast network of fenced block-house lines was woven over thousands of square miles of the theatre of war, which was thus split into a number of areas, which were one after another cleared by mounted columns. It was a long process of attrition, but it was an eminently successful one.[2]

In fact the war cost Great Britain two and a half years of hard fighting, and the expenditure of a hundred and fifty million pounds, before a population numbering little more than fifty thousand adult males was finally reduced to subjection. Furthermore, British military prestige received a very severe blow, and there was a great deal of sympathy with the Boers both in the Old World and in the New, but although in some countries Anglophobia was excessively virulent the war left British naval strength unimpaired, and so rendered foreign intervention too hazardous a proceeding to be attempted.

There were many lessons to be learnt, not least by the officers, and here history was showing a tendency to repeat itself. As far back as the reign of James II the French ambassador in London sent in a very damaging report to Louis XIV regarding the com-

[1] *The Rough Riders*, p. 98.
[2] *Cf.* Fuller, Major-General J. F. C.: *The Conduct of War, 1789–1961*, p. 140.

missioned ranks in the British Army. 'They are even ignorant', he wrote, 'of the most minor rules of war, and except for a few officers who have seen service in France and in Holland, the great bulk of them do not know even the first principles of the articles of war.' Some two centuries later, at the time of the South African War, a shrewd observer, also a Frenchman, could still write, 'The main defect of the British officer is that he is not what the French call *instruit* nor even disposed to become so; this has been his trouble historically and always. The successes of Great Britain in other times have been attained under this disadvantage. To meet difficulties as they arise, instead of by foresight, to learn by hard experience rather than by reflection or premeditation, are national traits.' To no inconsiderable extent it is to be feared that this attitude was a legacy from the days of the Duke of Cambridge, who was once heard to address a distinguished general of the time, 'I don't like Staff College Officers. My experience of Staff College officers is that they are conceited, and that they are dirty! Brains! I don't believe in brains. You haven't any, I know, Sir!'

The officers of the late Victorian and Edwardian era were mostly drawn from the upper and middle middle-class, and their whole code of behaviour was a reaction against the raffishness of their eighteenth- and early nineteenth-century predecessors, just as the Public Schools, from which the vast majority of them came, were a reaction against the anarchical establishments which preceded the reforms of Dr Arnold. It may be that the reaction was carried too far. For an officer to be seen travelling in anything but a first-class carriage was unthinkable; to be seen in the street smoking anything but a cigar was a thing not done; and a visit to the War Office could only be paid when attired in a frock-coat and a silk hat. Whether such a state of affairs was desirable may be regarded as a matter of opinion, even by those who feel that in more recent times the pendulum has swung too far in the opposite direction.

On the other hand, an officer, even in the Line, practically had to pay for the privilege of serving his country, for at the beginning of the South African War the pay of a Second Lieutenant in the infantry was 5s 3d a day, while obligatory mess expenses stood at from 6s to 8s 6d; even when the First World War came the pay had only risen to 7s 6d.

The tedious progress of the South African War, so incomprehensible to the ordinary citizen, stirred Britain to the depths, much as the revelations of the campaign in the Crimea had done some fifty years earlier. Even in the highest places it was admitted that all was not well; the Prime Minister, speaking in the House of Lords on January 30th, 1900, shortly after the Boer victories at Magersfontein, Stormberg, and Colenso, said:

> It is evident that there is something in your machinery that is wrong. . . . I do not think that the British Constitution as at present worked is a good fighting machine. . . . It is unequalled for producing happiness, prosperity, and liberty in time of peace; but now in time of war, when Great Powers with enormous forces are looking at us with no gentle or kindly eye, it becomes us to think whether we must not in some degree modify our arrangements in order to enable ourselves to meet the dangers that at any moment may arise.

As there was no General Staff it is not surprising to find that as late as 1901 there was not in the War Office archives, with a single exception, any comprehensive statement of the military resources of any foreign country in the world, or of the manner in which they might, in the event of war, be used against Great Britain. The mobilization section concerned itself chiefly with arrangements for defence against invasion, while the intelligence section collected foreign military information but was not responsible for making practical use of it. A few memoranda and minor schemes dealing with certain expeditions which might have to be undertaken were occasionally produced, but they did not contain, or pretend to contain, a complete survey of the resources of an assumed enemy, or anything like it.

The fact was that the Government was withholding from the Commander-in-Chief the powers which properly belonged to him, but at the same time it hesitated to abolish the office altogether and put something else in its place; so the farcical situation was produced that whereas the Duke of Cambridge, admittedly not a great soldier, was for nearly forty years accorded full powers of management, his successor, who had seen a great deal of service, had his authority cut down to the point of extinction. In 1901 Wolseley was replaced by Roberts, who was in any case a fighting soldier rather than an administrator, and advantage was taken of this change to bring the Adjutant-General once more under the Commander-in-Chief's control, and the other military departments were officially described as being under his supervision, but exactly what was meant by those vague terms, it is difficult to say. The Army, however, gained nothing, since the training of the troops, to give but one example, continued to be dealt with at headquarters by two junior officers of the Adjutant-General's branch, and was combined with such incongruous subjects as cooking, the school of music, and sergeants' messes.[1]

The Balfour administration did little or nothing to apply the lessons of the South African War, though there could be no question of the good intentions of St John Brodrick and Arnold-Forster, who were successively Secretaries of State for War during this period. The forces at home were allowed to remain a heterogeneous jumble of small units incapable of effective use, just as we have seen that the ships of the Royal Navy were scattered all over the globe in 'penny packets'. With the exception of the Aldershot army corps, so-called, the regular troops had no formation higher than the brigade which could have mobilized without changing its composition. The cavalry were short of horses, the infantry of men, the artillery of ammunition, and everybody of other requisites of war. The second line, the militia, continued to be bled for the regulars, and in any event only a portion of it was liable for active service abroad. The yeomanry and volunteers, which constituted the third line, were in most cases without any organization higher than the regiment and battalion. In these circumstances it is little wonder that, speaking in the House of Lords in July, 1905, Lord Roberts should have said, 'I have no hesitation in stating that our armed forces, as a body, are as absolutely unfitted and unprepared for war as they were in 1899–1900.'

[1] Cf. Robertson, Field-Marshal Sir William: *Soldiers and Statesmen, 1914–1918* vol. I, pp. 10–14.

In extenuation of the inaction of the Balfour administration it may be advanced that in the opening years of the century it was by no means clear what enemy the British Army would be called upon to fight, or where. Neither soldiers nor statesmen, even after the conclusion of the Entente with France, had yet sufficiently rid themselves of anxiety about Russia to admit of adequate attention being directed to Germany, and all the evidence goes to show that the German menace was appreciated earlier at the Admiralty than in the War Office. The numerous small wars in which the country had been engaged during the previous two or three decades had also served to contract the military outlook, and few people, if any, visualized a conflict such as the First World War.

The advent of the Liberals to power brought to the War Office the greatest Secretary of State for War that Great Britain has ever known, namely R. B. Haldane. His view was that the security of the British Isles demanded not only the possession of a powerful Navy, but the provision of appropriate land forces as well, and he realized that, in addition to meeting this first call upon its resources, the country ought to be capable of undertaking certain operations abroad. For this purpose the regular troops serving in the United Kingdom, together with the army reserve, were made to form the Expeditionary Force, while the militia was converted into a Special Reserve charged with the duty of training and providing drafts for the regular units at the front. These constituted the first line, and the second line, composed of the Yeomanry and Volunteers, became the Territorial Force of fourteen infantry divisions and fourteen mounted brigades for Home Defence.

As may be supposed, Haldane had many critics, among them Kitchener, who sneered at the new Territorial Force as a 'Town Clerk's Army', so it is hardly surprising that when the First World War came 'Kitchener's neglect of the Territorials was . . . a constant worry to Asquith'.[1] On the other hand, as in the case of Fisher and the Navy, Haldane received the enthusiastic support of the King. After the Territorial and Reserve Forces Act had received the Royal Assent he did what no other man, not even the

[1] Spender, J. A., and Asquith, Cyril: *Life of Herbert Henry Asquith, Lord Oxford and Asquith*, vol. II, pp. 132–133.

Prime Minister, could have done, that is to say he summoned the Lords-Lieutenant of the counties of England, Wales, and Scotland to a meeting at Buckingham Palace on October 26th, 1907, and made a speech impressing upon them the duty of energetically co-operating with the Secretary of State in launching the new County Associations. The new Act, he was careful to point out, revived much of the importance which formerly belonged to their office, and its success must depend on the public spirit of the nation which the Lords-Lieutenant and the County Associations were about to guide. He was confident that they would employ their best endeavours to carry out this great work. In the words of one who was present, 'The King played up magnificently.' The Duke of Norfolk then replied on behalf of his colleagues, and assured the Sovereign that he might rely upon them all to perform their new duties.[1]

Haldane was fully of conscious the value of King Edward's support, and he wrote to express his gratitude

> for the great impulse which he is certain has been given to the movement for the organization of a Territorial Army by the example which your Majesty has shown to the Lieutenants of the Counties. Mr Haldane believes that they have quitted your Majesty's presence with a new sense of their responsibility and with a greatly heightened realization of the nature of the national effort in which their King has summoned them to bear a notable part. If Mr Haldane is right in this belief, then the pains and trouble which your Majesty has bestowed in making the reception of today worthy of a great and historical occasion have not been wasted.

On November 18th the matter was carried a stage further when the King announced that in future no one would be made a Deputy-Lieutenant unless he had served for ten years either in the Forces or in connection with a County Territorial Association, and on the same day the War Office published the designations of the new districts and commands, as well as the names of the district commanders. After this the work proceeded apace, and the

---

[1] *Cf.* Redesdale, Lord: *Memoirs*, pp. 36–37.

very indifference of Parliament to the Army was of no small assistance in securing the passage of the measure. What cannot be stressed too often is the fact that Haldane had the full support and sympathy of the King, who thoroughly understood what was at issue, and the Secretary of State had no hesitation in declaring that 'there was no minister who had greater cause to be grateful to his Sovereign than himself'.

In this way was set up the machinery which in 1914 was able to put in the field the best-trained and best-equipped British Army that before or since has been sent overseas at the beginning of a war, and not the least curious aspect of the whole business is that this was effected by a Government whose ranks contained a large proportion of pacifists.

Of course it was not all plain sailing, as a modern military historian has pointed out:

It was the training of the soldier which, after the South African War, formed the field for the introduction of ideas and methods which signified a complete break with the bad old ways that had prevailed in the Army for close on two and a half centuries. Here again perfection was not attained, very far from it, partly because the ideal that was being set before officers and men was high and was perpetually being set higher still – like the poet's "margin of that untravelled world" which fades for ever as we onwards move; partly because the intellectual and abstract side of the soldier's profession could not keep pace with its concrete and practical aspects. This latter circumstance was, in fact, the source of the main weakness of the army that was coming into being. So it happened that excellent brigadiers, the men who must deal with situations in the field which they could "touch and see", were plentiful. The practical sense and the solidity of the national character here came into its own. But when the command of divisions and larger units was in question, it proved infinitely harder to find men who approximated to the ideal standard. The higher the appointment the more its holder must rely upon abstract thought as well as upon a trained imagination; the more difficulty might then be experienced in finding the required combination of moral courage, intellect, mental elasticity, and experience. Here lay the real disadvantage of that solid, phlegmatic, unimaginative British temperament.[1]

At this point is is not without interest to note the extent of British military resources in the middle of the Edwardian era. The British regular army was distributed as follows:

Home	142,328
India	75,031
South Africa	19,983
Egypt	4,008
Gibraltar	5,032
Malta	9,252
Cyprus	108
Sierra Leone, St Helena, and Mauritius	6,658
Ceylon, Hong Kong, the Straits Settlements, and Wei-hai-Wei	10,595
Bermuda and the West Indies	3,029
Not detailed	56
TOTAL	275,480

In addition there were the Reserve and Auxiliary Forces:

Army Reserve	94,770
Militia	96,603
Yeomanry	25,341
Volunteers	247,588

Finally, there was the Indian Army which amounted in all to 160,580 officers and men.

It was, however, not only the organization of the Army that was changed in Edwardian times, for the treatment of the ordinary soldier was revolutionized. For two hundred years the Army had been recruited mainly from the dregs of the nation, and the ranks had been filled with thieves and sharpers of every kind. The natural consequence was that the soldier was subjected to endless supervision, and he was not trusted to perform even the most

[1] de Watteville, Col. H.: *The British Soldier*, p. 211.

trivial task unless he were shepherded by a non-commissioned officer. So there could be seen the amazing spectacle of half-a-dozen grizzled old soldiers, whose total length of service might number over a hundred years, being supervised in the performance of a childish duty by a stripling corporal whose age might be round about twenty; even if a soldier left barracks on furlough, a lance-corporal had to go and see him into his train at the station. In 1909, Sir Horace Smith-Dorrien, who then had the Aldershot Command, made a start in the abolition of these archaic customs; he declared that henceforth the soldier would be placed on his honour, and accordingly the pickets which every night paraded the streets of Aldershot were abolished, with a consequent saving of the daily labour of seven hundred men. This trust in the troops, it may be added, proved to be thoroughly justified.

The ordinary amenities of life were also improved, and not before time, for they had fallen far below the normal standards of civil life. In London the chief centre for enlistment was St George's Barracks, which were in Charing Cross Road behind the National Gallery. It was a gloomy building by all accounts, with dark and dingy rooms, and it would appear to have been designed to quench in the ordinary recruit any martial ardour at the beginning of his career. There was still more than a little of the methods of Sergeant Kite about the way in which men were encouraged to enlist, and recruiting sergeants were much to the fore especially in the area of the Strand and Trafalgar Square; they wore the full-dress uniform of their regiment or corps, and the coloured ribbons fluttering from their caps denoted their duty. They could paint a very glamorous picture of life in the Army – smart uniform, horse to ride, good food and pay, and seeing the world: after a good day in London, and with his pockets nearly empty, many a country lad fell a victim to their blandishments. The fees they earned varied according to the branch of the Army for which they obtained their man: a recruit for the Foot Guards brought in five shillings, but one for the Household Cavalry was worth thirty.

The modern five-day week was unknown, and one of the chief features of life in a garrison was the church parade on Sunday, when units of all arms of the Service marched to church in full-dress uniform and headed by their band. No soldier other than officers' servants, Colour-Sergeants, and ranks above were allowed to wear plain clothes when off duty on any occasion, and there can be little doubt that recruiting was greatly helped by the sight of the smart uniforms which were everywhere.

The soldier in those days had to rely chiefly on his own resources for entertainment: the cinema was in its infancy, though there were music-halls in most of the larger centres of population, but many of the men never left their barracks for months on end except when on duty. The wet canteen was the hub of the soldier's social life, and on most evenings, especially over the week-ends, concerts of the music-hall type took place there: an old soldier acted as chairman, kept order, and announced the various turns, which were contributed by the troops themselves. The most popular ditties were those of a sentimental description, and if a performer failed to please he was left in no doubt of the fact, but the general atmosphere was one of conviviality and good fellowship. A Guardsman received 1s 1d a day, which was a penny more than the Linesman, but from this was deducted 3½d a day for messing and washing, and 1d a month for hair-cutting and barrack damages: the pay was increased by 3d a day according to service and musketry qualification. Beer was good and cheap at 1s a gallon, and for some years at the beginning of the century it was served in quart tin pots, and a soldier would buy a pot and share it at a table with two or more of his comrades, who in turn replenished it. This practice was in due course condemned by the medical authorities, but the custom of buying a quart of beer lingered on for some years, and it was canteen etiquette to buy not less than two pint glasses of beer at a time.

In most units the great majority of the men smoked pipes, but cigarettes could be obtained in the dry canteen, and there was also a regimental recreation room which provided a billiard table, newspapers, and games such as chess and draughts. The canteens were managed either under a regimental or tenant system: under the tenant system the contract would be let out to a firm of caterers for a year or more, and a proportion of the profits was paid to the unit; under the regimental system the canteen was managed by a committee of officers. Neither of these systems was very satisfactory, and they were generally replaced by N.A.A.F.I. at the end of the First World War. There was no unit system of messing in dining-halls, food being distributed from the cookhouse to the barrack-rooms to be eaten there, and by that time it was often cold. The A.S.C. provided a pound of bread and 12 ozs of meat a day for each soldier, and there was a messing allowance of 6d a day for groceries and vegetables. The Colour-Sergeant of each company kept the messing account for his company, and when the account got into debt, which was by no means an infrequent occurrence, it is to be feared that this was soon reflected in a diminution of the food and an absence of extras. No suppers were provided, and for tea a soldier had what remained of his pound of bread, and a small portion of butter which was issued at breakfast. Crockery was regarded as an effeminate luxury, and only plates and basins were provided. Sanitation at night was primitive, but there were tubs to be found outside the doors of the barrack-rooms.

Gambling in all its forms was very much in vogue, and nearly every unit possessed its own bookmakers in the form of a syndicate run by a few old soldiers. Crown and Anchor was played in the canteen and in the barrack-rooms, and although efforts were made to stamp it out they were not very successful. Discipline was strict, and punishments were severe. Punishment drills were carried out in full marching order with all movements in quick time. Court-martial sentences were read out by the Adjutant on the square before the whole battalion, and the soldier under sentence was marched on to parade under escort with fixed bayonets: if he was a non-commissioned officer, and the sentence included reduction to the ranks, his chevrons would be cut off his sleeves at the same time.[1]

As the King's reign drew to its close conditions were everywhere improving, and particularly was this the case where the

---

[1] This description of Army conditions is based upon a contemporary account of those existing in the Irish Guards, but there is no reason to believe that these were in any way exceptional.

housing of the soldier was concerned. Communal dining-halls formed an invariable feature of every new barrack-building scheme; washing facilities were multiplied until the cold, bleak 'ablution room' of the earlier days was hardly even an unpleasant memory; and the lighting of barrack-rooms became unrecognizable by those who could recall the isolated, hissing gas-burners, the swinging oil-lamps, and the tallow-candles of old. Libraries, reading-rooms, and writing-rooms too, were becoming the rule. Above all, the standard of cooking was raised, until it could truthfully be said that it was quite adequate and considerably more attractive. Anyhow, the day was long past when an officer who was walking across a barrack-square met an orderly carrying a steaming soup-can and ordered him to put it down and fetch a spoon. The orderly looked surprised, but obeyed. He came back, and the officer helped himself to a spoonful of the contents of the can. 'Goodness,' he exclaimed, 'what soup! It is more like dish water.' 'Sir, that's what it is,' replied the orderly, 'I was just taking it to the barrack-room to wash the plates.' There was to be no excuse for this type of confusion in future.

Even in those far-off days the British Army occasionally went outside the boundaries of the British Empire in time of peace, and one of these occasions was in 1904, when the Band of the Grenadier Guards played at the Great International Exhibition, or World's Fair, at St Louis. The idea of sending the Band seems to have originated with the King, who was always anxious to promote good relations with the United States, and the officer in charge of the party was George Jeffreys, later General the Lord Jeffreys, and Colonel of the Grenadier Guards in succession to Queen Elizabeth II. Fifty years later he wrote an extremely vivid account of the whole affair.[1] His difficulties, it may be added, were not diminished by the fact that at that time British troops were not subject to military law once they left British territory, so it was not until his party reached Canada on their return journey that Jeffreys had any very effective control over his men: in spite of this they appear to have behaved very well indeed.

On August 16th they all embarked at Liverpool in the Cunard

[1] In the *Household Brigade Magazine*, Summer Number, 1954, pp. 87–92.

S.S. *Ivernia* and reached Boston on the 24th, where the Band landed in Guard Order, and was given a cordial reception. Jeffreys was driven round Boston by the Mayor, but he 'found that there were disadvantages in wearing uniform, as people not only fingered it but even tried to cut off buttons as souvenirs'. The Band gave afternoon and evening concerts at Point of Pines, and on August 27th proceeded to St Louis, 'a long and dusty journey' which took from 10.45 a.m. one day to 6.30 p.m. the next.

St Louis proved as strange to the Guardsmen as they did to the inhabitants of St Louis. The President of the Exhibition, for instance, asked Jeffreys whether the Guards formed part of the British Army, and seemed greatly surprised when told that such was indeed the case. Their playing met with universal approval. One newspaper commented: 'The Grenadiers in the scarlet British Army uniforms and bearskin shakos have already scored a hit at the World's Fair.' Another reported that 'people . . . will perceive by looking at the Grenadier Guards band that we Americans do not resemble the English. . . . The somewhat astonishing blondness of the Grenadier Guards is their marked feature. . . . In interesting contrast to the English are the Musicians of the Garde Republicaine Band of Paris, who are nearly all dark.'

The Exhibition was a vast collection of buildings spread over many acres, as is the way of exhibitions, and each of the Great Powers had its own pavilion; the British one was apparently a reproduction of the Orangery at Kensington Palace. Jeffreys stayed at the Hotel Washington, but his sojourn there was marred by the fact that his room was broken into one night when he was asleep and his money, letter of credit, etc., stolen. He was not alone in his misfortune, for six other rooms in the hotel were similarly burgled the same night, but the thief or thieves got clear away. When Jeffreys complained to the police he found them 'casual, unhelpful, and uncivil', while to add insult to injury the Chief Police Officer attributed the crime to an 'expert gang of British thieves'. In any event Jeffreys seems to have formed rather a low opinion of the people of St Louis, for he found them 'very different from those of Boston, being of a much tougher type, and both sexes being given to chewing and spitting'.

At the same time he and Baden-Powell, who had come out from England as a balloon expert, were most lavishly entertained, but what seems to have impressed the British visitors most was an annual event called 'The Ceremony of the Veiled Prophet'. It began with a procession of emblematical cars through the streets, after which the 'Veiled Prophet', clad in robes of an Oriental type, entered the ballroom of the Hotel Washington at the head of a somewhat motley crew, and proceeded to crown the 'Queen of Love and Beauty': to her, and her three 'Maids of Honour', he then presented pieces of jewellery. The proceedings terminated with the dancing of a Royal Quadrille.

The beginning of October marked the end of the Exhibition, and the Band moved on to Canada by way of Louisville, Indianapolis, and Buffalo. From one point of view this made Jeffreys' task easier, for he was in a country where British military law was operative, but a General Election was in progress and this raised problems of its own. When the Band played in the evening of the day on which the results were announced the local manager wanted to arrange for the successful candidates to address the audience from the stage. Jeffreys objected to this very strongly on the ground that it would tend to identify the Band with politics, but it was only with some difficulty that he got his own way.

He was soon to have further light on the impact of politics upon the Canadian way of life.

I was given a glimpse of the influence of politics in the Army when, at the invitation of the Officer Commanding at Toronto, I went to luncheon at the Officers' Mess at the Barracks, which were old British barracks. Detachments of Regular Canadian Cavalry and Infantry were stationed there for the purpose of providing the necessary troops for Militia officers undergoing courses of instruction. After an excellent luncheon the Officer Commanding asked me if I would like to come round the barracks with him and see a parade. The barracks were not very clean and the parade was not a very good one, and the Commanding Officer, as we came away, said that he was sorry, and that everything would have been different had it not been for the election. I asked what the election had to do with it, and he replied that both the candidates for that division had been addressing the troops in the canteen, and standing drinks all round. I then asked whether he could not have refused them permission to do this, whereupon he said, "Refuse them permission! If I had tried to do that whichever one of them had got in would have had me out!" Which opened my simple European eyes a bit!

It is a tribute to the British Guardsman that the Band gave Jeffreys very little trouble indeed, although in the United States his authority over the men was slight, and some of them had received large offers of money to desert. He was, however, taking no chances and when the hour of sailing from New York drew near he found one man short, in spite of an order that no one was to go ashore.

I ordered one of the Band serjeants and two old soldiers to go ashore and go into every saloon on the dockside, and if they found him – no matter what anyone said – to bring him along. They went, and about half an hour before the ship sailed they returned with the man, who had got ashore by the crew's gangway right forward, and was now not very sober. Whether or not he meant to desert I don't know, but he had given trouble before, so I gave him a stiff fine in his share of the Band's earnings, and he was turned out of the Band when we got back.

As the ship cast off Jeffreys ordered *Rule Britannia* to be played, and when it was objected by the bandmaster that this might hurt American feelings he said that most of the Americans would not know what it was, and anyhow they were all on board a British ship.

CHAPTER IX

An Age of Transition

—————•◉•—————

WE have already seen evidence in more than one phase of Edwardian life that it was an age of transition, though few contemporaries, with the curious exceptions of Balfour and Laurier, appear to have noticed the fact. Outside what may be described as the ranks of the professional revolutionaries and prophets of woe it was comparatively rare to hear expressed views such as the following:

> The concentration of industry into great business firms is still proceeding. In retail trade the growth of great stores with branches in the country, and in manufactures and other industries the rise of big companies and the formation of trusts, seem to be the characteristic of the period. A big undertaking usually increases the economy of working, and the small man is unable to compete. A revolution is threatened in our fiscal system. But the most important sign of the times is a growing feeling against the present distribution of wealth, and even against the whole industrial system of the day. The increase in the popularity of Socialism on the one hand, and the renewed agitation of the wage-earners on the other, may possibly lead to great changes in our social organization. Whether such changes be desirable or undesirable, the times bristle with problems which our civilization must solve.[1]

It would be unrealistic to suggest that the death of King Edward VII represented a turning-point in the national life of his country. It neither opened the way to fresh currents nor diverted the course of those that were already in motion. A new world, which

[1] Salmon, S.: *An Introductory Economic History of England*, pp. 122–123.

both socially and politically would have been unrecognizable by the great Victorians, had been coming into existence before his accession, and had shown its characteristics strongly enough while he was still on the throne. Moreover, in the last four years of his life domestic politics, culminating in the People's Budget, and foreign affairs, restless and uneasy since the South African War, had already disturbed some men's minds with the sense that the foundations, as well as the surface, of a long-familiar world were moving. Whether events, either at home or abroad, would have taken a different course had the King lived longer is idle speculation.

Yet in retrospect is is impossible to resist the conclusion that even if it be admitted that the year 1910 was no turning-point it does seem to associate itself with an unwelcome change in the country's state of mind. From such beginnings as serious strikes unauthorized by the Trade Union leaders, the early demonstrations of the new movement for women's suffrage, and the platform extravagances of the 1909 Budget campaign, it grew until a temper of sheer fighting seemed to invade every aspect of the affairs, working up to the verge of civil war in 1914. The traditional Englishman, with his love of compromise, had become a relic of the past. It would not be fanciful to detect this development in other spheres than the political. In art (though in this field the attack upon old conventions has always been marked by a considerable amount of intolerance), the new methods of painting, the new conceptions of music, and the new exploitations of the stage were all more or less lurid – certainly violence of expression was an essential component. In social life the old steady penetration of the world of fashion by the world of wealth, only too pleased to maintain the old barriers once it was safely inside them, was giving place to a feverish, contemptuous construction of a new world of fashionable idleness, well attuned to a world of lurid art. Industry more and more took on the aspect of two massed opposed forces, and between them compromise became even more precarious. The result was that the period between the King's death and the outbreak of the First World War were very militant years.

Mr Douglas Jerrold well summed up the situation when he wrote:

> Yet the gravest reality was hidden. Men sensed no more than fatigue in high places, with a hint or two of corruption. That the great days of manufacturing supremacy and usury were nearly over was not realized in the least. Even the Tariff Reform campaign was preached not as a measure of reform, but as a measure of defence. Retaliation would improve the export trade.[1]

Seeing no threat, either politically or economically, from without the mass of the British people thought that they could afford the luxury of quarrelling among themselves, and this they proceeded to do with a bitterness unknown since the late twenties and early thirties of the previous century: the bitterness, it may be added, increased as the Liberal Government after 1906 took the first tentative steps towards the Welfare State. In consequence politics, at the King's death, were ceasing to be what they had been at his succession, namely a conflict of genuine principles dividing society vertically, with all classes represented on both sides, and were becoming a conflict between classes, whose divisions were determined by self-interest rather than by their estimate of the common good. The immediate consequence was to make some strange bed-fellows, for the merchant bankers and the shipping interests, anxious about Free Trade, found themselves allied with the popular party in support of a government which kept its majority together by fighting the battle of Welsh Nonconformity and Irish Home Rule, and which was making some very attractive promises to the proletariat. 'It is a hard thing,' Lloyd George was soon to say at Limehouse, 'that the poor man should have to fight his way to the tomb through the brambles and thorns of poverty. I am going to cut a new path for him, a longer and an easier one, through fields of waving corn.' On the other side were mainly the squirearchy, the county towns, and the professional classes, concerned immediately for what today is termed the Establishment, the security of capital, the revival of agriculture

[1] *England*, p. 97.

(of which they had come to despair under Free Trade), and the rights of racial minorities.

This development was accentuated during the Edwardian era by the extremely uneven distribution of wealth. As has been shown on an earlier page this was slow in making itself felt in terms of domestic politics. During the latter part of the nineteenth century the working classes as such were most certainly not predominantly Liberal, for unorganized Labour was traditionally Tory, for in those far-off days the Tories were the champions of the small man, and organized Labour was now turning to the new Labour Party. The backbone of Liberalism were the Nonconformists, the talking classes, and those big business interests whose prosperity depended, or appeared to depend, on Free Trade. It is true that the trade returns were extremely encouraging, but there was no corresponding benefit to the mass of the population.

To understand the situation existing sixty years ago it is necessary to forget that of today. Russia, India, and China were already the three greatest aggregations of population, and between them they comprised two-thirds of the total population of the world, but they were still peasant states. Outside Europe only the United States had approached anything like the full development of her resources. In effect, the world of King Edward VII was not one of industrialized states, each specializing in the industries most suitable to its talents, resources, and climate, and so producing in harmonious co-operation the maximum quantity of goods in the most efficient manner for mutual exchange: on the contrary the world of those days was in a state of economic transition in which Britain, France, Germany, and the United States were competing in the sale of manufactured goods to nations not yet highly industrialized; but they were each increasingly concerned, as the process of industrialization went on, to see that it was achieved with their machinery, supervised by their engineers, and financed by their capital. In this way each hoped that when the wheel should have come full circle, and the process of industrialization had been completed, they would be in a position to buy tribute in the form of interest on the vast potential resources of Latin America and of Asia.

It was only the upper and middle classes who derived any benefit from this competitive trade, and the prosperity it brought to Victorian and Edwardian Britain, for between 1896 and 1914 real wages fell substantially, while the money increase was at most 19 per cent while retail food prices increased by 25 per cent. The effect upon the countryside, as has been described in an earlier chapter, was catastrophic: the great prairie-lands of Canada and Argentina might produce wheat and beef more economically for the urban proletariat than could the British farmer, but it was not only British beef and wheat which was being thrown off the market, for home-produced butter, eggs, bacon, and market-garden produce met the same fate to the same detriment of the farmer and farm labourer. Nor was this all, for the writing was on the wall, and German competition was rapidly becoming a very serious menace. For example, in the period 1885–1889 Great Britain was producing on an average 7,600,000 tons of pig iron and 2,800,000 tons of steel per year, while German production lagged behind at 3,500,000 and 1,600,000 tons respectively; but by 1913 the German production of pig iron was 16,500,000 tons as against the British of 10,250,000, and German steel production was 17,300,000 tons as against British of no more than 7,650,000 tons. These figures, it may be added, were typical of industry as a whole.

The division of the country by self-interest with a class basis certainly began in King Edward's reign, but is was not carried to extremes until he had long been in his grave. The result was that the House of Commons still enjoyed much of the prestige it had known in the nineteenth century, and the same was true of the individual Member of Parliament, though whether he deserved respect of this nature is another matter. Certainly he tended to have closer local connections than is usually the case today, when any aspiring politician seems to consider himself or herself ideally suited to represent any constituency, urban or rural, in any part of the kingdom. Also prominent statesmen carried weight in large areas as the Chamberlains in Birmingham and Rosebery in Scotland, and so could influence a whole group of constituencies in a way now unknown.

The Edwardian era was definitely one of transition, but it is impossible to resist the conclusion that of all the changes it initiated the most revolutionary in every field has proved to be the triumph of the internal combustion engine.

Index